A Black Gambler's World

of Liquor, Vice, and Presidential Politics

A Black Gambler's World of Liquor, Vice, and Presidential Politics

William Thomas Scott
of Illinois, 1839–1917

Bruce L. Mouser

Foreword by

Henry Louis Gates, Jr.

The University of Wisconsin Press

The University of Wisconsin Press
1930 Monroe Street, 3rd Floor
Madison, Wisconsin 53711-2059
uwpress.wisc.edu

3 Henrietta Street, Covent Garden
London WC2E 8LU, United Kingdom
eurospanbookstore.com

Printed in the United States of America

Library of Congress Cataloging-in-Publication Data

Mouser, Bruce L., author.
A black gambler's world of liquor, vice, and presidential politics: William Thomas Scott
of Illinois, 1839–1917 / Bruce L. Mouser; foreword by Henry Louis Gates, Jr.
    pages   cm
Includes bibliographical references and index.
ISBN 978-0-299-30184-2 (pbk.: alk. paper)
ISBN 978-0-299-30183-5 (e-book)
1. Scott, William Thomas, 1839–1917.
2. African American presidential candidates—Biography.
3. Gamblers—Illinois—Biography.
4. African Americans—Political activity—History—19th century.
5. African Americans—Political activity—History—20th century.
6. Illinois—Politics and government—1865–1950.
7. United States—Politics and government—1901–1909.
I. Gates, Henry Louis, Jr., author of foreword.   II. Title.
E185.97.S37M68   2014
977.3´04092—dc23
[B]
2014007451

To

Martin N. Zanger and Darrel Dexter

Without the assistance of these two gentlemen,
I doubt that I would have attempted this project.

Contents

Foreword

Henry Louis Gates, Jr.

Bruce Mouser, in what will be the first major biography of William Thomas Scott, helps answer a question I (and I'm sure many other scholars of African American studies) are asked after class, during Q&A sessions, and at cocktail parties: If Abraham Lincoln "freed the slaves," and Lincoln was a Republican, why aren't the vast majority of African American voters still reliably for the GOP, and when did that shift begin to occur? What Mouser reveals in a painstakingly (and creatively) researched study has less to do with ideology than raw politics, at least in Billy Scott's case, and, as fascinating, it predates the New Deal Democratic Party revolution by a good half century.

As Mouser explains through the maneuverings of a single life, the groundwork for "the switch" was being laid as early as the 1880s and 1890s, when, in the decades after Reconstruction, the Republican Party took "the black vote" for granted to the point that it no longer felt it had to give anything back except to remain the lesser of two evils. The consequences of its indifference were driven home for blacks like Scott when the U.S. Supreme Court, made up entirely of Republican appointees, not only undermined the Fourteenth Amendment's promise of equal protection but struck down the Civil Rights Act of 1875 in the notorious *Civil Rights Cases* of 1883. That wasn't all. On a practical level (the raison d'être of political parties in the nineteenth century), Republican bosses were stingy with their patronage, even when blacks helped swing elections.

It took a man as pragmatic and ambitious as William Thomas Scott to sniff this out. As Mouser shows, Scott spent his life figuring out—and satisfying—men's interests with liquor, gambling, and women, and so, in turn, he was keenly aware of his own interests and refused to be complicit in backing politicians who took him and the broader base of first-generation black voters for dupes. As gifted a speaker as Scott was, he was, first and foremost, a businessman who'd made his fortune (apparently, at one time, the third largest in the state of Illinois) on vice in the former Union navy town of Cairo, Illinois, and over the years, greased enough palms to expect a fair shake in return. So, while Scott continued to have grave misgivings about the Democratic Party's treatment of blacks in the South, in his home state, and increasingly on the national level, he was willing to play ball (interestingly, he was an early and avid sponsor of the sport) even if it only meant pressuring Republicans to reform. Scott's was a gradual though "frenetic" evolution from Republican to Independent ("Negro-wump") to Democratic ally and patronage appointee, Mouser explains, and it was anything but fixed.

The high point of Mouser's drama occurs in 1904, that historic year of the Louisiana Purchase Exposition in Saint Louis, when Scott, at least for a little while, received the nomination for president of the United States on the National Negro Liberty Party ticket, a move he helped orchestrate by convincing his fellow conventioneers to undo their decision to back Theodore Roosevelt's national Republican ticket. Particularly intriguing were the issues at stake for Scott and his allies, including demanding pensions for ex-slaves, what we now call reparations. Many in the political press saw through this as pandering (really, what chances did it have of ever becoming law at the height of Jim Crow?), but with the generation of former slaves aging and dying off, it was, to many, both an offer of hope and an important symbolic reminder that blacks should vote with their wallets instead of out of blind loyalty to Lincoln men, themselves dying off (as Mouser shows, Theodore Roosevelt was anything but sympathetic in reviewing blacks' military pension requests; to T.R., apparently, emancipation itself had been enough of a reward). Obviously, the Liberty Party ticket lost the 1904 election. In fact, Scott only lasted a day on it before the law caught up with him, which is only part of the intrigue of Mouser's book.

As Mouser makes clear throughout his account, Scott was anything but a promising, or even recognizable, politician, because there was no way for him to conceal his past. From his early days as a riverboat steward to his triumphs as a gambling hall operator and hotelier, Scott had made a killing in the liquor and vice industry, and he wasn't interested in reforming himself, despite changing political winds (though he did emphasize his other credentials as owner of the *Cairo Gazette*, the first black daily in the Midwest, and as a real estate maven). In the wake of the 1883 *Civil Rights Cases*, Scott saw the political game for what it was: a game of power, especially to offer and withhold appointment, and in the era before robust civil service reform, he was a major voice in encouraging blacks to think twice before handing their vote over to one party and in showing them they were better off using their vote (even splitting it) in close elections to back candidates who would reward them with jobs and policies and protections against Jim Crow.

Few, if any, today have heard of William Thomas Scott (despite ten different newspapers carrying his obituary), but, after reading Mouser's biography, I realized that Scott deserves more than a footnote. He was a captivating figure of his time who, against all the classic types, was neither a member of the *Up from Slavery* generation in search of respectability like Booker T. Washington nor a college-educated professional in the vanguard like W. E. B. Du Bois. Instead, Colonel Scott was a tough, street-smart, and (because of his business dealings) behind-the-scenes political boss—a "puppeteer" with money, as Mouser describes him—who anticipated interest-group politics and embraced them. While Scott was controversial then, he is all but forgotten now, which is why Mouser's extremely well-researched and well-written narrative strongly merits publication.

Where most historians would be daunted by the lack of primary records (diaries, letters, etc.), Mouser makes valuable use of an array of newspapers now searchable digitally, and he has the discipline and years of experience as a scholar of Africa and the United States to know how to set the proper context while refraining from venturing beyond what his sources will permit. Combined with Mouser's 2011 treatment of Scott's political associate, George Edwin Taylor (and the man who replaced Scott at the top of the Liberty Party ticket), we now have a set of biographies that captures the first pair of black presidential candidates. *A Black Gambler's World* may not appeal to the casual reader, but it will be a valuable source for scholars and devotees of American political history looking to understand the roots of African American party affiliation. It's a cautionary tale and one that should be allowed to illuminate and inform the "Grand Old" story.

Henry Louis Gates, Jr., is the Alphonse Fletcher University Professor at Harvard University and director of the W. E. B. Du Bois Institute for African and African American Research.

Preface

William Thomas Scott's name first surfaced while I was doing research for a biography I was writing about George Edwin Taylor of Ottumwa, Iowa. Scott was nearly twenty years older than Taylor, and he and Taylor had collaborated on many issues at the end of the nineteenth and beginning of the twentieth century. But the story was more complicated than that, and Taylor was as much a part of Scott's history as Scott was of Taylor's. Both were from small cities in the American Midwest, and both were newspaper owners and editors. Both had transitioned from Independent Republican to Democrat at a time in America's history when few of America's black leaders were willing to identify themselves with the political party that had vigorously defended slavery. Scott was vice president and Taylor was president of the National Negro Democratic League between 1900 and 1902, and they had joined arms in numerous other regional and national leagues, serving high offices in most of them. Republican newspaper editors described them as traitors to the party that had liberated blacks from slavery, while Democratic editors hoped that they represented the beginning of a tidal shift from political identification linked solely to emancipation.

Scott's history is one of a complex person who rose from modest origins to national prominence and who involved himself in businesses that could have deprived him of public office and respect. And they did. Scott was a gambler, a bondsman, a hotel owner and operator, a real estate broker and landlord, and an operator of liquor- and vice-related businesses that brought him censure as well as wealth. For a time, others considered him the third wealthiest black person in Illinois. It was he, not Taylor, who was the candidate that the convention of the National Negro Liberty Party chose in 1904 to head that party's ticket for the office of president of the United States, and yet his name is still conspicuously absent from African American political history. The tumult that accompanied his abrupt removal from the National Negro Liberty Party ballot soon after the party convention concluded its business demonstrated that opponents would use his reported misdeeds against him in any political campaign he might attempt.

Searching for information about Scott presented its problems. There were no surviving accounts of businesses he operated and no personal diaries, letters, photographs, or family mementos. He published no books or articles. None of the newspapers he owned and edited survived. Only one article was published about him, and that was written as a guide for Illinois's secondary school teachers and as a lesson plan that could be used in classrooms. Powerful African American voices in large urban centers in the upper Midwest and upon the East Coast overshadowed his accomplishments. He was arrested dozens of times on charges that ranged from selling liquor without a license, to illegal gambling, and to operating "houses of ill repute." In nearly all cases, however, police charges were settled quickly within a city's magistrate court, where minimal records were kept. The only times he spent in jail occurred when he was unable or unwilling to pay a fine.

Despite those significant deficiencies, Scott was not without publicists. Scores of newspapers and their editors printed accounts of his political and especially his nonpolitical adventures because he was an anomaly and because editors as well as readers found him fascinating, audacious, and sometimes startling. He owned a gun, and he used it. He was at the forefront of attempts to move black voters away from blind allegiance to a Republican Party and to set them on an independent course to vote only for candidates and parties that championed issues important to blacks. He was a prominent figure in midwestern black politics in the late nineteenth century and was able to parlay that regional success into considerable influence at the national level. He was well known among black Democrats and became an influential voice within that group at a time when nearly all black voters were Republicans. He founded the Negro Free Silver League of Illinois and the National Negro Anti-Imperialist League and cofounded the National Negro Democratic League, the National Negro Liberty Party, and the National Negro Anti-Taft League. He served on the executive board of the National Negro Democratic League for most of the period between 1888 and 1916. He was an avid convention attendee and an excellent public speaker. He owned and edited the *Cairo Gazette*, which most believed at the time to be America's first black daily newspaper.

This book relies heavily upon newspaper reports for the bulk of information about daily events and for their chronological sequence. Twenty years ago, it might have been possible to read every line in a few newspapers for a span of years, but to claim that one had read through a dozen or more newspapers would have been challenged. That has now changed—at least to a degree. Recently produced databases that contain thousands of the nation's newspaper titles and that are digitally searchable have added considerably to the number of newspapers and accounts that can be consulted for a given event, person, or period and to the volume of information that can be used in this type of historical reconstruction. While searchable databases are fallible, they increase options by drawing attention to opposing sources and interpretations of events. The volume and variety of newspaper reports enhance the value of using newspapers in historical reconstruction. In Springfield, Illinois, where rival papers competed for readers, it was possible to observe how party affiliation influenced reporting, but in small towns, where competing papers did not exist or survive, it was more difficult to see options.

Fortunately, and opportunely, large portions of the *Washington Bee* (African American [hereafter abbreviated as AA]), *Broad Ax* (AA), *Cairo Bulletin*, *Indianapolis Freeman* (AA), *Illinois State Register*, *State Capital* (AA), *Illinois State Journal*, *Inter Ocean*, and *Saint Louis Republic* are included in searchable databases and are sufficiently covered to produce a reliable chronology for onsite study within smaller papers that often reported events in greater detail. More than thirty African American newspapers were consulted for collateral coverage of events within the national black community. The Abraham Lincoln Presidential Library in Springfield, Illinois, has a collection in microfilm format of nearly all Illinois newspapers that have survived. Few of these are included in searchable databases. In this narrative, I have attempted to identify newspapers' political attachments and, as much as possible, to keep newspapers and their writers from becoming participants in Scott's history.

Reports of interviews with Scott about events during his lifetime were complicated. Being a journalist, Scott was protective of information about himself, yet he seemed unconcerned about consistency in what he told reporters. There were two times, however, when Scott lowered privacy barriers that he maintained for most of his life. One of those occurred after his election as chair of the executive committee of the National Negro Democratic League in midsummer 1888, less than three years after declaring his newspaper a Democrat paper. In that interview with the *Indianapolis Freeman* (AA), Scott narrated a story of his youth that tied together the bits and pieces that he had told others. The second came after his appointment as custodian to the Democratic cloakroom at the Illinois legislature in 1905. In that interview with the *Daily Illinois State Journal*, Scott candidly discussed the circumstances following the Civil War that helped him to amass significant wealth and property in Cairo, Illinois. Even his autobiographical entries contained errors that were unexplained.

Nearly every student of nineteenth-century history acknowledges that churches, schools, and fraternal and sororal societies were the three most influential institutions in black society. Leadership in any of those placed one in an elevated status, presumably the black middle class. Preachers called for educational reform and, by default, became spokesmen for their congregations when negotiating with local school boards. Fraternal and sororal societies served as bridges between congregations and as informal schools where men and women learned and practiced skills of communication, community, and politics. Scott acknowledged his membership and leadership in many such societies. Unfortunately, nearly all of these were societies whose membership rolls and rituals were surrounded by secrecy. Rather than deal with his memberships, I chose to focus on Scott's political and commercial achievements.

I have attempted to present a biography for an individual who achieved financial success in business ventures associated with liquor and vice and who was an initiator of independence for black voters at the end of the nineteenth century. At times, it was difficult to identify positive attributes, for he was so certain that his course was honorable, legitimate, and praiseworthy. At the same time, Scott consistently operated businesses that often landed him in court. Scott was practical. He was a hustler who lived in a real world ruled by whites and governed by rules that denied him full membership. He limited himself to a black setting where he could play the game without a racial ceiling. He relied upon his wit, his wealth, his willingness to travel, his speaking ability, and his charm, all of which provided him independence and allowed him to speak his mind. He was as unabashedly interested in patronage as he was in service to constituents. That was the way politics was played in Scott's time and space. He was satisfied to be kingmaker rather than king. And he was willing to reevaluate and move in a different direction—more than once.

This biography is organized along lines that reflect both his place and the nature of what was acceptable in or understandable of the time. The introduction reviews Scott's formative years in Ohio, his work as a barber onboard riverboats upon the Ohio River before the Civil War, and his service in the Union navy at Cairo, Illinois. These were formative years when Scott's adult character took form and when he learned lessons that served him well for most of his career. Chapter 1 focuses on occupations that were open to Scott in Cairo, his early successes in the world of liquor, vice, and gambling, and the alliances he forged in an emerging political world. Chapter 2 covers the golden period of the 1880s, when Scott reached his greatest level of economic success and was secure enough to branch out into journalism and to reevaluate his alliances within the Republican Party and options outside of it. Chapter 3 examines Scott's rapid rise within the ranks of national black Democrats, his attempts to reinvent himself within a national context, and the impacts of temperance and antivice movements upon his economic world. The effects of the Panic of 1893 upon his commercial enterprises, his continuing political activities, and his early attempt to reestablish his commercial base briefly in Chicago and then in East Saint Louis are described in Chapter 4. Chapter 5 details the history of the National Negro Liberty Party, the Saint Louis Convention of 1904, and the debacle of the election campaign. The last chapter deals with Scott's attempts to recover following the 1904 election, his move to Springfield, Illinois, and his statewide and national activities until his death in 1917.

Acknowledgments

I am indebted to institutions and persons with special knowledge of times and places who read my imperfect drafts and gave me suggestions. Murphy Library at the University of Wisconsin–La Crosse permitted me complete access to its collection and its connection through Universal Borrowing to resources throughout University of Wisconsin libraries. This permitted me to conduct research from the comfort of my home and removed the financial burden of frequent visits to distant archives. Especially helpful were personnel at the La Crosse Public Library, whose databases were particularly useful. During the course of data collection, I visited public libraries and archives in Springfield, Belleville, Carbondale, and Cairo in Illinois and relied upon the assistance of others in Granville and Newark, Ohio, to locate obscure sources. Personnel at the Abraham Lincoln Presidential Library in Springfield, Illinois, were very accommodating to my requests. Those at the Special Collections division, Morris Library, Southern Illinois University–Carbondale readily opened their doors and files for my use. Marsha Davis and Monica Smith at the Cairo Public Library shared the secrets of their city. Without their assistance, it would have been significantly more difficult to conduct this research.

I cannot adequately express my appreciation for the assistance of readers who gave me the benefit of their expertise and experience. Retired colleagues from the University of Wisconsin–La Crosse were particularly helpful. These included John Betton, Charles Haas, James Parker, William Pemberton, J. Richard Snyder, Martin Zanger, and Joan Yeatman. Isabel Garcia-Ajofrin Romero-Salazar (Complutense University of Madrid, Spain) commented on international readability. Those who read and commented on the Ohio material were Nikki Taylor (University of Cincinnati), Stephen Middleton (Mississippi

State University), and Rita Jackson (Ohio University–Newark and Denison University). Edwin Hill (archivist, Area Research Center, University of Wisconsin–La Crosse) read parts that covered riverboats and commerce on the inland rivers. Several historians of Cairo made it possible for me to capture the history of black politics in that city. These were Darrel Dexter (Cairo historian), Shirley Portwood (Southern Illinois University–Edwardsville), and Rachel Ensor (Southern Illinois University–Carbondale). Preston Ewing, a life-long resident of Cairo who has read all of Cairo's newspapers for accounts of blacks in that community, critiqued the full manuscript and made invaluable suggestions. Without their help, tolerance, and critical comments, I could not have completed this study. Charles Lumpkins (Pennsylvania State University) provided helpful suggestions regarding black settlement in East Saint Louis, Illinois. For the evolution of black politics in Illinois, I was fortunate to receive comments from Roger Bridges (Illinois State University), David Joens (Illinois state archivist), Christopher Reed (Roosevelt University–Chicago), and Sundiata Cha-Jua (University of Illinois–Urbana). All submitted suggestions, many of which I incorporated. I am responsible for all errors.

Several persons read the full manuscript toward the end of the writing process and provided last-minute suggestions, for which I am very grateful. These include Roger Bridges of Illinois State University; Christopher Reed of Roosevelt University; Joan Yeatman, Martin Zanger, William Pemberton, James Parker, and Laura Godden of the University of Wisconsin–La Crosse; Patrick Killeen of La Crosse, Wisconsin; and Muriel Tillinghast of Brooklyn, New York.

As always, I am most indebted to my wife, Nancy, who tolerates my obsessions and listens to my daily recitations. Without her indulgence and willingness to read, I could not have completed this task.

Abbreviations

AA	African American
AME	African Methodist Episcopal
FBSA	Free Benevolent Sons of America
GUOOF	Grand United Order of Odd Fellows
NAACP	National Association for the Advancement of Colored People
NAAL	National Afro-American League
USS	United States ship
WCTU	Woman's Christian Temperance Union
YPTA	Young People's Temperance Association

A Black Gambler's World
of Liquor, Vice, and Presidential Politics

Introduction

Scott's Foundational Years

It is now time for the Negro papers to speak out, and show that Scott is put up for sale. God save us from them.

Saint Louis Palladium, 16 July 1904

While William Thomas Scott was preparing to attend the second session of the National Negro Liberty Party Convention in Saint Louis, Missouri, on Thursday, 7 July 1904, the front page of the *Saint Louis Republic* was advising that day's visitors to the Louisiana Purchase Exposition to expect a continuation of "unsettled and showery weather." Wednesday had been a warm, rainy, and humid day, and perhaps that, or the fact that more than three hundred delegates from thirty-five states had crowded into the meeting hall at Saint Louis's newly opened Douglass Hotel, explained why delegates of this new political party had selected a ticket unacceptable to Scott.

Scott was the host and chair of this convention, and he should have had a greater impact on its deliberations and decisions. On the positive side, delegates had adopted a number of platform planks important to black Americans, including one that supported a bill then circulating in the U.S. Congress to give pensions to ex-slaves as reparations for condoning slavery. Then living in nearby East Saint Louis, Illinois, Scott had announced that the party would select candidates for the offices of president and vice president of the United States and surely had thought that delegates would choose candidates who were black and who would give black voters an opportunity to express their independence and their manhood. Instead, delegates endorsed the ticket of the national Republican Party, headed by Theodore Roosevelt, who was white and the sitting president of the United States. Delegates either ignored or were unaware of the fact that only a year earlier Roosevelt had summarily dismissed a delegation of

3

black leaders seeking pensions for black veterans of the Civil War, stating that it was enough that blacks had obtained their freedom in 1865 and the right to vote in 1870.

Scott likely obtained only a few hours of sleep between the Wednesday and Thursday sessions, spending much of his time huddled with like-minded delegates and convincing others to reconsider their votes when the convention reconvened. He was, after all, in his own hometown and still the chair of the convention. The ambience of the hall and the convention—and its composition—had changed dramatically by Thursday morning. Delegates had been certified in the first session, but an additional hundred or so delegates had arrived during the night, and that detail was either overlooked or ignored for the second session. After spirited debate, delegates reconsidered Wednesday's votes, removed Roosevelt's name from the party's ticket, and turned to the task of nominating someone who would stand separately as the party's standard-bearer. Those who had supported Roosevelt and the Republican ticket quit the convention in dismay, leaving behind only those enthusiastic for independence. By the end of the day, the convention had selected a different ticket, and this one was led by Scott for the office of president and W. C. Payne of West Virginia for the office of vice president of the United States. The editor of the African American and Republican *Saint Louis Palladium* certainly was impressed enough to sound an alarm and ask his colleagues in the black press to join arms against both the party and its candidates.

How that person—William Thomas Scott, 1839–1917—came to obtain the support of enough political activists to lead the National Negro Liberty Party's ticket in 1904 is the subject of this work. This is the story of a small-town midwesterner's political journey from Republican to Democrat and finally to Independent in a time when black Americans voted Republican and when white Americans chose to forget the promises they had given blacks at the end of the Civil War. It also is an excursion into the crude but lucrative world of liquor, gambling, and vice, which much of American society tolerated in 1865 but sought to eradicate forty years later. It is a voyage through a time when black males obtained equality at the ballot box, only to have those rights denied and their manhood questioned by the end of the century. It personally connects the drama of the Civil War to the tragedy of pre–World War I race riots.

William Thomas Scott was born a free black in Newark, Ohio, on 28 April 1839. His was a large extended family consisting of his grandfather Samuel Scott; his mother, Lucy; his father, whose name is unknown; and his siblings, Henry, Hiram, Wilson, Ann, and Jane. By the time of his birth, the Scott family had lived in Newark for nearly twenty years.[1] Arriving in Ohio before 1820, the

Scotts were among the first blacks to settle in Ohio's Licking County, but that did not necessarily mean that they were welcome there. Neither Newark nor Ohio was a friendly place for free blacks. From the time of statehood in 1803, Ohio's legislature had attempted to block their migration into the state and had passed a number of restrictions that collectively became known as the Black Laws.[2] Ohio's constitution had declared slavery, involuntary servitude, and long-term indentures illegal, but it had identified only white males as voting citizens and did not establish a doctrine of equality or equal treatment. It did precisely the opposite by treating its black residents as sojourners or strangers who enjoyed none of the rights of citizenship, ignoring its free black residents completely. A law—An Act, to Regulate Blacks and Mulatto Persons (1804)— required each black male entering the state to obtain written proof of his non-slave status and to register with a county clerk of the Court of Common Pleas. It stipulated a fine of from $10 to $50 for a person who hired a black who had not obtained a certificate of free status issued by a local official.[3] Blacks already in Ohio at the time of statehood were required to register as well, including the names of all their children. That same law made it unlawful to harbor runaway slaves, and it established procedures for their return to owners in the South.[4] In 1807 the legislature expanded legal restrictions to require newly arriving blacks to secure sponsorship from two whites willing to agree to provide a surety of $500 to guarantee their "good behavior" (that they would not become a burden upon the state) and increased the fine to be levied against an employer hiring uncertified blacks.[5] Blacks were not permitted to marry whites, they were not allowed to serve in the state militia (1829) or on a jury (1831), and they could not give testimony against a white citizen (1807).[6]

The state issued similar restrictions regarding education. Until 1829, schools were privately operated and funded through gifts and tuition, which kept many families of any ethnic origin from sending children to learn the basics of mathematics and grammar.[7] To correct that deficiency, Ohio's legislature in 1829 passed a law that established a statewide and publicly funded school system but at the same time, according to historian Stephen Middleton, "restricted schools to white youths."[8] In the 1830s the Ohio Supreme Court grappled with determining what the word "white" meant and settled on a definition that stipulated more than 50 percent "white blood" and a more indefinable and interpretive one of no "visible admixture."[9] Application of those descriptions was left to the discretion of local authorities, which meant that enforcement varied significantly and depended upon whether that determination was made in the northern part of the state or in the southernmost part, where people from Kentucky and Virginia had settled and where the number of black residents was far above the state average.[10] There, the problem of escaping slaves was constant and vexing to owners and political elites, since that part of Ohio shared a border with two slaveholding states, Kentucky and Virginia.

Located in the geographic center of the state, Licking County, with Newark as its county seat, occupied the middle ground between Ohio's northern and southern regions.[11] Internal district and county politics also reflected that division. Even towns within Licking County took on decidedly different political positions on the question of black residence and migration during the period of Scott's young life. With a population of 4,675 in 1860, Newark leaned to the Democratic camp, although a moderate Republican, William B. Woods, served as its only Republican mayor in 1856 and 1857. From 1858 to 1863, however, years that included the period leading up to the Civil War and the first years of it, Democrats occupied Newark's office of mayor. They opposed the antislavery rhetoric of the abolitionists, but they also opposed the right of states to establish laws contrary to those passed at the federal level. In sharp contrast, the neighboring town of Granville, with a population of 1,285 in 1860, was a hotbed of antislavery sentiment, although a majority of rural residents in the township that surrounded Granville were neutral or leaned to the South on the issues of slavery and states' rights. Granville was located less than ten miles west of Newark, and it had the largest settlement of New Englanders in Licking County.[12]

Two events that occurred in the decade before Billy Scott's birth and two after it illustrate the inconsistent attitude of Licking County's citizens about the presence and status of blacks. The first occurred in Newark in response to decisions made by officials in cities along the Ohio River to enforce the 1807 requirement that incoming blacks obtain the guarantees of two white persons. Between 1807 and 1829 that law had not been strictly applied statewide, and many incoming blacks were unaware even of its existence.[13] Officials at Portsmouth, which was located on the Ohio River, were among the first to apply that law, forcing eighty of their noncompliant blacks to leave that city in January 1830. Officials in Cincinnati gave its black residents thirty days to obtain sponsors or be removed by force.[14] About the same time, two of Newark's three-member board of trustees issued an order that noncompliant blacks should vacate Newark within twenty-four hours. In that instance, Newark's entire black population rushed to the town square, where they obtained the support of A. E. Elliott, the third member of Newark's board of trustees. Elliott convinced the others to rescind the order, at least temporarily, a delay that "became indefinite."[15]

The second was the formation in Licking County of chapters of two antislavery organizations and a physical confrontation between their members in 1836. In 1835 the Anti-Slavery Society, which had strong connections to New

England abolitionists who were demanding that slaves be freed immediately, formed a chapter in Licking County, with the largest number of its members living in Granville. Many residents of Licking County believed that these abolitionists only increased tensions on both sides of the slavery debate through their abrasive language and confrontational tactics and that they were delaying rather than encouraging meaningful resolution of the slavery question. In response to that chapter's formation, a rival group met in November 1835 in Granville to form a chapter of the American Colonization Society, whose members believed generally that whites and blacks could not live harmoniously and as equal citizens within a single polity and that the solution to the slavery issue and the country's Negro problem was to free slaves gradually and to settle them upon Africa's coast, which members believed to be slaves' natural home.[16] Colonization would solve Ohio's problem and provide a destination for all of its black residents. While both societies supported an end of slavery and considered it a "great & growing evil," their solutions to the problem were very different.[17]

Physical confrontation between the groups within Licking County occurred in 1836 when Ohio's Anti-Slavery Society organizers selected Granville as the site of their first statewide convention.[18] Even before the convention convened, however, Granville town officials and sixty-nine other residents who supported colonization as a more reasonable solution signed a petition to prohibit the society's use of Granville's public spaces, with the consequence that organizers moved the convention's meeting hall outside the town boundary and into a barn belonging to one of its supporters. Meanwhile, several hundred opponents from within Licking County—some of whom were likely states' rights advocates who believed that slaves should only be freed at the choice of slave owners—"formed themselves into a mob and drilled up and down the main street [of Granville]," a common enough practice of the day.[19]

When the conference concluded, delegates to the convention and those opposed to it were prepared for battle. Armed with metal hoop rods that had been cut in half, 192 of the convention's delegates marched into town, supposedly as an escort for female delegates who were returning to Granville's Female Academy, located on the opposite side of town. James G. Birney of Columbus, who had been a speaker at the convention and who was to become the Liberty (and antislavery) Party's candidate for president of the United States in 1840 and 1844, rode his horse "slowly and proudly" through the subsequent melee "amid showers of [rotten] eggs which poured in from every side."[20] The Anti-Slavery Society described the battered delegates as "aggrieved victims" of "Mobocracy" and of slavery's proponents and used this event to produce Ohio's first martyrs to the cause of immediate emancipation.[21]

Three years after the so-called Granville Riot and the year that Scott was born, the differences within Licking County and Ohio between those who advocated abolition and those who accepted slavery as a part of the national fabric were made even clearer when Mr. Flood, a representative from Licking County, proposed a series of resolutions in the Ohio General Assembly. These resolutions stipulated five principles: (1) that the Constitution of the United States had been the product of a grand compromise and had given states jurisdiction over slavery within their own boundaries in exchange for a certain date set for the end of slave trading between Africa and the United States; (2) that any action in nonslaveholding states in opposition to slavery was a "violation of the faith that ought ever to exist among states"; (3) that the schemes of abolitionists were "wild, delusive, and fanatical"; (4) that any attempt within Ohio to change the slaveholding system within another state was "in violation of the Constitution of the United States"; and (5) that it was "unwise, impolitic, and inexpedient" to grant equal rights to free blacks then living in Ohio. These resolutions passed the assembly on a resounding vote of fifty-eight yeas and five nays.[22]

The third event, two years after Scott's birth, involved a black man named John who was believed to be a runaway slave. Authorities in Newark arrested him as required by law and brought him before a Licking County court, which was expected to order that John be returned to his rightful owner. In that case, however, abolitionists rallied in support of John and obtained a change of venue from Newark to Granville, where Judge Samuel Bancroft ruled that it was the county's responsibility to prove that John had left his owner illegally and that, having failed to do so, he was therefore a free person.[23] As in the case of the Granville Riot, abolitionists used this incident statewide to generate enthusiasm for their cause. They printed an exaggerated account of abolitionist attorney Samuel White's advice to his client when the trial ended: "Knock off those shackles! No fetters here! John you are a free man! Run, John, run [to Canada] for your life and liberty!"[24]

A fourth event involved representatives from Licking County who were participants in 1850 and 1851 in Ohio's constitutional convention, which came only months after passage of the national Fugitive Slave Act (1850) and when Scott had not yet reached his teen years. Passage of that act effectively marked the beginning of the collapse of the Whig Party at both the state and national levels and the dramatic rise of the Republican Party to replace it. The convention had generally avoided the status of blacks within Ohio, but it did not avoid controversy. Abolitionist delegates from the northern part of the state who were outnumbered by colonizationists and opponents of the antislavery movement placed three motions before the convention, requesting specifically that the word "white" be deleted from those sections pertaining to the militia, suffrage, and public schools. Had those motions passed, they would have granted full legal rights to all of Ohio's male residents, regardless of color. All of Licking County's twenty-three convention delegates voted against these motions.[25] Essentially, a significant majority of Ohio's white residents were unwilling in 1850–51 to even consider equal treatment for blacks and accepted the premise that "the longer the two races occupy the same soil, the greater will be their revulsion and the stronger the prejudice."[26] Those who advocated colonization in Africa or elsewhere held that attitude, as did those who still supported states' rights and constitutional limits on federal powers to regulate slavery in member states. By 1850, 3,836 blacks lived in the northern half of the state, while 21,443 were located in its southern half. Only 128 were living in Licking County, with more than half of those in Newark.[27]

In consequence of the first three of these events and the enthusiasm they created among abolitionist supporters and their opponents, Newark's black population became sufficiently energized in 1844 to form the Colored Citizens Union Society of Newark and Vicinity, although members described it carefully to avoid alienating friendly whites who opposed the divisive rhetoric of the abolitionists and supported colonization and emigration as a more viable solution to the slavery issue. This new society claimed that its purpose was to tend to the "mental and intellectual elevation of the colored people in general" and to guarantee that "the sacred charters of humanity which our ancestors have once sealed with their blood may be forever preserved from the deadly grasp of slavery."[28] Unfortunately, no records from the Newark society have survived to indicate its membership or its attitudes about conditions for blacks within Newark.

Assuming that Newark followed patterns common to the region, public schools, which were mandated in 1829, were open to whoever could afford the luxury of sending children who were otherwise healthy or old enough to enter the workforce—but only if they were white. According to the 1830 census, Billy Scott's grandfather was head of household to a family of six unidentified children under the age of ten and two between the ages of ten and twenty-three.[29] That Scott's children were allowed to attend schools (they were listed in the census as blacks) was highly unlikely. But there is some indication that an unofficial "Newark high school," operated by R. K. Nash as a tuition/subscription and "common" school in the 1830s, was open to the few black students found in Newark. Edward James Roye Jr., the son of a black barber and born in Newark in February 1815, claimed that he had attended high school in Newark during the 1830s.[30] Roye went on to attend Ohio University in Athens, to migrate to West Africa in 1846, and to serve as chief justice of Liberia from 1865 to 1868 and as that country's president from 1870 to 1871.[31] Roye received educational training while in Newark, but whether it was a result of an enlightened community's willingness to violate the spirit of the 1829 law or a consequence of private schooling is unknown. The census for 1850 listed only Samuel Scott within his family as unable to read and write.[32]

But there also was another venue for black education in Newark. That occurred within the Newark branch of the Trinity African Methodist Episcopal Church. William Henry and George Roots, both African Americans and barbers, opened a common and Sunday school attached to Trinity AME in 1844, and that school remained operating—off and on—until blacks generally became accepted in the public schools.[33]

In 1849 the question of education for Ohio's black children was legally clarified. The 1849 law mandated separate schools in areas having significant black populations and ordered that equal tax funds be expended for that purpose. But the 1849 law also permitted mixed-race classrooms in towns where the numbers of black students were small (twenty or less), so long as no white student or a parent objected to black students in classrooms. That law, and the election of a moderate board of education in Newark in 1850, should have opened Newark's schools fully to black enrollment, but that apparently did not occur.[34] Of a total population of 3,528 persons counted in the 1850 census, 822 of Newark's children were attending schools, and only one of those children was listed as a person of color.[35] By the time of the 1860 census, however, those figures had changed, with six students listed as mulatto and one black student, Lorenzo Morgan, attending school, although surviving records fail to indicate that those schools were the same as those established for white students.[36]

Perhaps of equal importance for understanding the importance of Newark and Licking County as foundational for Billy Scott was the presence of several individuals in Newark who shaped the antislavery debate between 1842 and 1862. The most influential of these was Samuel G. Arnold, a New Englander and an aggressive abolitionist who purchased the *Newark Times* in 1855, when Scott was fifteen years old. Arnold renamed it the *Newark North American* and transformed it into a voice of antislavery advocates.[37] A native of New York State, Arnold had obtained some literary fame before moving to Ohio and had run for the United States Senate from Rhode Island in 1853.[38] Arnold did little to gain new white supporters for abolition, especially after he reported in 1860 that Salmon Chase had said that "it was the destiny of the white and black races on this continent to amalgamate and out of that union, was to grow the most mighty and perfect people the world ever knew"—a totally unacceptable solution for nearly all of Licking County's white citizens.[39]

But Arnold did obtain some success among Newark's blacks and within the Scott family. Arnold was the source of a controversial petition produced in Newark and delivered in January 1860 to state senator James Monroe of Oberlin, who was to present it to Ohio's General Assembly, despite a prohibition of such petitions from Ohio's nonvoting blacks. Twenty-eight persons, twenty-one of whom were black residents of Newark, had signed that petition. It asked the Ohio General Assembly to enact legislation that nullified application of the national Fugitive Slave Act of 1850 within Ohio. Among the signers were three of Newark's black barbers, among them William Henry, the partner of Henry Robinson, with whom Billy Scott was taking his barber apprenticeship and one of the organizers of Newark's common school in 1844, and John Clark, who boarded with William Henry and worked in Robinson's barbershop. More importantly, Scott's elder sister Ann also had signed the petition. The *Coshocton County Democrat* printed the names of all of the petition's signers supposedly to satisfy the curiosity of a Licking County farmer but more likely to remind Newark's blacks that they had violated a state prohibition and to warn them that white Ohioans were recording their activities.[40]

Another influential antislavery voice belonged to James Falconer Wilson, who was born in Newark and who practiced law there from 1851 to 1853. Wilson then had moved to Iowa, where he entered politics and served as the Republican congressman from Iowa's First Congressional District from 1861 to 1869. He supported the Radical agenda during Reconstruction. He was considered for appointment to the United States Supreme Court during President Benjamin Harrison's administration.[41]

Another was Willard Warner, a native of nearby Granville, where he was born in 1826. Warner operated the Newark Machine Works in the mid to late 1850s. He was a Republican and a close friend of Salmon Chase.[42] Warner achieved the rank of brigadier general in the Union army during the Civil War and moved to Alabama, where he became that state's United States senator in 1868. He supported the agenda of Radical Republicans during Reconstruction and became one of the Republican Party's most contentious and divisive voices, focusing most of his efforts on securing patronage for his friends.[43]

Salmon Chase was a lightning rod who energized those in Newark who opposed slavery as well as those who supported the principle of states' rights. His was an immoderate voice by any measure. And Chase's connection to Newark is a part of the mythology attached to Newark's education. Folklore still places him as a teacher in an early Newark common school when another famous African American Newark son was obtaining his education.[44] That person was Edward James Roye Jr., who later became the president of the Republic of Liberia.

Between 1839, when Billy Scott was born, and 1856, when he left Newark to practice his newly acquired trade as a barber, his personality and character were formed largely by his environment in Licking County, the circumstances surrounding and following his father's death in 1846, and his nearly ten-year apprenticeship with Henry Robinson.[45] Robinson was a successful barber who reported assets of $3,250 in 1860, a tidy sum for that day (approximately $88,000 in 2010 dollars), which placed him in the ranks of middle-class businessmen, surely enough to have sponsored Scott in a tuition-based school.[46] Robinson had weathered the discomfort of Ohio's Black Laws during the 1830s and 1840s, but national circumstances changed in the 1840s and 1850s, and the position of blacks in Ohio had actually deteriorated with the growth of abolitionism and the passage of new laws at both the state and national levels. Still, Robinson and Scott's elder brother Henry, also a barber, had learned to accept whatever station was given them; otherwise, their professions as barbers in Newark would have been jeopardized. Their customers had been whites, and they remained barbers after Billy Scott left Newark. Robinson and Henry Scott also would have known Edward Roye and the promise of colonization, even if that was to be realized in a faraway land. Scott indicated in 1905 that he had attended high school in Cincinnati, a circumstance that likely would have placed him in close proximity to Peter H. Clark, a noted black educator and political activist.[47] He also claimed in his brief autobiographical sketch, printed in W. H. Hartshorn's *An Era of Progress and Promise* in 1910, that he attended Newark's common school.[48]

Youths, however, regardless of race, tend not to hold tightly to tradition or permit themselves to be restrained by threats of reprisal or economic failure for involving themselves in debates dividing the larger community. William Henry, John Clark, and James Pointer, barbers who worked in Robinson's shop, and Scott's sister Ann certainly were willing to sign a petition in 1860 that a majority of Newark's voters would have considered extreme and risky. Billy certainly knew of the Granville Riot, at least that version that produced martyrs to the cause of abolition. His critics in the Democratic *Cairo (IL) Daily Bulletin* placed him "of old . . . at the feet of [William Lloyd] Garrison and [Charles] Sumner" and described him as a "New England advocate of human rights."[49] Those characterizations were made in 1876 with deliberation and apparently with some knowledge about the circumstances of his youth. It is doubtful that the editor of the *Cairo Daily Bulletin* knew the relevant histories of either Newark or Granville.

While the details of Scott's education and a full list of those with whom he associated in Newark may never be known, there was ample opportunity for Scott to have developed a personality that was self-assured, determined, abrasive, and demanding. His models were not his parents, but Billy was not without mentors. Small-town barbershops are known in male culture as places where politics is always discussed and problems are solved. Whether in Newark or Granville, there were numerous intemperate voices. Two of the most vocal within Newark's black community, obviously, were those of William Henry (Robinson's partner) and Scott's sister Ann.

After finishing his barber apprenticeship with Robinson in 1856 and at age seventeen, Scott operated a barbershop in nearby Coshocton, Ohio, but he remained there for only six months. In 1857 he moved to Cincinnati and in 1859 obtained work as a barber on riverboats that carried passengers on the Ohio and Mississippi Rivers.[50] During the decade before the Civil War, many riverboats were known for their luxurious construction, ornate ball and dining rooms, and magnificent food. Nearly all of the fancy boats had barbershops and, of course, a bar.[51] They were the playgrounds of the wealthy, especially southern planters who sought the diversion, recreation, and pleasure of a cool river excursion during the hot summer months common to the South.[52] On the grander boats, one could expect to be served in grand style by black barbers, stewards, bartenders, and room servants.[53] Some travelers also sought out riverboats for games of chance and general excitement.[54] Such boats attracted professional gamblers/sharpers and pickpockets, although these men, who often traveled in packs, were being made unwelcome in river towns because gamblers used many tricks to fleece their victims, many of whom then sought the assistance of local authorities to recover their lost wagers. River towns increasingly passed laws prohibiting gambling, primarily to rid themselves of crimes that seemed to follow gamblers whenever and wherever they appeared.[55]

The local police and courts viewed riverboats, moreover, as operating on federal territory and therefore outside their jurisdictions, unless the boats were moored to their shorelines and docks. That meant that a riverboat's captain effectively became the legal authority when the boat was in motion, and, as likely as not, he was eager to make his boat popular and free of restrictions for his passengers.[56] Most captains posted signs warning travelers to beware of unscrupulous card sharpers and pickpockets, and captains regularly overlooked the presence of professional and known gamblers and high-class prostitutes.[57] Customers who were interested in the excitement of gambling actually sought out the professionals and the boats that carried them either for the entertainment that they brought to a voyage or to become participants in the game. Gambling also was a great equalizer. According to historian Henry Chafetz, "Europeans who traveled on the riverboats [during this period] were astonished at the equality that existed among traders, plantation owners, the boat's barber, members of Congress, clerks, army officers. One man was as good as another if he had enough money to pay."[58] Gamblers and passengers seemed eager to "bet on anything; they cheated at everything."[59]

Blacks working on riverboats also were participants, but in a different context. A professional gambler quickly learned which bartender would mix drinks to loosen up the gambler's victims while supplying him with drinks that left him unintoxicated. The bartender also was generally the keeper of a fresh deck of cards, which, of course, the gambler had likely supplied in the first place. Mirrors and glassware at the bar were carefully positioned to provide the sharper with an opportune glance at his opponent's hand. Since dining rooms were often used for gambling, stewards produced the environment that best suited the gambler for his game. A room steward or the porter taking luggage to a stateroom was the first person on board that a prospective player would contact. All of those services came at a price. The wealthy tipped handsomely for information, and the gambler tipped for assistance rendered. But the gain often was greater than that. On some boats, blacks received a portion of winnings because blacks were necessary for the game to be successful.[60]

During the time when Scott worked on riverboats, his models were different from those of Newark or Coshocton, and his income was higher than that earned by a barber. He was trained in the tavern business, for many riverboats were little more than floating saloons and gambling halls. Thus, he learned a trade that also was often legal on land, that tolerated the types of persons that accompanied that trade, and that accommodated itself to rules governing the world of liquor, gambling, and vice. The riverboat was a place where pickpockets, con men, and prostitutes collected because victims were many and the risks of getting caught and punished were low. As long as there were many boats plying the rivers, it was easy to depart at the next port before victims realized they had been swindled or their pockets picked and to join a new boat where a new set of victims waited to be fleeced or serviced. If one was caught, restitution generally was sufficient to quiet the anger of victims and satisfy the ship's captain.[61] Or a fine might be imposed, a minor inconvenience easily overcome. At some point, Scott returned to Newark with sufficient assets to build a house for his mother.[62] That certainly could not have happened without income from a source other than wages earned onboard as a barber.

But there also is the possibility that Scott became a gambler in his own right, for, according to historian Thomas Buchanan, "workers played cards, craps and other games of chance with abandon." Worker games generally occurred after payday and probably included blacks of all ranks. Passengers generally found these games a part of the amusement on board and treated the games as entertainment. Seldom did blacks gamble with passengers.[63]

When the Civil War began in 1861, Scott's days on riverboats ended, along with the leisurely excursions upon America's inland rivers.[64] The Union considered the Mississippi River and the Ohio River as front lines in the upcoming war, and it blockaded commerce on both to curtail the smuggling of war matériel southward to the Confederacy. That brought, at least temporarily, a serious economic recession to towns along rivers that had built their commerce upon riverboat trade. Scott established residence in Cincinnati, likely in 1861.[65] Perhaps it was there that he obtained his political voice, for those within Cincinnati's Union Society who supported either immediate abolition of slavery or gradual emancipation and colonization were vocal and public in their disagreements. Scott also was within a larger community where his models increased in numbers and included successful entrepreneurs in businesses other than barbering.[66] Cincinnati also was a center of black education in Ohio, with several schools producing a generation of black leaders, among them Pinckney B. S. Pinchback, who became governor of the state of Louisiana during Reconstruction.[67]

How Scott earned a living during this period is unknown, although a commentator later alluded to his "dark deeds in Cincinnati."[68] But it is known that he married Nellie, likely in 1861 or 1862, and that they had a son, William Edward Scott, who was born in January 1863.[69] Scott obviously was a supporter of the Union when war commenced with the secession of southern states in 1861. Once it became possible for him to join the war, he volunteered for the Union navy, which in 1863 was recruiting in Cincinnati. The navy sent him to Cairo, Illinois, to serve as wardroom steward on board the receiving vessel USS *Clara Dolsen*, a "magnificent" 939-ton side-wheel steamer. Scott was responsible for planning meals and supervising waiters in the officers' mess.[70]

The Cairo that Scott encountered when he arrived at the Ohio River docks and its naval depot in 1863 was very different from the Newark and Cincinnati that he had left behind in Ohio. By the time that Scott arrived to take up his post, the fate of Cairo had already been settled. It had become a fortified camp of Union forces, "second in strategic importance only to the District of Columbia."[71] When war commenced in April 1861, Governor Richard Yates of Illinois had responded quickly to fortify Cairo against rebel seizure and against the real possibility that the most southern part of Illinois, called "Egypt," might attempt to secede from the state and the Union and join the Confederacy as a separate state, with Cairo serving as its capital.[72] Southern Illinois had been a stronghold of Democratic sentiment in the lead-up to the war, and many of its residents defended the principles of states' rights as strongly as did voters in slaveholding states in the South. Yates sent a large detachment of troops from Chicago to Cairo, an act that began a Union occupation and Cairo's transformation into "a haven for Confederate refugees and spies, [and] a vast supply depot for the [Union's] Army and Navy."[73] Large numbers of troops moved from Indiana and Wisconsin into southern Illinois, partly to hold that region against attack and partly to secure valuable transportation networks that would carry the war into the South.[74] If Cairo and Egypt fell to the Confederacy, access to the lower Mississippi River would be closed to Union troop movement. With Cairo in Confederate hands, the upper Mississippi would be open to raids against Saint Louis in Missouri, a slaveholding state that remained within the Union. In consequence, Union strategists considered Cairo as the "key in the West to the conquest of the Confederacy."[75]

By the time Scott arrived in Cairo in 1863, the presence of large numbers of Union troops in or near Cairo also had transformed Cairo's economy. As the southernmost terminus of the Illinois Central Railroad, Cairo became the principal rendezvous for tens of thousands of troops who rode the trains carrying war supplies southward from northern industrial centers.[76] Antebellum plans to develop Cairo as the nation's principal intersection of rail and riverboat commerce for the cotton-based economies of the North and the South were postponed.[77] Rumors circulated constantly about planned rebel raids upon the town, with the consequence that Cairo received enormous political and military attention, and along with that came corruption and financial opportunity. The army designated Cairo as the headquarters of its operations in the west, with nearly twelve thousand troops stationed there by mid-1861.[78] In August 1861 Gen. Ulysses S. Grant moved his headquarters to Cairo.[79] The southernmost tip of the juncture of the Ohio and Mississippi Rivers was transformed into the massive military Camp Defiance.[80]

The character of the camp was unique. Since there were no existing barracks or fortifications at Cairo, arriving troops had to build their own shelters and buildings. Most of the arrivals were freshly recruited with little military training, and they spent much of their time marching and drilling in ankle-deep mud. Nearly everyone believed that the war would be quickly fought, and troops were eager to prove their manhood in battle before the Union and the Confederacy resolved their differences. Local entrepreneurs quickly recognized a potential market for services, whether those included shoes, notions, or libations, boarding, baths, or female companionship. The town changed quickly and radically in response to these new opportunities. The one prewar economy that survived and thrived under these changing circumstances was that relating to liquor, gambling, and vice.[81]

Northern occupation of Cairo transformed it. Before the war, it had been a river- and railroad-driven town of 2,188 inhabitants at the juncture of the two mighty rivers.[82] It was a "rough sort of hamlet," and it smelled mightily, because swamps surrounded it on three sides.[83] Water seepage occurred whenever the rivers flooded, muddying Cairo's streets. Only an elaborate system of elevated plank boardwalks made the town's center passable. Mosquitoes and semitropical fevers abounded. Charles Dickens, writing in his *Life and Adventures of Martin Chuzzlewit* (1843), certainly found Cairo unimpressive, describing it as located

> on ground so flat and low and marshy, that at certain seasons of the year it is
> inundated to the house-tops . . . [making it] a breeding-place of fever, ague, and

death. . . . A dismal swamp, on which the half-built houses rot away: cleared here and there for the space of a few yards; and teeming, then, with rank unwholesome vegetation, in whose baleful shade the wretched wanderers who are tempted hither, droop, and die, and lay their bones; the hateful Mississippi circling and eddying before it, and turning off upon its southern course a slimy monster hideous to behold; a hotbed of disease, an ugly sepulchre, a grave uncheered by any gleam of promise: a place without one single quality, in earth or air or water, to commend it: such is this dismal Cairo.[84]

While Cairo might have been an unpleasant town, it did take on the character of a military post that expected a bit of class and decorum for its army and navy officers. Military wives demanded comforts—and they got them. Stores opened to service those demands, and some described the city as "a place of fashionable resort," perhaps an exaggeration but nevertheless indicating a new town different from that which had existed before the war.[85] Local government seemed to disappear as the town was overrun with "captains, colonels, generals," and speculators.[86] Prices went up, as did rents and property values, and investors erected "a hodgepodge of high-rent shacks" to accommodate the influx of new residents attached to Grant's headquarters.[87] The Union army, as a principal investor, expected the war to last only a brief time, and many buildings seemed built "with the view of early abandonment."[88] Parades were common, as were dances and balls to celebrate a victory or the arrival of someone important. Corruption in the supply of military goods was rampant.

In general, Cairo's prewar promise of becoming someday "an eminent city, a colossal center of progress and business; in a word, to become the key of all the commerce of the south, west, and northwest" was forgotten and replaced with schemes common to towns dominated by the military.[89] Newspapermen reported that "every other house on the levee" was a tavern and that "gambling saloons and bawdy houses" flourished.[90] Newspaper reporters who traveled to Cairo, where they expected an important battle to decide the war's direction, seemed fascinated by Cairo's disorder, its mud, its lack of discipline, and, of course, its "liquor/vice complex."[91]

Scott reported that while in Cairo he worked as a wardroom steward on board the *Clara Dolsen*, a "receiving ship" that was docked permanently at Cairo's Ohio River levee and that was connected to the naval station's recruitment efforts. Newly arriving recruits were processed through a receiving ship before assignment to a crew on one of the many ironclads and tinclads that in 1863 patrolled the tributary rivers draining into the Mississippi River and that were assigned to the Cairo naval depot. The life of a wardroom steward also meant that Scott spent nearly all of his time on board a ship and in close proximity to those in command. A steward was part of "a well-defined skill group" and was similar to a domestic servant who managed accounts and purchased small order supplies.[92] The rank and pay of a wardroom steward was lower than that of a cabin steward but considerably higher than that of a landsman and boy.[93] Scott had enlisted only for an eighteen-month tour, and he was permitted to leave the navy late in 1864 or early in 1865.[94]

Cairo had risen overnight to become one of the largest military posts of the war, and when the war ended, it collapsed nearly as quickly as it had boomed. Cairo's resident population had increased from 2,188 in 1860 to 8,569 in 1865, or nearly 400 percent, only to stabilize at 6,267 in 1870. The military population fluctuated daily as troops moved through the city but approximated an additional ten thousand persons, most of whom were stationed at Fort Defiance. The black population of Alexander County, with Cairo as its county seat, rose from 55 in 1860 to 2,296 in 1865, a whopping 4,000 percent, despite the closure of the Cairo camp for freed slaves in 1863.[95] By the war's end, more than five thousand steamboat dockings had been recorded at Cairo, carrying food and coal and troops and freed slaves either into or out of the war zones. Arthur Cole in his history of Illinois during this period termed Cairo the "Ellis Island" of a migration that brought boatloads of farmers northward.[96] The majority were blacks who crowded the levees in September 1862. The editor of the *Cairo Gazette* sarcastically reported that there were so many blacks in Cairo that "pedestrians found it difficult to peregrinate without lanterns."[97] More than a million men had passed through Cairo, which had become a place where "2,000 'lewd' women gathered on street corners" and where "drinking, brawling, and brutal crimes" were common.[98]

Cairo was unique. Nearly all of its white residents were southerners who held racial attitudes similar to those living in the southern parts of Ohio and Indiana. Its location placed it south of the capitals of the slaveholding states of Kentucky and Missouri and even south of Richmond, Virginia, one of the capitals of the Confederate States of America. It was within thirty-five miles of the Tennessee border and sixty from that of Arkansas, both of which had joined the Confederacy in secession. Yet it became one of only three Union recruitment "yards" along the Ohio River and certainly the most southern point and town of the Union.[99] Had Cairo been left to decide its own fate at the beginning of the war, it likely would have joined the Confederacy as the capital of a divided Illinois. The state and congressional election of 1862 saw an overwhelming Democratic vote in Alexander County: of 863 votes cast, 550 were for Democratic candidates.[100] Instead of following that path, however, it became a command location of both the Union army and the Union navy. That made it the key pin for control of interior waterways and for dividing the Confederacy. That transformation was profound.

A Gambler's World of Liquor, Vice, and Hometown Politics in the Post–Civil War Era

> We never before saw just such a lot of darkies in our life. Uncle Toms, Aunt Cloes and Topseys were abundant. There were about 500,000,000,000 baby darkies.
>
> *Cairo Daily Democrat*, 21 August 1862

When the Civil War ended in 1865, nearly everyone in the North believed that they had preserved the Union and had freed the slaves—and that it was time for their troops to go home. For many, the Union army answered the promise of returning its soldiers to farms and towns in the North almost immediately. It released full regiments one after another and loaded them on river transports or trains for a rapid retreat from the South. But some—and certainly Scott was one of those—found a return to a certain place no longer appealing. Cairo was an attractive option and had more opportunities for success than places left behind when the war began. Cairo had changed and was no longer solely a white town. Nearly all of its population in 1864 and 1865 was connected in some way to military occupation and to a belief that prosperity would continue indefinitely. People had accumulated significant and quickly acquired wealth in businesses that catered to soldiers and their wives and later to newly employed nonmilitary personnel, often in the form of "small, highly specialized establishments" that sold "shoes, clothing, hardware, and other non-perishable items."[1] Billiard halls, drinking saloons, "bawdy houses," gambling rooms, and restaurants also had flourished thanks to Cairo's gender imbalance, caused by the presence of large numbers of single military and river commerce personnel.[2] Even bowling alleys and gymnasiums became popular during and after the war.[3] For William Thomas Scott, Cairo represented a venue where a black man with experience in the liquor and vice businesses just might succeed.[4]

Cairo's commercial world was in transition when the war ended. The war had altered the city's racial composition and had produced a sizable population of 2,083 blacks, a figure large enough to support black-operated enterprises and certainly large enough for a newcomer such as Scott to engage in politics—if blacks were to obtain the right to vote.[5] His customer base was adequate, and his supplies were reliable. Business opportunities—within limits and so long as permissions were obtained from those whites who regulated them—remained, as did the protection that came with a continuing military presence and new rules being applied during a period of national reconstruction and reconciliation.

Still, Cairo had been an occupied city, and it remained so when the war ended, "a southern city, not only geographically but racially."[6] Its total population was nearly a quarter black in 1865, and the divide between the races was palpable.[7] John M. Lansden, who was the Republican mayor of Cairo between 1871 and 1873 and the author of Cairo's standard history, described a prevailing attitude of resignation and paternalism that dominated the thinking of Cairo's white community when he published his history in 1910: "The colored people are here to stay, just as they are throughout the South. The situation is not of our nor of their making. To make the best of it, both races should do all that can be reasonably expected of them. The white people claim to be the superior race. Let them prove their superiority by showing that they can do more than the other race for the situation, concededly more or less difficult and embarrassing."[8]

In his 394-page history, Lansden devoted only two pages to the city's black residents, despite the fact that blacks accounted for nearly 39 percent of Cairo's population in 1900, concluding that "there are a large number of worthless and debased negroes in our population."[9] Another of Cairo's historians made that condescending and dismissive attitude even plainer in 1883: "Cairo was always 'diabolically Democratic,' at least until the 'man and brother' from the cotton-fields and jungles of the South parted company with the swamp alligators and toothsome possums of that region and came upon the town like the black ants of his native Africa."[10]

Precisely when Scott was mustered out of the navy is uncertain, although a newspaper report from 1889 indicated that he had enlisted in 1863 for an eighteen-month tour, and an account from 1866 described an incident in which a woman shot her husband on 26 May 1865 outside a saloon that Scott was operating on Cairo's Commercial Avenue.[11] Cairo also was one of only a few places in the North where the Freedman's Bureau maintained an office, and that may have influenced Scott's decision to remain in Cairo. In 1864 the bureau had built a separate and segregated school for blacks and a hospital specifically to serve Cairo's black population.[12] Also, perhaps the birth of a daughter,

Wilmina, on 11 May 1864 encouraged him to stay put, for Wilmina was un-healthy and died there on 2 May 1865, less than a month after Gen. Robert E. Lee's surrender at Appomattox Court House in Virginia.[13] W.T., as he was generally known in Cairo, and his wife, Nellie, had four children. William Edward was born in Ohio before Scott enlisted in the navy, and their daughters, Wilmina, A.D., and Jessie, were born in Cairo. A.D. was mentioned only once in the records consulted.[14] While pregnant with Jessie in 1869, Nellie was an entrepreneur in her own right. She and T. Smith operated a Ladies' Hair Salon at 121 Commercial Avenue in Cairo's business district. They sold perfumes and hairdressing supplies, as well as Barrett's Vegetable Hair Restorative, which was guaranteed to "promote the growth of hair, prevent the hair from falling out, eradicate dandruff, and keep the scalp healthy."[15]

Scott may have begun his professional career as a barber in Ohio, but he never practiced that trade in Cairo, unless it was a part of his assignment as wardroom steward while attached to the *Clara Dolsen*. Once he was mustered out of the navy late in 1864 or early in 1865, however, he involved himself in businesses that required little inventory and that thrived in military towns and river ports. Within a year of his discharge, he was operating a profitable saloon that served a black clientele, but not exclusively so, and, according to an inter-view Scott gave in 1905, "for a long time he conducted one of the largest colored gambling houses in the country."[16] Within five years he had opened the Metro-politan Hotel, which he advertised in 1870 as "the only first-class place of enter-tainment in the West for the accommodation of colored guests."[17] Within the hotel were an ice-cream parlor, a dancehall, and a billiard parlor. Scott invested in real estate and "shortly controlled considerable wealth."[18] Scott also was a "bondsman," a profession at which he "made considerable money."[19]

In a 1905 interview, Scott admitted that the person most responsible for his financial success at Cairo was Capt. William Parker Halliday, a white Ohioan and a Democrat who was ten years his elder and who became one of Cairo's wealthiest merchants, bankers, and hoteliers following the Civil War. Halliday had been a steamboat captain on the Ohio River before settling in Cairo in 1860. His brothers operated passenger and freight "steamers" out of Cincinnati.[20] Halliday and George Washington Graham, his business partner in Cairo, ac-quired considerable wealth during the war by obtaining a "perpetual" lease and a rental payment of $1,000 per month for the Union's use of their large wharf-boat as headquarters of the western navy. It was docked alongside the *Clara Dolsen* on the Ohio River levee at Cairo.[21] Halliday also owned many steam-boats that carried supplies and troops in and out of the war zones. He claimed to own assets of $80,000 ($1.38 million in 2010 dollars) by 1870. In 1865 he built the Riverlore Mansion, which still stands as a Cairo landmark.[22] According to the 1905 account, Scott approached Halliday directly for advice and obtained repeated loans, "often amounts as large as $3,000 and $5,000," to finance his bondsman business at a time when few blacks could obtain loans from any white-operated bank or lending operation.[23] Scott claimed that he had sought a Republican partner, but every Republican he contacted had turned him down.[24]

When the census enumerator interviewed Scott in 1870, he claimed he owned real estate valued at $1,500 ($26,000 in 2010 dollars) and personal property at $2,000. While considerably less than Halliday's, these sums were substantial for a black man who was thirty years old in 1870 and more than the reported wealth of dentist A. G. Holden and physicians W. R. Smith and Joseph Hennard, all of whom were white.[25] And the amount was in stark contrast to the majority of Cairo's blacks, who reported wealth of less than $50 per household. Underreporting of wealth in census records was common, then as it is now, with less than 10 percent of all of Cairo's residents reporting any wealth at all. Only one other black resident, Thomas Freeman, a "saloon-keeper" and Scott's lone black competition in Cairo's liquor/vice complex, approximated Scott's gross worth. Only seven blacks indicated that they owned real estate in 1870.[26] Scott's business success gained him respect and status within the black community and recognition within the white. Editor John Oberly of the *Cairo Daily Bulletin*, the city's principal Democrat newspaper, certainly noticed, describing Scott in 1870 as "one of our most energetic colored citizens."[27]

Tavern management and bondsman were common professions available to blacks in the Midwest, especially in those towns where large numbers of blacks had settled.[28] In 1865 the urban Midwest was, after all, still an ethnically diverse part of the nation, with new immigrants still speaking their own languages and enjoying their favorite brews in taverns operated by their own countrymen. Tavern management only required a small economic investment, for there were minor overhead costs and a limited inventory of goods waiting to be sold. Saloon owners also could purchase liquor on credit from suppliers, which meant that they generated sufficient profits through sales to cover costs before payment to suppliers became due. In Brooklyn, Illinois, near East Saint Louis, Saint Louis's sister city on the Illinois side of the Mississippi River, saloon ownership was "popular" among the black "political elite" and was considered, according to historian Sundiata Cha-Jua, "one of the few lucrative avenues easily accessible to Black entrepreneurs."[29] The same circumstance prevailed in Chicago with Daniel Webster, a black saloon keeper who operated a tavern on the levee and was a bondsman who also "made money by having his corrupt police friends arrest the patrons of his saloon, whom he would then charge to get them bailed out of jail."[30]

The profession of bail bondsman, on the other hand, did require a greater investment. Essentially, on request, the bondsman provided the court a sum of money to guarantee that an accused person would appear in court for a trial or a judgment. Once that bond was paid to the court, the accused was free to move about until his or her presence in court was again required. When the accused appeared in court, the bondsman concluded his business by collecting his bond filed with the court and the fee charged for his service. In Scott's case, his likely arrangement with the court allowed him to appear in the client's stead as the defendant's lawyer, to plead his client guilty as charged, and to pay the client's fine. In such an arrangement, the bail bondsman would collect one fee as bondsman and another as his client's lawyer. If his client appeared in court without a lawyer, the bondsman still collected his fee as bondsman. To ensure that the bondsman not lose his bond or fee, the bondsman, as in Scott's case, generally collected his fee or fees in advance, as well as the known fines to be given by the court, before the bondsman provided the court with the requested bail.[31] In this arrangement, the return on investment for his services was large, constant, and hardly traceable.

Black and white attitudes in the late 1860s and 1870s about saloon owner-ship and alcohol consumption among blacks were ambivalent.[32] Abolitionists had generally argued that slave owners had used alcohol as a "sedative" to produce a passive slave and to keep him or her from developing skills of self-restraint and self-control and the will to rebel. Those were not attributes aboli-tionists wanted in a liberated black. This attitude contrasted with that held by slave owners who believed that alcoholic consumption led to rebellion, crime, and aggression. For the most part, Cairo's blacks after 1865 accepted the premise of "controlled toleration" because saloon ownership provided employment and an infusion of income, neutralized the city's gender imbalance of men to women, and served a societal need.[33] Moral considerations were reserved for a later day. Besides, vice in Cairo was restricted to the city center, the levee, and Commercial Avenue and away from the city's schools and residential areas.

Scott's entry into the "underworld" of liquor, gambling, and bondsman services—and vice, which by default surfaced around and within his businesses— was contingent, however, upon his adherence to rules and obligations established by others who governed that sector of Cairo's economy. Historian Herman Lantz described that sector as providing Cairo's "most stable and predictable source of revenue" before the Civil War, and it increased its relative impor-tance during and after it.[34] One advantage of this sector was its immunity to economic downturns that affected manufacturing and consumption. The high numbers of transient young males living in boarding houses near the city's levee meant that demand for its products and the services associated with those products remained high.[35] Still, it was not a sector that one could enter without risk or without regulation. Saloon owners in Cairo formed a trade association or syndicate that decided who could open a saloon and under what circumstances. During the war, military authorities attempted to curb the growth of this sector but failed primarily because of high demand and because it was impossible to control the influx of vagrants, pickpockets, thieves, and prostitutes that saw economic opportunity and took it. The majority of Cairo's prostitutes operated from street corners or within or outside businesses where they and their pimps paid the owner a fee for the privilege of soliciting customers.[36]

Nor was Cairo's city government in a mood in 1865 to eliminate this sector from its economy. In 1865 saloons provided vital revenue to the city, with license fees increasing from $50 in the 1860s to $100 and $200 in the 1870s, reaching a high of $500 ($11,200 in 2010 dollars) per annum for each of the seventy taverns operating in the city in 1883.[37] The city's revenue report for 1887 indicates that more than half of Cairo's governmental revenue came from saloon license fees.[38] Cairo also received income from fines imposed by the city's courts. Most of these involved misdemeanor offenses associated with vagrancy, drunkenness, fighting, disorderly conduct, and prostitution. Cairo's police sent most of those arrested to the magistrate or police court, where the presiding judge almost always found the person guilty, imposed a fine and costs, and set the person free so he or she could return to practice his or her trade. Few of these cases made it to the circuit court, which required a trial and produced a felony record.

Cairo's police force was small and inadequate to control the large numbers of saloons and other businesses that made up the city's liquor/vice business. Yet policemen tolerated and even encouraged it. They essentially ignored minor legal infractions and concentrated on problems that involved violence and drunkenness, which generally ended up with fights or loss of life. Some policemen were investors or participants in the liquor/vice complex and were reluctant to enforce laws that would interfere with this economy. They also accepted bribes.[39] Economic success soon after the war helped establish Scott's credentials in Cairo.

Scott's business success, however, was far removed from the political role he was later to play in Cairo and the state. Two issues that dominated black objectives in the 1865 to 1870 period were voting rights for the city's black males and the quality of schools for Cairo's black children. In 1869 the Fifteenth Amendment to the United States Constitution, which would grant voting rights to black males, was making its way through the states for ratification, and everyone in Cairo knew that its ratification would dramatically change Cairo's political landscape. Almost all Democrats opposed the amendment, with those

Democrats in nearby Indiana campaigning on a party platform that bluntly stated that "government was formed *for* white men, in the *interest* of white men . . . *by* white men," leaving little doubt that neither blacks nor women should campaign for voting rights in that state.[40] California and Oregon initially opposed the amendment because they believed it would grant voting rights to Irish and Chinese immigrants. Ratification was a principal condition for re-entry to the Union for the states of Georgia, Texas, Mississippi, and Virginia, and that alone may have been sufficient to guarantee the twenty-eight ratifications necessary for it to be accepted as a part of the nation's Constitution. Yet, even with that stipulation, Members of Georgia's legislature voted against ratification in July 1869 and waited until 2 February 1870, only one day before a sufficient number of states had agreed to the amendment's provisions, before changing their minds and ratifying it. Other states were equally reluctant. Delaware finally ratified it in 1901, followed more than half a century later by Oregon in 1959, California in 1962, Maryland in 1973, Kentucky in 1976, and Tennessee in 1997. Cairo's Democrat *Evening Bulletin* wrote in July 1869 that Radical Republicans were forcing "negro suffrage upon an unwilling people."[41]

Republicans as a party were a numerical minority within Cairo and Alexander County before the war, and that changed little in the years immediately following it. The internal workings of that party were tightly controlled by a select group of lawyers and businessmen who either had their origins in New England or had received federal appointments at Cairo during the Lincoln and Johnson administrations. They bided their time, waiting for a tidal change that surely would come with black enfranchisement and that would increase the number of voters in Cairo by more than a third. In anticipation of that change, and to maintain their control over its consequences once it happened, party officials began to search for blacks who could bring these new voters to the polls as Republicans and who could keep them there. They met with black leaders, including Scott, in July 1868, nearly two years before ratification of the Fifteenth Amendment, to encourage organization of Republican clubs that would tie new voters to the party.[42]

The churches were one of the natural places to find such leaders, but Cairo's black preachers were controversial and contentious. Cairo's black churches were divided historically and regionally into those that leaned to the North and were populated by people from the upper Midwest who had never been slaves, and those who came from the South who were aware of and sympathetic to issues important to people from small towns and farms. One issue that should have brought agreement among Cairo's black preachers was the lack of schools for Cairo's numerous black children, but even that brought discord. In the fall of 1867 the Reverend Thomas Jefferson Shores of the First Missionary Baptist

Church, whom historian Christopher Hays described as most "influential among migrants from the rural south," met with Alexander County officials to discuss education. When that meeting ended, Shores believed that he had received assurances that county and public support for a separate black school would be forthcoming. Shores rushed to form a board of directors and establish the Colored Union School, which would be located in his church, with himself as its principal and teacher, at least until others could be hired. Not to be left out, the Reverend Thomas Strothers of the African Methodist Episcopal Church (AME), who "appealed to natives of the North" and who, according to Hays, "had [already] engaged in numerous bouts of public character assassination" with Shores, announced his intention to open a similar school in his own church.[43] At that time Strothers was working with other black leaders at the state level for similar purposes and was one of the organizers of the State Convention of Colored Men, which met in Galesburg, Illinois, in October 1866 to discuss the same problem.[44]

When officials failed to deliver support for Shores's school, a large group of Shores's black students and parents staged an occupation of Cairo's Thirteenth Street Grammar School in October 1867 and demanded that either their children be admitted to that school or that adequate support for a separate school be delivered. The reaction from Cairo's white community was swift. Shores's life was threatened, and nothing changed. The *Cairo Daily Democrat* of 17 October made its position, as well as that of a majority of Cairo's white residents, perfectly clear: "Every negro in Cairo of ordinary reasoning faculties knows that the time will never come when white and black children will be educated under the same roof, in the same room, and by the same instructor. Natural, mental, and physical differences and incompatibilities render this impracticable—forever impossible."[45]

With the churches and their ministers so contentious and identified by the white community as troublemakers, Republican leaders also turned to persons who were not so involved with church business and who were still known and had levels of respect as leaders in Cairo's black community. Among those were John J. Bird and W. T. Scott. Bird was born in Cincinnati, Ohio, in 1844, but he had spent several years in Windsor, Ontario, Canada, before moving with his wife and children to Cairo, where he became a close associate of the Reverend Strothers. He also was active at the state level with black groups that dealt with disabilities and education, and he had accompanied Strothers to the Colored Convention held at Galesburg in October 1866.[46] He had received his formal education in Cincinnati before the Civil War.[47] Cairo's blacks respected him, and he had political ambitions in the city. He was studying to become an attorney. Editor Oberly of the *Bulletin* was impressed, describing Bird as a scholar, an eloquent speaker, and an intelligent politician and in 1869 as "a black bird with good strong wings . . . [who] is sure to fly high."[48] Bird and Scott represented different constituencies within the black community, but both were articulate, and, at least for a time, they were willing to work together and to submit to the white leadership of the county's Republican Party.

But the greater worry among all of Cairo's white politicians was the possibility that Scott, Bird, and other politically attuned blacks, once they obtained the right to vote, would form an "out and out Negro ticket" and that black voters, when they numbered nearly a third of the eligible voters, might vote only for black candidates. Even Democrats had warned that 1870 might bring "the last white man's election."[49] On 4 February 1871, after ratification of the Fifteenth Amendment to the Constitution, Editor Oberly of the *Bulletin* (Democrat) reported that Scott, whom he described as a "prominent colored Radical," Thomas Shores, "an unscrupulous nigger politician" who was considering a run for the office of mayor, the Reverend Jacob Bradley of the Second Baptist Church, running for alderman, and John Bird, "a vindictive colored cuss" running for city clerk, had combined to form a "Colored Man's Party," which would "put into the field a full ticket."[50] That prompted a letter from a Democrat writer who appealed for all whites—whether Republican or Democrat—to unite against any "colored" party that "'Bill' Scott, Bradley and Shores" might lead.[51]

Editor Oberly echoed that sentiment, identifying Scott as "one of the leaders of the Republican party of Cairo" and warning that "nearly all of the votes of the negroe [*sic*] electors" would be cast for a "colored" ticket if such a party or list of candidates were to emerge.[52] To emphasize that point, Oberly noted that Republican leaders would be forced publicly to support Scott for city marshal, otherwise "he will go back on them hereafter."[53] Certainly in an attempt to forestall such an outcome, the *Bulletin* published a list of candidates belonging to its own and quickly fabricated "Citizens' Ticket," which contained only the names of whites and included several prominent Republicans among them but excluded Scott's name and any of his fellow black candidates.[54] When votes were tallied on 28 February, the Citizens' Ticket had won every contest. Scott had obtained 334 of 1,079 votes cast for the office of city marshal, approximately 30 percent, which roughly was the percentage of total black voters in the city.[55]

Scott's defeat at the polls in 1871 was the least of his worries for that year. His daughter's birth in 1870 may have led to complications for his wife, Nellie, for she was no longer mentioned in the record after Jessie's birth. Indeed, on 22 April 1872, Scott married Lizzineky Jenkins of Massac County in the town of Metropolis.[56] Lizzy was twelve years W. T. Scott's junior. There is no indication that he and Lizzy had children, but Lizzy was responsible for young Jessie, who apparently was not healthy and died on 27 August 1876 at age six.[57] The status of William Edward Scott, W.T.'s son, who was nine years old in 1872, could not be determined by current research.

Meanwhile, John Bird quickly recovered from his first defeat in politics. Rather than compete at the local level, he focused his activities at the state level and attended, as a delegate-at-large for the state of Illinois, the National Colored Convention, which met in Saint Louis, Missouri, in September 1871 to determine a day on which to celebrate the Emancipation, to discuss education for blacks, and to determine a strategy for the upcoming 1872 national election.[58] A month later, Bird was one of four delegates from Alexander County to attend a special state Republican convention called to fill a seat vacated in Illinois's First Senatorial District.[59] Bird's acceptance as a regular voting delegate rather than as an alternate caught the attention of the *Bulletin* (Democrat), which now demonized him as a "venomous fellow" who "domineers over his fellow-citizens of the blackcolor" while being "domineered by the white radical clique."[60] Bird was becoming a team player.

Scott also learned lessons from his first forays into politics, lessons that built barriers against rather than opportunities for cooperation with whites within the Republican Party. The most important lessons were that blacks could not depend upon white allies to support black candidates and that alliances would always place black leaders in subordinate positions within established parties. If Scott hoped to become a player within local politics, he would have to accept that as given and assume that patronage, respect, and rewards would eventually flow downward to him and other blacks in exchange for that support. Race constituted a critical factor, because a substantial number of whites, whether Democrat or Republican, would never vote for black candidates. Nor could Scott depend upon black colleagues to form a cohesive, temperate, and reliable alliance. Shores, for example, had indicated his interest in the office of mayor, but he withdrew his name twice, in 1871 and again in 1872, both times within days of the elections. The Reverends Shores and Bradley, moreover, were bitter rivals.[61]

Scott also carried negative baggage that would keep him from obtaining any elected position in city and county government. While he was involved in several businesses in which black people were allowed to participate, these businesses nevertheless were ones that gained him little respect within either the black or the white community, especially among those groups opposed to his enterprises on moral grounds—unless, of course, he made generous contributions to those groups' causes. The police arrested him occasionally, though as long as he paid his fines and court costs, they permitted him to resume his business until the next time. Shores, in contrast, had the support of a large constituency of churchgoers and the goodwill of those who opposed gambling and alcohol consumption.

The year 1872 began calmly enough, with Shores and Scott joining forces on a question of increasing black participation in Cairo's public schools. Illinois's new constitution, ratified in 1870, had stipulated that blacks were to have equal access to education, and in 1872 the state legislature had spelled out that provision more plainly in an "equal education" law.[62] To test that law and to guarantee greater black access to Cairo's schools, Shores and Scott announced in April 1872 that Shores would become a candidate for director of Cairo's schools and Scott, a member of its board of trustees. Both reluctantly withdrew their names from consideration, however, when Col. John Wood, the Republican candidate for mayor of Cairo in 1872, exerted pressure on them to remove their names from the ballot.[63] Oberly of the *Bulletin* used this dustup to at least encourage a division between white and black Republicans, suggesting that Wood believed that "colored men should not aspire to any office and ought to be satisfied with the privilege of voting."[64]

Later in that year, the divisions within the black community and within the local Republican Party in Cairo and nationally became even more visible when the national Republicans fractured into two parties, with one supporting the reelection of sitting president Ulysses S. Grant and the other the candidacy of newspaperman Horace Greeley, editor of the *New York Tribune*, who had long been an opponent of slavery and an early supporter of Reconstruction. Greeley, along with Charles Sumner and others, had broken with President Grant in 1872 over the issues of corruption and mismanagement and Grant's failure to "renationalize" whites in the South. Greeley was convinced that Grant was the captive of a small group of advisers who had isolated him from the realities of Reconstruction, which Greeley thought was crippling the South. Greeley also accused Grant of bankrupting the country through lack of control over pensions and patronage and of manipulating currency at the cost of farmers and workers, all issues that dominated the way that politics operated following the war. Without major reform and an end of Reconstruction, according to Greeley, the South could not develop. Nearly all Democrats agreed. Following the Republican Party's Philadelphia convention, which selected Grant as that party's candidate for a second presidential term, Greeley supporters and Grant opponents met in Cincinnati, where they formed an opposing Liberal Republican Party and produced their own slate of candidates, with Greeley as the new party's standard-bearer. Remarkably, the national Democratic Party, then in disarray, endorsed the Greeley ticket and its liberal platform, and it ran no person of its own for the national office in 1872.[65]

The Cairo branch of the Republican Party supported Grant for reelection partly because his official residence was at Galena, Illinois, and partly because he was still considered to be the hero of Cairo. Oberly of the *Bulletin* described Bird and Scott, who were building their leadership roles among black Republicans, as subservient "tools" to lead Cairo's new black voters to the Grant ballots at the polls.[66] But not all of Cairo's blacks remained loyal to either Grant or the main party. Shores supported Greeley's candidacy and carried with him most of his "southern" black constituency. At the Alexander County Administration Convention (Republican), which convened in Cairo in mid-July 1872 to select delegates for the upcoming congressional district convention, blacks outnumbered whites, and Scott, according to the *Bulletin*, "had the effrontery" to participate directly in debate and demonstrate his independence and the newfound importance of the black vote. For his loyalty to the party and to President Grant, Scott, according to the *Bulletin*, "was thrown the empty honor—a sop you know—of alternate delegate" to attend the district convention.[67] Whether the gesture was a sop or not, Scott was becoming a player in the game.

A direct confrontation between Scott and Shores came a few days later at a barbecue benefit for Cairo's AME church. One of several speakers, Scott openly criticized Shores for his support of Greeley and accused him of splitting the black vote for a candidate that Democrats also had endorsed. Scott was a street fighter who overreached in this instance "by attacking Rev. Mr. Shores' reputation for chastity while he was in the army."[68] Shores responded with an equally intemperate letter printed in the *Cairo Daily Bulletin*, comparing Scott to the biblical Balaam and Judas. Shores wrote:

> This Scott is a fiend in human shape to abuse a man who never did him wrong. . . . I need not refer to his dark deeds in Cincinnati and St. Louis. His moral character is known here. . . . I would not trust such a man at the Lord's supper; he would steal the meal and run away with the table cloth. He appears to be like Saul of Tarsus, who, while he was persecuting the Christians did not know he was fighting against God; and Scott, in his present course, is either villainous for gain or in ignorance is sinning against light. He will find that he will fail. Light is stronger than darkness, and the good cause will triumph in spite of all the corrupt and ignorant Scotts in the country.[69]

Editor Oberly, a Democrat, gleefully printed all letters, enjoying the spectacle of a black gambler and a black divine battling it out in print. Oberly now elevated Scott to the rank of lieutenant in "Captain [Patrick H.] Pope's Bedouins" and, while describing him as "a really sharp and money-getting fellow," also claimed that Scott and his fellow Bedouins or black party enforcers were threatening blacks with violence if they voted for Greeley.[70] At the time, Pope was head of the county's Republican Party. Once convinced that Scott had acquired status within the party, Oberly focused his pen upon Scott and left it there.[71] That focus had the unanticipated effect of improving Scott's status within the party and his acceptance as a leader in Cairo's black community.

Scott's confrontation with Shores also affected Scott's businesses. Cairo's black community was already split between two Republican Parties, and many disapproved of Scott's verbal and public battle with Shores and Scott's threats. He had enemies who had lost money at his establishments, even though gambling was illegal—although it was generally ignored by the police. He also was a bondsman, a profession generally considered as exploitive. The building containing Scott's tavern, billiard room, dance hall, ice-cream parlor, and Metropolitan Hotel was set afire on 27 November 1872, but firefighters arrived quickly enough to save the structure. Scott would not again become a hotelier until late December, when he reopened at Hickey House on Fourth Street.[72]

A second fire, this time at Hickey House, was set three months later, on 19 March 1873.[73] In that instance, the house burned to the ground, and Scott's loss was "in the neighborhood of $1,000," approximately $19,000 in 2010 dollars.[74] Scott did not fault Shores's followers for this fire. Instead, he brought legal charges against three black men, among them Thomas Freeman, Scott's major commercial competitor, who owned a tavern and dance hall large enough to host minstrel shows traveling up and down the rivers. During the trial, one of the defendants testified that he had attended a show at Freeman's dance hall, but he had taken a room at Scott's hotel because "Scott had all the women." The court ruled that there was insufficient evidence to prosecute any of the defendants.[75] But Scott's troubles were not yet over. Two days after the fire, Scott was charged with "maintaining a gambling house" and set free on a five-hundred-dollar bond to await a trial by jury.[76] Rather than withdraw from his businesses, Scott chose to increase his investments by purchasing the land where the Metropolitan Hotel stood on Commercial Avenue and building an even grander hotel that would contain most if not all of his enterprises. That building was completed in July 1873 and was celebrated with a reception in its "grand ball room" with free lunches and fine wines and liquors.[77]

Despite these significant setbacks, Scott and his allies were not so intimidated that they retreated from their political ambitions. Bird, who was ingratiating himself at a different level within the party than was Scott, announced that he would run for one of the two offices of police magistrate (a four-year term) in the 1873 city election, and he won that contest in a four-man race with 398 votes out of 991 votes cast, the approximate number of blacks voting.[78] While a relatively minor post, the police magistrate was the judge that received defendants directly from the police department and dealt with issues such as civil disorder, drunkenness, and assault. Oberly of the *Bulletin* had only good words about "Squire" Bird's court in the months following his election despite numerous calls from citizens and even policemen for nullification of Bird's election on the grounds that only a white magistrate should judge whites.[79] Mayor John Wood, a Republican, refused to change the established pattern of assigning cases to the two magistrates on an alternate-day basis regardless of race, and Oberly agreed with Wood. On 5 June Oberly reacted aggressively and negatively to an editorial that appeared in the *Mound City Journal*, a nearby Democratic paper that accused Oberly of being a "Negropholist."[80] Southern Illinois, after all, was still a part of Egypt and was very southern in its approach to questions of race.

Bird's election, and the failed attempt to nullify it, marked a turning point for Bird and Scott and for black voters in Cairo in general. Responding to changes in Cairo's politics and growing demands from the black community for patronage to the party faithful, Illinois's Republican governor, John L. Beveridge, had already appointed Bird as a trustee of the newly created Illinois Industrial University, the early name for the University of Illinois, a position he held from 1872 to 1880.[81] Until that time, most whites had assumed that blacks were incapable of governance and that they could not win elections when a significant majority of voters were white. Yet in less than three years after ratification of the Fifteenth Amendment, a black person in Cairo had been elected to a public office and had been appointed to a patronage post that interacted directly with white clients. And the sitting mayor and the influential editor of the *Cairo Bulletin* had defended Bird when his election was challenged by white voters. Those were major accomplishments both locally and statewide. Black voters also had demonstrated that, if they voted as a bloc and if there were more than two persons running for an office, they might win elections. Those lessons were not lost within Cairo's Republican leadership. If the party expected to retain those voters, it would need to recruit and involve more black leaders within the party structure.

Nor was that lesson lost on Editor Oberly of the *Bulletin*. In March 1874 Oberly reported that an assembly of several hundred blacks had met at Scheel's Hall to commemorate the death of Senator Charles Sumner of Massachusetts, who was author of the civil rights bill then working its way through Congress. Scott, Bird, John Williams, and John Gladney spoke to the crowd on national issues because Sumner had been a national rather than a local figure.[82] Oberly was impressed. When Thomas Freeman, Scott's old adversary in the tavern business, wrote a scathing letter attacking Scott and accusing him of intending to announce his candidacy for a position on the city's council only among black voters and to "slip into the council" before opposition against him could be organized, Oberly replied with a rejoinder:

> It will be seen by Mr. Freeman's card published in another column, that Mr. William Scott, the colored saloon man, will be a candidate for the Council in the first ward. Mr. Scott is, as Mr. Freeman has said, a sly gentleman. He is a necessity to the republicans of this city, and will probably receive the support of the leading white men of that party. Major Munn dare not oppose him, and Mr. Pope will not. Mr. Fisher may. We think he will. Mr. Scott attempted to elect a colored man to Mr. Fisher's seat in the board of education, and Mr. Fisher may come to the conclusion that revenge is sweet, and support a white man against Mr. Scott.[83]

Nor was the lesson of Bird's election lost on Scott. Bird had proven that blacks could be elected to public office if the candidate were right and if there were more than two persons contesting for the seat. Scott, however, made his living in businesses that attracted attention, most of which was negative. He also had made enemies in 1872 when Cairo's blacks split their votes in the presidential campaign. Scott, moreover, was aware that the temperance movement was gaining ground locally and was openly characterizing his dance hall and tavern as "dens of iniquity" that were frequented by "lewd men" and "lewd women" who were controlled by "erring brothers" and "erring sisters," all of whom were still capable of being saved.[84] Instead of contesting for elective office, Scott chose to involve himself at a deeper level—behind the scenes as a puppeteer within Cairo's black community.[85]

That strategy paid dividends almost immediately. When local Republicans met in convention in August 1874, party leaders confirmed Scott's change of tactic and permitted him to participate fully in its deliberations. Whether as a result of some designation given him by the party or a rank that Oberly arbitrarily assigned him, the *Bulletin* recorded him as "Col. Wm. T. Scott."[86] Nearly everyone within Cairo's Republican leadership had served as officers in the Union army during the war, and they openly flaunted their ranks to gain voters and deference. Perhaps Scott's new title was little more than a promotion from captain to colonel within the ranks of "Pope's Bedouins" or an attempt to give him honorific status and membership among fellow party leaders. Perhaps, as Cairo folklore suggests, it represented nothing more than a clever transposition of the "col.[ored]" that regularly appeared in Cairo's city directories from the back to the front of his name.[87] Whatever the explanation, the designation of "Col." stayed with Scott through much of his political life. Scott also was elected as an alternate delegate to the district conference to be held in nearby Mound

City, where the party would select candidates for legislative seats at the state and national levels.[88] Still, there must have been discomfort and a certain sting when Oberly wrote that Pope, the leader of Cairo's Republicans, "pulls the wires and makes Bird, Gladney and Scott dance to the political tune he whistles."[89]

The years 1875 and 1876 proved difficult for Scott, despite passage of the civil rights bill at the federal level in 1875. In January 1875 he "pled guilty to [an] indictment for gambling," although everyone in Cairo—including the courts and police—knew that he permitted gambling at his tavern, "and was fined by the court one hundred dollars and costs."[90] That was not the first time he had been arrested, and apparently the fine was not sufficient to encourage him to change his profession. It was merely a cost of doing business. However, in September he faced charges once again, except this time the circuit court judge would hear his case.[91] In December 1875 a fight broke out in the dance hall above Scott's saloon between two gamblers, a steamboat roustabout and a local black male, and the local man was stabbed.[92] None of those events were particularly helpful for someone attempting to establish a positive and public political presence, unless that position was away from public eyes and within the party structure itself.

The 1876 presidential election did not set well with most blacks. The nation was deeply mired in a recession that had started with the Panic of 1873, and there was little interest in the North for continuing an expensive and unpopular military occupation in the South or for enforcing federal law. This was the Reconstruction era's first real opportunity to change the nation's ruling party. Presidential election results in the 1876 campaign indicated that the national Democrats had won a majority of the nation's popular vote but lacked sufficient electoral votes to place their candidate in the White House. With the election results uncertain when the new and still Republican-dominated Senate sat and a numerically tied House convened early in 1877, an electoral commission composed of five congressmen, five senators, and five Supreme Court justices (seven Republicans, seven Democrats, and one Independent) met to determine who had won the presidency. In a grand compromise, that commission chose Rutherford B. Hayes, the Republican Party's candidate, but with an understanding that federal military occupation of the South would end and Congress and President Hayes would relax restrictions placed on southern states.[93] Within two years of the Great Compromise of 1877, Democrats held majorities in both houses of Congress.

That July brought the first known physical confrontation between Scott and a white person. The Scotts were returning by train from a celebration at Mound City. Lizzy, who was lighter complexioned than W.T., was the first to enter the first-class coach, and Scott had hesitated for some unstated reason. When he tried to enter the coach to join her, however, the conductor told him that the coach was full and that he would need to take a seat elsewhere. Scott believed that the conductor had violated Scott's legal right to equal access to accommodations, and he refused to accept that as an adequate answer. In the ensuing pushing and shoving, Scott claimed that someone threw him "against the brake," and "the brakeman then got in front of me and began to kick me in the face, head, and breast."[94] Scott brought a suit in the U.S. District Court against the Cairo and Vincennes Railroad and the conductor and brakeman for damages—he had suffered a broken tooth—and for denying him privileges guaranteed in the 1875 Civil Rights Act. The court ruled that the railroad would offer equal access but assigned no punishment to those named in the suit.[95] This incident, however, differed from those that had occurred before. Scott had often jostled with authority, but nothing that was physical or of this scale.

The year 1876 also brought a change within Scott's family and his platform. His only remaining daughter, Jessie, died on 27 August, which must have had an important impact upon his life.[96] That summer also placed Scott on a larger platform and introduced him to politics at the state level. His successes in Cairo and those of his friend John Bird had been noticed statewide, and the state's Republican leadership asked Scott and Bird to campaign for Republican candidates throughout the state.[97] Among those running for office was John W. E. Thomas of Chicago, contesting for a seat in the Illinois legislature as representative from the Second Legislative District; he would be elected Illinois's first black legislator.[98] Cairo in 1876 was somewhat unique in the state. Everyone knew of Cairo because of its Civil War history. Its black community accounted for nearly 30 percent of the city's population, also an anomaly; and it had gained some fame by being among the first to elect a black person to a public office. The city of Cairo also had produced several speakers who were able to energize black audiences anywhere in the state.

The message that Bird and Scott delivered in 1876 at the state level was reasonable and simple. Both believed that there should be a direct and reciprocal relationship between voter participation and patronage or appointed positions. If elected office could not be won at the ballot box because of the issue of race, public jobs could be obtained through delivering large numbers of black votes with the expectation that jobs would be forthcoming. Essentially both men argued for political leverage. As a businessman, Scott was motivated by a reasonable return on an investment. In politics, the dividend could come in the form of patronage jobs, in position and status within the party structure, or in policies a party espoused. A group from Cairo made that point more directly and without apology in 1878, when they met with Governor Shelby Cullom to discuss the prospects for the appointment of a black commissioner at the state penitentiary, located at Chester, Illinois, about an equal distance between Cairo and East Saint Louis on the Mississippi River.[99] A few months later, the Cairo group made the same argument to both state and national politicians, this time with reference to black schools, emphasizing that blacks could exercise free choice at the ballot box and would do so depending on proffered rewards and services.[100]

If personal quandaries existed for Scott between 1876 and 1880, they likely related to the nature of his businesses, his linkage to the Republican Party, and the impact of both on his reputation and standing within Cairo's community. Other black leaders had begun as tavern owners and still had maintained their "political influence."[101] By their natures, however, taverns and dance and gambling halls attracted a rowdy crowd, and Scott's enterprises were no exception.[102] But it was not until the 1870s that newspapers and reformers focused on the activities of Scott's customers. In 1871 the *Cairo Bulletin* lavishly reported accounts of two women slashing each other while in Scott's saloon and followed their trials, setting in play intense public interest in the saloon/vice commerce.[103]

While newspaper readers might have chosen to avoid such places, accounts of professional gamblers/sharpers who visited Scott's halls enthralled them. Colorful characters such as Limber Jim, Red, Bud Weaver, Green Neal, and Charleston appeared among those arrested and brought to trial. Readers were equally fascinated with reports of ladies who frequented his establishments— Jennie Rose, Annie Harris, Lucy, Jane Gerold, Harriet Benard, and Harriet Buncy. Editor Oberly varied his terms when describing the latter for his readers: viragoes, damsels, wenches, rapscallions, bawds, whores, gaudy triggers, courtesans, and "throat-cutting vagabonds."[104] Scott defended himself in court in these years on charges of perjury, selling beer in the park on a Saturday without a license, operating a gambling table, and maintaining a dance hall, all of which were described in the *Bulletin*. Nor was Oberly's pen kind to Scott's Congress Saloon, which Oberly described as a "resort of all the lowest and vilest among the black and white Bohemians that come to town," an "intolerable nuisance," a "disgrace to the city," a "den," a "haunt of vice and wickedness," and "a notorious resort for men and women of doubtful character."[105] The term "resort" was used in Cairo to identify a place of "pleasure." But these were times when newspaper editors and writers entertained as well as informed, and readers delighted in an editor's ability to be witty and extravagant in word choices. Nevertheless, none of those descriptors were helpful for a person considering a political role within a community or a state.

The party of Lincoln—to which Scott had attached his political future— also was becoming a problem for him. As a party, it was supporting a policy of tight money with high interest rates and stringent credit arrangements that favored business and capital investments at the expense of the laboring class.

And it was forgetting those it had liberated during the Civil War. Republican leaders who had led the charge of Reconstruction in the South in the decade following the war, championed equal rights legislation in the Congress to force meaningful reforms in the North, and expected that blacks would be grateful to the party by supporting it at the polls were now retiring, dying, or retreating from politics. Leaders with economic rather than social agendas were replacing them. Nor was the local Republican Party in Cairo open to the prospect of black-shared governance. Although Republican victories in southern Illinois depended on the black vote, whites remained the partisan puppeteers for the likes of Scott, Bird, and others emerging within the black community. The rewards coming to blacks and black leaders from that alliance seemed increasingly insufficient for the investment made.

For Bird, interacting with whites either within his magistrate court or within the party was not an overriding problem. It was a part of his employment. He owed his job to the party, and his job allowed him to engage in other activities, including black-focused ones, at the city, state, and national levels. He was a leader among blacks in Cairo and was often the secretary who announced meetings and kept records. He participated in statewide and regional Colored Conventions where he became known as a team player and an articulate speaker.[106] In December 1873 he was appointed one of several delegates from Illinois to attend the National Colored Convention in Washington, DC, to devise measures to enforce provisions of the Fourteenth Amendment to the U.S. Constitution.[107]

For Scott, the alternatives to the Republican Party were problematic, although they had their attractions. He had learned through experience that blacks were electable only under certain conditions: when and where their numbers were large, when the white vote could be splintered into factions, when blacks overcame divisions among themselves, and when a plurality rather than a majority of votes cast was sufficient for victory. John Bird had won his office of police magistrate and Scott had been denied his seat on the council under those conditions. With few exceptions, however, Scott also knew that an independent party comprised only of black voters would have little chance of winning elections when a single party of whites opposed it. Numerous third-party movements that emerged in the 1870s offered attractive agendas, but each had problems similar to that which would likely have come to an independent "Colored Men's Party" should it find itself in a two-party race: unelectability. Those parties also tended to be single-issue movements that supported easy money, farmers, reform, and temperance.[108]

The Democratic Party as an alternative was awkward for obvious reasons. Historically, it had been the party that had supported slavery and states' rights. At every turn it had opposed the principle of equal rights and enfranchisement for blacks, arguing that racial equality had not been covered in the Constitution and that it was unconstitutional for the federal government to legislate on issues not specifically given it in that document. Nor had the Constitution spelled out rules for voting privilege. As late as 1868, the official policy of Illinois's Democratic Party was to restrict suffrage to white men.[109] In the 1870s the Democrats also were leading the charge to dismantle Reconstruction in the South and to establish a white-black relationship not unlike that existing in the North between employers and workers.

Yet, and despite those significant problems, elements within the Democratic Party championed low interest rates and easy credit, the rights of the working class, an eight-hour workday, "the dignity of labor," and government ownership of railroads, all issues that ought to have appealed to black voters, a vast majority of whom were listed in the censuses as "laborers."[110] The most outspoken of voices in support of labor and of Cairo's Trade Cooperative Union was John Oberly, editor of the *Cairo Bulletin*. Almost universally, employers, in contrast, allied themselves to the Republican Party and essentially transformed it to champion the interests of capital and business owners.

The dilemma for Scott and for black labor in general was the fact that white labor barred black workers from numerous trades, and, during economic downturns, with jobs scarce and pay low, laborers collectively stood at the mercy of employers who sought to destroy any efforts made by workers to organize for their own economic interests or to obtain dignity in their work. White labor held the unshakable belief that blacks degraded the value, status, and dignity of work and that close affiliation with black workers would adversely affect their own status within the general and larger society. Employers in hard times also found it easy to hire cheap labor from the ranks of underemployed or newly arriving black workers who were only too eager to obtain a job at any wage. Resident blacks in Cairo even formed a group in 1879 to intercept and divert newly arrived blacks and pay "their passages to St. Louis or elsewhere."[111]

For most voters in the black community, however, there was no dilemma. Republicans had freed them from slavery and had fought to secure equal treatment through the civil rights acts. Nothing could change that reality. And nothing could convince them to vote Democratic—perhaps for a third party, but surely not Democratic.

Covering His Past
with Rebellion and
Journalism, the Early 1880s

> It was only when blacks began to flirt with the Democratic party that
> either party moved realistically towards political rights and equality.
>
> Roger D. Bridges, "Equality Deferred"

By 1880 black voters were reaching a crossroad. Nearly all had remained loyal to the party that had liberated them from slavery and that had fought for their civil rights in the decade after the war. Through their votes, blacks in the North had shifted the balance of political power in a few areas where their numbers mattered. To obtain their support and to keep them attached to the party, Republican leaders had promised reforms and patronage but had been slow to deliver on either, claiming that blacks were not yet ready to hold appointed office and that segregated schools were better, at least until a later day. Many in Cairo's black population had accepted those explanations and promises and had waited with growing impatience for conditions to improve. And, to a degree, they had. A black school was in place, and several blacks had been given city jobs. But by 1880 white Republicans had basically forgotten those guarantees and had moved on to other issues that reflected a changing party and time.[1] Cairo's blacks had not.

Scott's crossroad in 1880 was more personal than that. His arena until 1880 had been primarily Cairo, where his business and political experiences were grounded, but that too was changing. He had been active in secret societies and had attended the national Prince Hall Masonic Convention in Wilmington, Delaware, in May 1878, where he was Illinois's lone recognized delegate and chair of that convention's committee on credentials. He was elected a vice president of the national society, a post he began to take as a given if he were the only delegate from Illinois attending a convention.[2] While his business interests remained centered in Cairo, his political focus gradually came to include activities at the state and national levels. Scott was a master at keeping these two worlds separate. A popular speaker, Scott often addressed Emancipation Day audiences outside of Cairo. In 1876 he and John Bird traveled the state in support of Republican candidates, making his name and face known throughout the state and region. Railroads joined Cairo to Chicago, Saint Louis in Missouri, and Vincennes in Indiana, with Cairo the center of a vital north–south rail network. That made it possible for him to move about quickly and often.[3] People listened to him and to his message of reciprocity, which translated generally as a demand for rewards in exchange for votes cast. And he was questioning whether the party he had supported for better than a decade was willing or able to deliver on any of its promises.

The Colored State Convention, also known as the State Convention of Colored Men, which met in Illinois's capital city of Springfield in mid-July 1880, was the fourth of its kind in Illinois. It also was the most important event to mark the beginning of Scott's transformation from Republican to Democrat, although Scott claimed in a 1905 interview that Captain Halliday's willingness to invest secretly in a black man's bondsman business in the 1870s had weakened Scott's affinity for the Republican Party: "It told on me and before long I got to working for the Democrats in local matters."[4] Both Scott and Bird had signed the initial convention call in 1880 and represented Cairo as official delegates to that meeting.[5] Convention planners presented an agenda that included state-wide and black-centric issues of school quality, training and testing of teachers, membership in the Republican Party's leadership, and patronage jobs to loyal party voters. Theoretically, this was to be a nonpartisan forum, but since all delegates were declared Republicans, most expected that delegates would remain loyal to the party of Lincoln and to its platform.[6]

By 1880 patronage was a major issue for blacks in Illinois politics and within the nation. It was the way that politics was played across the board in the later part of the century. Officeholders and parties rewarded their supporters with jobs without much concern for their qualifications. Party leaders made promises in districts and cities where the number of black voters was large enough to determine election outcomes, yet they never delivered jobs in proportion to votes cast. Legislator John W. E. Thomas, the first black member of the Illinois General Assembly, complained in 1877 that blacks "do not feel that we ask too much when we ask for representation in the various city and county departments, for we always vote one way." It was a matter of race: "We think it is a burning shame for these [Republicans] to treat us as they have in the past. They are very careful to select from every nationality but the black American."[7] And it was a special issue in Chicago, where patronage was a pervasive institution and where northern Democrats were making concerted efforts to weaken the attachment of blacks to the Republican Party.

It also was an issue that divided Bird and Scott and all delegates to the 1880 Colored Convention. All agreed that the party had failed to provide enough patronage jobs, but they disagreed in degree and how aggressively to press for more appointments. Most agreed that the best opportunities for progress remained within the Republican Party, for the Democrats had opposed antislavery and black suffrage and in 1880 were reclaiming states in the South and attempting to undo accomplishments made during Reconstruction. The difference was in northern cities, for example, Chicago, where an African American Democrat Club was organized in 1879 and where patronage opportunities were tied to precincts and precinct bosses as well as to parties.[8] The delicate path for black Republicans was to demand change without threatening outright to leave the party for other options. In a sense, all were Independent Republicans, but some were more independent than others.

No one signing the call for the July 1880 meeting knew in advance that the Republican National Convention that was to be held in nearby Chicago in June would turn out to be such a contentious affair, with the potential to split the national party again, as had been the case in 1872. The Illinois party was already divided into warring factions, with Chicago and Independent Republicans in rebellion against Illinois's U.S. senator, John Logan, who was the heavy-handed boss of the Illinois Republican Party. The convention that the state party held to select delegates to the national convention in 1880 had increased rather than decreased those divisions. The initial presidential candidates at the national party's 1880 convention included Ulysses S. Grant, the hero of Cairo and a resident of Galena, seeking an unprecedented third term after three years out of office and by far the candidate whom a majority of Illinois's black leaders favored.[9] It took thirty-six ballots for delegates at the national convention to choose the party's standard-bearer, however, and that person was James A. Garfield of Ohio, who had joined the contest only on the thirty-fourth ballot. He won because the remaining convention delegates were tired, stubborn, and hopelessly deadlocked. Garfield followed a "laissez-faire" philosophy and believed that the primary duty of government was "to keep the peace and stand out of the sunshine of the people." But he also supported civil service reform.[10] At least for the moment, the national party would unite behind a compromise candidate, and the internal struggle between bosses for party control would be postponed.

When the Colored Convention convened in Springfield on 20 July 1880, a similar divide existed among its delegates. Most were dissatisfied with the reforms that party officials had brought to black Illinoisans, and few who had signed the convention call were interested in a policy of "less" government or of less action on concerns that were important to the black community.[11] Even before the convention met, rumors circulated that some signing the convention's "call" believed that they were being "ignored by the republican party" and were considering a "bolt" to the Democratic Party or to another party if meaningful reforms were not forthcoming. Known as Independent Republicans and Negrowumps, these delegates, including a large contingent from Chicago, wanted a black person added to the party's leadership.[12] That accusation was mostly levied, however, against delegates from southern Illinois and in particular against those from Alexander County and Cairo.

Essentially, all claimed to be Independents, but that term lacked definition in 1880. Some were critical of party policies but rigorously supported the party at election time. Others proposed that blacks should vote only for issues important to the race and for whichever party and candidate supported their positions on those issues. Some believed that "African American leaders often had to make alliances with white leaders," while others, like Scott, were willing to avoid alliances altogether.[13] And a faction was prepared to break with the party of Lincoln. The *Boston Advocate* (Republican) wistfully concluded, however, that "it is safe to presume that the Negro Independents will do in the future as in the past; talk Democracy—vote Republican."[14]

One hundred twenty-six delegates attended the Springfield convention, and both Scott and Bird played prominent roles in its deliberations. Delegates selected John G. Jones, a Cook County lawyer and adversary of John W. E. Thomas, as permanent chair and Bird as one of five vice chairs. Jones was on particularly good terms with Carter Henry Harrison Sr., who served as Chicago's Democratic mayor from 1879 to 1887 and who "gave the race substantial patronage in the police and fire departments, hired the city's first Black public librarian, and appointed a Negro as a city health inspector."[15] The convention's resolutions focused upon five issues. Delegates emphatically affirmed that Democrats had not called the convention, nor were they paying for it.[16] Speaker after speaker pledged his loyalty to the Republican Party, with a Mr. Hutchinson of Mattoon striking a chord acceptable to most but not all delegates: "Some say, vote as you please. That is wrong."[17] They passed a resolution that said in part: "We disclaim any intention to give aid or comfort to the democracy [Democratic Party], either by thought, deed or action."[18] But delegates also demanded more influence within the Illinois Republican Party and in local and state government through appointments to public offices "in proportion to the number of their votes."[19]

Led by Bird, delegates denounced the dismal conditions within the state's black schools and demanded that all teachers in black schools be "competent" and required to fulfill the same preparatory requirements as those for teachers in white schools.[20] At Bird's suggestion, they asked that a statewide and nonpartisan Convention of Colored Men, with its own state executive committee, be established as an organization to "advance their interests" through "joint action" and that each town and county organize branches of that new association. A committee chaired by Bird was to produce a constitution for later adoption and establish committees assigned to study issues mentioned in the resolutions. And they invited "southern refugees" to settle on "untilled land" in Illinois.[21] None of those items were friendly to the notion of laissez-faire. Bird was elected to the executive committee for this new and as-yet-unformed association.

The most contentious issue at this convention, however, was the formation of a statewide executive committee. Some delegates considered that proposal as a direct challenge to Republican leadership within the black community and to represent possibly "a separation from the Republican party." That resolution passed, but only by a vote of thirty-one ayes to twenty-six nays. The convention concluded with a series of speeches, all of which reminded delegates sternly that Democrats had bought and "sold blacks" and had "bound them in slavery."[22]

The 1880 meeting captured the attention of the state's Republican leaders, who questioned the "real purpose" of "the signers of the call" and their plan for possible "joint action" outside the framework of the Republican Party.[23] But the full impact of that meeting and of "joint action" was not fully understood until the group's executive committee met in Bloomington on 14 October to adopt articles of organization for the new nonpartisan group. While there, and voting by districts, delegates endorsed the candidacy of John H. Oberly, who was then living in Bloomington, for Illinois secretary of state in the upcoming election by a vote of sixteen ayes and three nays, effectively ignoring the earlier convention's resolution to support only Republican candidates for office. Oberly was a Democrat and a supporter of workers' rights, an issue of interest to Scott.[24] Oberly also had been editor of the *Cairo Bulletin* in the 1870s and, while opposing the Republican leaders at Cairo, had maintained a reasonably civil working relationship with both Bird and Scott. In 1882 the statewide Republican Party responded to the convention's demand that a black man be added to the party's leadership by appointing Dr. James Magee, head teacher at the "colored school" in Metropolis, to the party's state central committee.[25]

Scott and Bird returned to Cairo energized and ready to implement the convention's recommendations. In a hastily called meeting of Cairo's black

Republicans, Scott and Bird explained their votes and were especially critical of a quarterly report from Republican congressman J. B. Thomas of the Illinois Twentieth Congressional District, which Bird characterized as "not satisfactory to the colored voters in this section of Illinois."[26] But their status and influence as leaders in the party of Lincoln had changed as a result of the 1880 convention and the endorsement of a Democrat for Illinois secretary of state by delegates at the Bloomington meeting.[27] Scott and Bird, nevertheless, supported the "Oberly Boom" and became Cairo's principal advocates for the ability of blacks to vote independently for candidates who supported black issues. Bird remained firmly allied, however, with John W. E. Thomas of Chicago, who had been the lone black Republican in the Illinois General Assembly between 1877 and 1879.[28]

Still, Cairo remained a place where blacks could cooperate in the early 1880s. It was a fertile ground for educational reform because most of its black residents, who accounted for nearly 37 percent of its population in 1880, believed that Cairo was not offering equal opportunity to its black children. In 1874 demands and protests had resulted in the building of the publicly funded and segregated Greeley Grammar School, but Greeley, which had five teachers for 220 blacks, was a wooden building of two stories and five grades, and its quality was hardly equal to that offered to Cairo's white students, who were served by a high school and three grammar schools.[29] By 1880, moreover, middle- and upper-class whites were moving to the northern sections of the city and out of its center, which dated from its Civil War period. That part of Cairo being left behind was becoming industrialized and compressed and was becoming, according to historian Joanne Wheeler, "synonymous with homicide, prostitution, and other forms of vice," none of which were conducive to improvements in publicly sponsored educational changes.[30] Demographic changes continued throughout the 1880s and 1890s and further eroded the willingness of Cairo's white leaders to modify the prevailing system.

Cairo was not unusual among Ohio River towns and cities where large black populations lived. Industrialization after the Civil War had brought an influx of labor, and with that came compression, with many people living in close proximity to industrial plants. Poor internal transportation also encouraged the working class to live in the city center. Compression brought increased crime, poverty, stress, labor disputes, and the flight of capital from town centers, where those characteristics were most common.[31] By the 1880s those holding political power generally resisted reforms because they were immune to those issues by virtue of residential patterns and wealth. They sent their children to private academies. If there was stress, it came largely restricted to those who were captive to a system that produced increased distance between those who exercised power and used capital and those who lacked the ability to do either.

Cairo's location as the southern terminus of the Illinois Central Railroad and as a river town with easy access to information also accelerated change within Cairo. Cairo's blacks were aware of the return of whites and Democrats to power in many southern states. Newspapers published in river towns moved quickly along the river. The Colored Convention movement was spreading from state to state, and information about its deliberations appeared widely in the black press. Improved railroad communications linked Cairo with Chicago, Indianapolis, and Saint Louis, all of which had active black reform elements that were questioning aspects of Republican rule. Essentially, the Industrial Revolution, which had arrived in the lower Ohio River Valley by the late 1870s, had joined Cairo's blacks to those of other cities, demographically as well as ideologically.[32]

Scott understood the "information revolution" and had the foresight to realize its influence and usefulness. In 1881 Cairo had only one African American newspaper. Aleck Leonard and Martin Gladden published the first issue of the *Three States* on 9 October 1881, but they dissolved their partnership over political differences in February 1882, and Gladden continued its publication as a loyal Republican newspaper only until February 1883. In the meantime, Leonard, the more independent of the two editors, joined in a business arrangement with Bird and Scott and traveled to Saint Louis, where he purchased equipment for a print shop that he would operate in Cairo.[33] Leonard was the only person with printing and newspaper experience in this new partnership. In any case, all partners became coeditors when they printed the first issue of the *Cairo Gazette* on 23 April 1882 as an "Independent" rather than a "Republican" newspaper.[34]

Unfortunately, no copies of the *Gazette* have survived. Newspapers of that day regularly and loudly proclaimed their political philosophy, with Irving Penn, the first writer to survey black newspapers in the country, reporting that "Scott's politics do not meet the approval of many."[35] It certainly did not meet the standards of coeditor Bird, who publicly "relinquished his connection" with the *Gazette* in December 1882, less than eight months after it began publication.[36] Weekly attacks upon Scott, Leonard, and then their newspaper appeared in the March through May 1883 issues of the *Massac Journal* and *Barton's Free Press*, Republican papers published in nearby Metropolis and Carbondale. Both accused Scott of unfairly holding the Republican Party hostage to demands for more patronage and of threatening to support Democrats if those demands were not met.[37] Gladden and Leonard verbally assaulted each other in their competing newspapers, much to the delight of readers of the *Cairo Bulletin*, which reported that they "call each other naughty names, and tell ugly stories on one another." Leonard, for example, called Gladden, who was a "six-footer," the "pumpkin-colored giraffe."[38]

Those characterizations may have come in recognition of serious divisions among Cairo's Republicans, whether black or white, that surfaced directly during a county party convention in June 1882. In May Scott had made his position absolutely clear. He believed that white voters, whether Republicans or Democrats, would always join forces to defeat black candidates for office and that the only certain way for blacks to obtain offices was through appointments rather than elections. He also indicated that he "would not pledge himself to support the Republican ticket in the coming election" unless he knew the positions of its candidates on the question of patronage.[39] Such a bold position indicated a significant rift between Scott and John Bird, with whom Scott had collaborated on many questions.

The most contentious issues facing delegates at the June convention of Alexander County Republicans, however, were the selection of a candidate to place on the ballot for Illinois's reconfigured Twentieth Congressional District, which included Alexander County, and the selection of a permanent chair who would govern the June convention and its selection of delegates to the upcoming district convention, which would convene in Cairo a month later. The Independents championed the candidacy of Judge J. M. Damron of Carmi, Illinois, a progressive, in opposition to incumbent congressman J. B. Thomas, who was supported by the party Stalwarts. Even Bird had indicated earlier that Thomas's "report" to his congressional district was unsatisfactory.[40] Scott supported Damron and was particularly critical that black voters in southern Illinois had repeatedly sent Thomas to Washington, DC, but had received no patronage positions in return.[41] But first, delegates needed to choose a permanent chair for the June convention. Neither side would compromise. When it became apparent that the convention was hopelessly and nearly evenly divided, delegates, in effect, split the convention into two bodies, with each choosing separate chairs and separate delegations for the upcoming district convention, and each passing separate resolutions.[42] Only one delegation could be seated at the district convention, but others would have to make that choice. Scott positioned himself to lead the Damronite faction, while Bird, according to the Democrat *Cairo Bulletin*, allied himself to the Thomasites and the party's bosses and introduced within his faction a series of successful resolutions "endorsing Captain Thomas and instructing the delegates . . . to vote for that gentleman 'first last and all the time.'"[43]

The district convention, which convened in Cairo's Opera House in July 1882, was even more contentious than the June meeting had been. Scott packed the visitors' gallery with noisy Damronites, and the Thomasites rallied supporters both inside and outside the hall. Maud Rittenhouse, the teenage daughter of a prominent white Republican who was a leader in Cairo's Thomas delegation, attended that meeting and wrote a lively diary account:

In spite of all the little despicable tricks, the bold cheating, the dishonesty and bribery of the Damron party, right triumphed. . . . Even people who went to that convention as Damronites were so disgusted at the unfairness displayed that they favored Thomas instead. There were two delegations from Alexander County (which caused the greatest trouble) each claiming to be the authorized delegation and they had to come up before the committee on credentials. The Thomas delegation contained sixteen of our best and most respected citizens, the Damron delegation consisted of a number of darkies (one the keeper of a gambling-hell and worse [Scott], the meanest man in town and one or two others his bar-tenders), two men (one a gentleman, one a rascal) working for the post-office, and some other office seekers. By a system of palpable frauds, which aroused the indignation of the entire populace, the Damron delegation was admitted, throwing Thomas out of sixteen votes, fairly and honestly belonging to him. . . . I was so angry I wanted to choke one contemptible old beer-barrel. They called him Jumbo (the name of Barnum's biggest elephant) and it suited him.[44]

The credentials committee deliberated and initially seated the Damron delegation, much to the dismay of the Thomas group, which actually represented a majority of delegates who had attended the Alexander County convention. When the district convention ultimately selected Thomas as its candidate, however, Scott "demanded recognition for his race and politely declared if they did not receive it the Republicans could no longer depend on the solid colored vote of the Twentieth district."[45]

Scott had won a minor victory, but it came at a cost. The party in Alexander County appeared seriously splintered.[46] But there also was a growing divide among black Republicans. Some, like Scott and Leonard, supported a progressive and independent agenda, while a majority continued to unquestioningly support the apparatus ruled by party bosses. In August 1882 George Tanner, a young teacher and "prominent colored politician" from Cairo, became so upset with the confrontational tone of Scott's newspaper and the debate within the June and July conventions that he stabbed Aleck Leonard, who was on a boat bound for Metropolis to attend Emancipation Day celebrations.[47] Leonard's injuries were minor.

There is little doubt, however, that 1882 and 1883 were important years for Scott, with several developments in both Cairo and the nation consuming his attention. First came the conventions demonstrating that Scott was increasingly separating himself from the mainstream within the party and from Bird. Then came a fire that burned the *Gazette* in November 1882, with lasting effects into 1883.[48] Certainly the disharmony of the county and district conventions added to his displeasure. The third event involved the city of Cairo and its schools. Neither Scott nor Bird had been silent on the issue of Cairo's inferior black schools, and friction between Cairo's board of education and black parents increased steadily after 1880. In addition, the devastating Mississippi River flood of 1882 damaged Greeley Grammar School, and Cairo's board of education still had not made repairs. On 3 March 1883, in the midst of yet another time when floodwaters were testing Cairo levees, Pastor Nelson Ricks of the Free Will Baptist Church led 125 children and their parents to Cairo's all-white Thirteenth Street School and demanded that repairs to Greeley be made. When the board of education refused to make that promise, Ricks and his group staged a sit-in at the Thirteenth Street School and escalated their demands to include better teachers for the black school and grades extending beyond grade five. In place of that, Ricks indicated his willingness to accept full admission to Cairo's white schools for all black children.[49]

That sit-in lasted a full week and profoundly changed the dynamics of racial relations in Cairo. At first, the board of education threatened to close Greeley but relented when blacks indicated that they would desert the Republican Party if the board did so. Taking a conciliatory stance, the board agreed to repair Greeley and to add a library. The board also authorized funding for a separate and segregated high school, named after Charles Sumner of Massachusetts, the author of the 1875 Civil Rights Act. But the black uprising of 1883 infuriated whites in the community, who increasingly abandoned the city center and changed the voting patterns within the city, giving black voters a greater hold on wards, on city government, and on city patronage positions.[50] It was during this time that Scott sought and received a costly contract to print the city's official documents.[51]

In the meantime, Scott and his editor, Leonard, were staking out an Independent and Democrat-leaning course of their own. Early in January 1883, and with Bird no longer affiliated with the *Gazette*, Leonard had affirmed that, while he and Scott were in serious disagreement with Republican policies and practices, they were not yet ready to declare the *Gazette* a Democrat newspaper: "We don't believe in leaving the party at present, but if the Republican party demonstrates the fact that we are not wanted, then it will be time enough for us to go to another promised land. . . . The colored people of this country must give the Republican party to understand that they are no longer political slaves, but are free American citizens."[52] And a month later, Leonard continued that theme: "We still believe the President means to do what is right [patronage], and will wait a little longer before we join in the chorus [singing for independence]. But we beg leave to respectfully remind President [Chester] Arthur that the time is at hand for him to do something proper for the ever faithful allies."[53]

That conversion was nearly complete in July 1883, when Scott attended the meeting of the National Colored Press Association in Saint Louis, Missouri, where he represented himself as associated with two African American newspapers published in Cairo. Names attached to the *Cairo Gazette* were those of Scott and Warren Wims of Cairo, Joseph Houser and Robert M. Mitchell of Chicago and Cairo, and J. Milton Turner of Saint Louis. Scott and Houser were the sole names listed with another newspaper, the *Palladium of Cairo*, which was mentioned only once in sources.[54] On the second day of that meeting or conference, Scott read a paper titled "Journalism as a Business."[55] That convention also passed resolutions, one of which asked black voters to vote on issues rather than be "tools of any existing party and be tied to any political kite." Scott, above all, was a businessman who expected that an investment pay a bonus; in this case, he was suggesting that votes should bring jobs. And the conference asked that editors print the word "negro" with a capital letter *N*. The Colored Press Association elected new officers, selecting Scott as its first vice president.[56] Not only had Scott weathered the storms engulfing Cairo that year, but within a year of beginning the *Gazette* as a weekly newspaper, Scott had entered the national scene as a critic of Republican dominance and had been recognized sufficiently to address a national convention. He also had taken his confrontational approach to politics to the July meeting. His election as first vice president came as a surprise to at least one delegate from Michigan who bitterly accused Scott of loading the meeting hall with his own supporters, thus assuring his election to a high and undeserved office. The *Cairo Bulletin* essentially agreed with the "Michigander," describing Scott as a "shrewd" maneuverer who "got there '*allee samee* [whatever it takes],' as he generally does in races for political honors."[57] On 15 June 1883 the *Quincy Herald* (Democrat) noted that Scott on 14 June had attended, as its grand master, the state convention of the Grand United Order of Odd Fellows of Illinois in Quincy, Illinois, and, prematurely, that by that date the *Cairo Gazette* was "Democratic in politics."[58]

A series of events late in 1883 accelerated that conversion. The first was a continuing debate at the federal level over the constitutionality of the 1875 Civil Rights Act and of an impending ruling by the United States Supreme Court regarding that act. In anticipation of a negative opinion from the court, Scott, Bird, and others issued a call for a conference led by nonpartisans and Independents to meet in Springfield in October to discuss that question. Before that conference convened, however, Scott, Leonard, and John Gladney of Cairo attended the National Conference of Colored Men held in Louisville, Kentucky. In September Scott was elected a member of that convention's national executive committee and a vice president representing the state of Illinois in its permanent organization.[59] Frederick Douglass had issued the conference call, billing it as the first national meeting since Reconstruction and expecting to produce from it an umbrella organization through which state-based Colored Conventions would convey their demands or memorials to officials in Washington, DC.

Dissention plagued even that conference from the start. Some were attending as official delegates, while others, such as Scott, were not. Was the Louisville meeting a conference, or was it a convention? Black Republicans were in a mood to be argumentative. "Independence was in the air."[60] Conference attendees were divided into those who represented a generation of elders and were firmly attached to the Republican agenda (the "thick and thin Republicans") and those who were upstarts ("young rebels" and Independents such as Scott).[61] Despite the expectation that so-called delegates would quickly and unanimously select Douglass as the meeting's permanent chair, they spent the first day "wrangling" before electing Douglass by an unexpected vote of 190 to 74.[62] Eastern delegates accused those from the southern and western states of attempting to dominate the meeting, and Independents believed that party Stalwarts were trying to transform it into a Republican fest.[63] Douglass addressed the delegates and asked them to be cooperative but also to be aggressive in their demands and, taking a more independent stand, to question the agenda of all parties, for "parties are made for men and not men for parties."[64] And he added: "If parties do right, stand by them, but when they do not uphold their principles laid down in platforms, down with them. Follow no party blindly."[65]

What followed Douglass's speech was "a scene of confusion."[66] Delegates vigorously debated the substance and language of Douglass's speech, which Scott wanted to send to Congress as a formal resolution. The thick and thin group interpreted Douglass's comments as nothing less than an attack on the Republican Party. Delegates "referred to committee" a resolution endorsing the Republican Party and tabled one supporting the administration of President Chester Arthur.[67] That meeting also exposed a significant divide among black activists at the national level and ended with little accomplished except to agree to meet again in Washington, DC, in late December, when a "memorial" would be adopted and sent to Congress. As permanent chair, Douglass appointed Scott to chair a civil rights committee of eight persons whom Calvin Chase, editor of the *Washington Bee*, later characterized as the "weakest and most obscure set of men that could have been found."[68]

When delegates to the Illinois Colored Convention converged on Springfield in October 1883, they were in a combative mood. Newspapers described its sessions as "inharmonious," "red hot," "boisterous," and "stormy." Independent Republicans had issued the convention call, and party Stalwarts had opposed it, assuming that its sessions would be used to criticize and "harm" the Republican

Party. By that date, moreover, Bird had firmly allied himself to the Stalwart wing of the party, led by John W. E. Thomas, while Scott had become an ally of the Independent Republicans, led by Chicago lawyers John G. Jones, Ferdinand L. Barnett (future husband of Ida Wells and editor of the *Chicago Conservator*), and Lloyd G. Wheeler (from Little Rock, Arkansas, who had joined Jones's legal firm in Chicago in 1879) and the Reverend Charles Spencer Smith (an AME minister in Bloomington). With battle lines between Stalwarts and Independents drawn, however, and with both the convention's chair and its agenda at stake, delegates engaged in protracted parliamentary maneuvers to seize and control the convention. For a time, it appeared that either Bird or Scott might be selected as the convention's permanent chair, but Bird stepped aside in a continuing power struggle between the two camps. Delegates elected Thomas by a vote of twenty-two for Thomas, seventeen for Scott, and one for Bird. Delegates then, at Thomas's insistence and despite the impressive support for Scott, selected Bird as first vice chair. Scott was selected second vice chair, and Thomas T. Brown, an Independent from Springfield, was chosen as secretary. According to historian David Joens, "Thomas had effectively taken over the convention for Republican loyalists."[69] But Thomas became permanent chair of a convention that had already selected members of important committees, with Wheeler as chair of the committee on resolutions; Barnett, the committee on civil rights; Charles Smith, the committee on education; and Scott, the committee on state organizations. The convention also passed a report creating a central executive committee, dominated by Wheeler and his allies, that included Scott.[70]

On the second day of the convention, the United States Supreme Court issued its ruling, which was broader than expected and more devastating in its implications.[71] In the majority opinion, which ruled the 1875 Civil Rights Act unconstitutional, Associate Justice Joseph Bradley included a sentence that effectively set the course of civil rights legislation for decades to come: "When a man has emerged from slavery, and by the aid of beneficent legislation has shaken off the inseparable concomitants of that state, there must be some stage in the progress of his elevation when he takes the rank of a mere citizen, and ceases to be the special favorite of the laws, and when his rights as a citizen, or a man, are to be protected in the ordinary modes by which other men's rights are protected."[72] That ruling and sentence ended the period of civil rights legislation. But they also energized the Independents and transformed the Springfield convention. Delegates now "were angry at the Republican Party."[73] Even Thomas, who was leader of the Stalwarts, "was outraged."[74] Committees controlled by Independents brought resolutions to the convention floor that established a state central committee and appointed its members, most of whom were Independents; condemned the Republican Party; questioned Republican commitment to civil rights; and declared that blacks should vote only for those candidates who recognized the importance of the black vote.

The resolution that drew the greatest attention was what became known as the Cairo Convention Resolution:

We, the colored citizens of the State of Illinois, in convention assembled, have been the patrons of the Republican party, and during its existence since the war have rendered valuable services in perpetuating its power.

But, while thanking it for its protection, we are forced to the opinion that it has not been actuated entirely by disinterested motives. Its actions are such as to convince all fair-minded men that it welcomes the negro to the ballot-box only.

Elsewhere in the walks of life of American citizenship he is not so desirable a companion.

Therefore, be it

Resolved, That, while we are proud of the noble record of the Republican party in the past in the interest of the negro race, we solemnly pledge ourselves to not vote for any man for office who will not give us that recognition to which we are justly entitled.

Resolved, That this convention enters on record its solemn protest against the manner in which competent colored men in this State have been refused appointments by the State officers and Federal officers in the central and southern parts of the State.

Resolved, That we will not vote for any man for office in the future who has not shown a disposition, while in office, to act honorably and fairly toward colored applicants for political preferment [patronage].

Resolved, That we recognize in the Douglass Louisville speech a "new departure," the principles of which are the underlying elements of the future success of the negro race of this country; we therefore adopt it as our idea of right and justice.

The following preambles and resolutions were passed in convention in the Twentieth Congressional District [Cairo], September 20, 1883:

WHEREAS, It is known that there are 2,500 colored voters in this Congressional district, and the district is only Republican by 800 majority, while the district would be Democratic by 1,800 majority without the said colored voters; and

WHEREAS, In the three Federal departments, situated at Cairo, of this district, that of the Collector of Revenue, Collector of Customs and Post Office, the said 2,500 colored voters are completely ignored, not a single representative of the race is found in these departments, that have been Republicanized by their votes; we therefore, in unmeasured terms denounce this policy of the heads of the departments for their refusal of representation, and would recommend the inadvisability of the Administration further retaining or sustaining such men, who make a direct discrimination on account of color; however, we recommend the removal of these men for the harmony and perpetuity of the party in this district, and that such men be appointed that will not make these undue discriminations; and

WHEREAS, This State, with 20,000 colored voters, has never had a single colored delegate to the Republican National Convention; and

WHEREAS, the said 20,000 colored voters have never had a representative on the State ticket or appointed to any position of trust by any of the Executives of this State;

Resolved, That we denounce the bosses and managers of the Republican party in this Congressional district, in the State, as well as those who manage and "boss" the National Republican Party.

Resolved, That we indorse the foregoing resolution as adopted in convention held in the Twentieth Congressional District at Cairo, Ill., September 18, 1883.[75]

To the dismay of Bird and Thomas, the delegates adopted each of the resolutions "until the Cairo convention resolution was reached," when there was "a wild scene for a few moments."[76] Bird was doubtlessly surprised. This resolution was similar to one supported by Scott and adopted by the Damronite faction at the June 1882 Alexander County convention, the convention that had split the party at Cairo and that effectively had ended Bird's collaboration with Scott and his association with the *Cairo Gazette*.[77] Nor had there been a district convention in September 1883, unless it was one to which Bird had not been invited. A motion to table the Cairo resolution was offered, and, in a standing vote of twenty-five ayes to twenty-two nays, the motion to table passed, although the reporter from the *Springfield State Register* thought that the totals were the opposite to those officially recorded. Scott asked for a roll call, which Chair Thomas refused. Scott also asked for a reconsideration, which Thomas again denied. "The action of the officers was denounced loudly."[78] The Democrat *Cairo Bulletin* more directly reported it "tabled by force of official power."[79]

Scott left the October convention defiant, and not without some success. The reporter from the *Chicago Evening Journal* described Scott as

the wily manipulator for political preferment. It will be observed that [as chair of the committee on organization] in addition to himself he put on the Central Committee his clever partner in the ring, L. G. Wheeler. Wheeler secured the

Chairmanship of the State Central Committee. Editor Scott was wise enough to have his faction in the majority on the committee. The name of his opponent, Judge J. J. Bird, of Alexander [County], was added to the list by the convention. This manipulation of the convention by Scott was so well contrived and executed that only a few of the Thomas party were keen enough to see how successfully they had been hoodwinked and beaten by their crafty opponents, and the true state of affairs came to them too late for remedy.[80]

Black Republicans had rejected Scott's most radical call for change, but the vote had been close. His comradeship with Bird, which had been seriously weakened by the chaos of the Alexander County convention of June 1882, was forever broken, and Bird had emerged the victor in a struggle between the established leadership and those who had accused him and others in his group of "bossism." But the 1883 convention also had been personal for Bird. No longer attached to the *Cairo Gazette* nor apparently even reading it, Bird received a letter informing him of an open letter that had appeared in the *Gazette* in November 1883 and that had been written by Robert M. Mitchell of Chicago, an opponent of Thomas. Mitchell accused Bird of being sent to the Springfield convention as an appointed "assassin" of Scott and as an enemy of the *Gazette*. Mitchell also accused Bird of advocating "Industrial Education," of encouraging "co-operative business enterprises," and of equating patronage with the "barter and sale" of political influence. Bird replied simply: "I am guilty[,] and let the gentleman (?) make the most of it."[81]

Scott's choices were clear. He could remain a worker within the party as an Independent Republican, he could publicly break from the party and declare himself an Independent without party affiliation, or he could become a Democrat. In any case, he could continue to remain a part of the Jones-Wheeler-Barnett-Smith-Scott coalition. The *Cairo Bulletin* cleverly described Scott's *Gazette* as "now neither fish nor flesh, but is, so to speak, a crowd to itself."[82] Before he made that choice, however, Scott attended several more conventions in 1883 and 1884 nominally as an Independent Republican. The first was a follow-up to the Louisville conference, which convened in Washington, DC, on 15 December 1883, with Col. W. A. Pledger of Georgia presiding. Douglass attended and addressed its delegates, and nearly all deliberations dealt with the Supreme Court's decision of October. Scott chaired the committee assigned to prepare a resolution on civil rights, and he asked that the committee be expanded to include prominent black voices from the East Coast. Calvin Chase of the *Washington Bee*, Judge James Dean of Florida, Frederick Douglass, Senator Blanche Bruce of Mississippi, J. T. Wilson of Virginia, and William Murray joined the committee, and some of these men participated in its deliberations.

Scott also was appointed to a committee that would "present the memorials adopted to Congress." The Honorable James E. O'Hara of North Carolina, the only black member of Congress in 1883, also attended the convention, and it would be he who would carry the committee's resolution to the floor of the U.S. House of Representatives.[83] The conference also passed resolutions supporting equal education and asking that "platforms of the different political parties" be considered and that support be given only to those "who shall give them their rights civilly, politically, and that recognition due them as citizens."[84]

Scott returned from Washington, DC, enthused and ready to expand his influence nationally. On 10 January 1884, Wheeler, as chair of the newly established Illinois state executive committee, announced a meeting of the executive committee to be held in Chicago, and he distributed a "circular" to members that outlined a proposal for an interstate convention of participants from ten northern states to be held in Pittsburgh, Pennsylvania, on 1–2 May 1884 to discuss "united action . . . so as to wield the balance of power which we hold in the states above mentioned [Indiana, Ohio, Pennsylvania, New York, and Massachusetts]."[85] At its 30–31 January meeting, Scott, who had cosigned the original call, moved to adopt the substance of Wheeler's circular, which called for a national meeting of invited participants and the establishment of a committee to organize clubs throughout Illinois to implement the committee's recommendations. That motion passed, and Wheeler appointed Scott to the committee of statewide organization.[86]

The actions taken by the executive committee brought swift condemnation from John W. E. Thomas, who summoned a meeting in Chicago for 22 March. Wheeler's defense of the committee's resolutions was "powerfully eloquent" but without effect. This meeting passed, "in the midst of the wildest confusion," a resolution stipulating that "members of the State Central Committee of Illinois . . . had exceeded its authority" and that "the delegates who would go to Pittsburgh would be there as individuals and not as [elected] representatives of the colored people [nor of the Illinois convention]."[87] But this meeting went further, condemning the Pittsburgh meeting as little more than a conference and for "discriminating" against blacks in southern states, who were not included in its call. It concluded that "these gentlemen by ignoring the rights of the people of this State [Illinois] by not allowing them to select delegates to represent them in *this* convention or conference . . . have offered a direct insult to the intelligence of the people of this State, and we here resent and hurl back the insult from whence it came, and again declare that these gentlemen do not represent the people of this State in said meeting."[88] Civility was becoming a scarce commodity among Illinois's black Republicans.

When the Pittsburgh convention convened on 29 April 1884, Scott and sixty self-appointed and invited participants from eleven northern states and the District of Columbia were present. While the meeting was billed as nonpolitical, nearly all those attending were Independent Republicans, but several were declared Democrats and Socialists. T. Thomas Fortune from New York, George T. Downing of Rhode Island, and Douglass from Washington, DC, were noted participants. Wheeler, who had issued the meeting's call, was selected as its permanent chair, and he set its tone with the statement: "Our plain duty is to battle in a manly way for our rights and grant no favors to any party or individual who is not willing to reciprocate honorably and honestly. This is not a struggle for offices, but for human rights for all without regard to color." Nearly all endorsed that sentiment and agreed that blacks should have voting options; at least that was the case until the Reverend Charles Smith of Bloomington, Illinois, offered a resolution that "it was inexpedient at this time to endorse any party or any presidential candidate." That resolution was adopted after "sharp, acrimonious, and even angry debate."[89] Douglass objected to a resolution condemning the United States Supreme Court for its decision regarding the Civil Rights Act of 1875, but even that resolution "was adopted by an almost unanimous vote."[90]

The Washington and Pittsburgh meetings radically changed the platform upon which Scott operated and narrowed the philosophical distance between Independent Republicans and black Democrats. Until then, Scott had been successful at the city level and to a significant degree at the county, district, and state levels. Party Stalwarts had successfully overruled or rejected many of his proposals and his agenda, but he had positioned himself as a supporting member of a group in opposition to the status quo and party bosses, whether they were white or black. His group had attempted to control the October 1883 Springfield convention but had failed. Through clever planning and strategic maneuvering, however, Scott and his allies had obtained positions as chairs of important committees, including chair of the convention's executive committee, and they would remain in place until a new state convention would be held. At the state and national levels, Scott had been selected vice president of no less than three national associations, and he represented state fraternal organizations at national meetings either as grand master or as a delegate sent by a state organization. By year's end, he had been selected one of the many state-based vice presidents of the Louisville conference and chair of its civil rights committee, which included national leaders in black politics and black journalism. The atmosphere of Washington and Pittsburgh was far different from that of Cairo and Springfield. When party leaders met to select delegates to represent Illinois at the 1884 Republican National Convention scheduled for Chicago, Scott's name was not mentioned, because Scott by that time had likely already labeled himself and his *Cairo Gazette* Democratic. Bird, Smith of Bloomington, and Thomas of Chicago were considered for delegates-at-large from Illinois, but in the end, no blacks were included in Illinois's delegation.[91] And, thanks to the large number of Independent Republicans who either changed parties or voted Democrat in 1884, Grover Cleveland, the governor of New York State, was elected the first Democrat president of the United States since Reconstruction.[92]

Cleveland's election and changing attitudes in Washington, DC, regarding patronage and public support for education for black youths led Wheeler, who was still chair of the convention's executive committee, to call yet another state convention. It was billed as nonpartisan and would meet in Springfield in October 1885. The fracture among Illinois's black Republicans, however, was evident from the outset. The *Daily Illinois State Journal* (Republican) described those attending as "practiced caucus manipulators" and identified four by name as "eloquent speakers": Wheeler, Scott, Jones, and Frederick McGhee, the latter a young lawyer from Chicago and a member of Thomas's Stalwart camp. The first day's session was "stormy," "troublesome," and "turbulent."[93] Wheeler, as the person responsible for calling the convention, delivered the opening speech, in which he addressed the continuing complaints about segregated schools and patronage, but he also added criticism of protective tariffs on foreign-made goods, which was a major plank of the national Republican Party, and vigorous criticism of Senator and former governor Shelby Cullom for disbanding one of the few black units in the Illinois militia.[94] At one point, "two hours of utmost confusion prevailed, there being constantly ten or fifteen delegates on the floor shouting to the chair and asking to be heard on points of order."[95] The *Illinois State Journal* noted that "everyone is loaded with words, words, words, and appears anxious to fire them off."[96]

The candidate for the convention's permanent chair, James H. Magee of Metropolis, delivered a blistering speech in which he defended the Republican Party and accused the convention's organizers of attempting to turn the convention into a Democratic event. Essentially, Magee, who was a member of the statewide Republican executive committee, argued that the notion of separate Colored Conventions had been maliciously misused by Independent Republicans and that more progress would come through joint action within the Republican Party than through any nonpartisan convention or conference:

> What can the colored people do without the whites? The white men have the wealth, the power, they own the railroads, the mills and the factories, and we must be, in a measure, dependent upon them. Without them we can do nothing. . . . The Independent Republican is really a dependent Democrat. They are men who have sold themselves to the Democratic party for an appointment.

> Such a man is a wolf in sheep's clothing. I thank God the rank and file of the colored people are grounded in the Republican faith and the powers of hell cannot change them.[97]

More directly, Magee accused "Democratic Bill Scott of Cairo" of seeking the patronage position Magee then held as third assistant grain inspector at Chicago, which paid him a salary of $1,300 per annum, or $5 per day. "This brought Scott to his feet to reply, but he was shut off by the [temporary] chair." For Scott, the convention had become intensely personal, and Magee's attack was a reflection of the animosity then being directed against Scott's newspaper in Cairo and against him within the convention. When Magee finished, Scott replied in kind: "I have a right to express my opinion, and I now say that if you elect Dr. Magee [as permanent chair] you will elect a chairman whose hands are tied by a Republican salary, and who cannot do justice to the wishes of the colored people."[98] The convention was evenly split, but delegates reached a compromise by rejecting all candidates then contesting for permanent chair. Several persons were nominated from the floor, but all declined to have their names placed before the convention. No one wanted to be chair of such a fractious and embittered meeting. In frustration but in a spirit of compromise, Charles Smith of Bloomington, who was a prominent voice within the Independent camp, suggested that delegates accept John W. E. Thomas of Chicago, who had remained aloof from battles being fought on the floor, and delegates elected him chair by a unanimous vote.

The consequences of that choice should have been expected but apparently were not. Thomas was not nonpartisan by any measure. As in 1883, he had again obtained control of a convention that had been called by Independents, but this time Independents had been appointed to minor positions on committees that mattered and chairs of those that exercised little executive powers. Thomas suffered a defeat when he attempted to have Frederick McGhee selected as chief secretary; the Independents were able to place their own candidate in that position. Thomas did not make the same mistakes he made in 1883. Scott was assigned to the education committee. The *Illinois State Journal*, even though it was a Republican sheet, did have kind words for Scott, listing him as "managing editor of the Cairo *Gazette*. He is quite an influential politician, and quite a wealthy man."[99]

Reinvention
as a Respectable Democrat,
1884 to 1893

W. T. Scott, proprietor and editor of the *Cairo Gazette*, the only paper
edited and printed by colored men in Illinois, was in the city yesterday
attending the colored celebration. Mr. Scott's paper is gotten up to good
style, is well edited, Democratic in politics and is the official paper of
Cairo.

Quincy Morning Herald (Democrat), 15 June 1883

Scott was not yet a declared Democrat in 1883 and perhaps not even in 1884,
although his and his editor's opinions, published in the *Gazette*, certainly
appeared to suggest as much to the editor of Quincy's Democrat *Morning
Herald*. Dr. Magee of Metropolis was certain of Scott's identity as a Democrat
by 1885. No copies of Scott's newspaper have survived to date precisely when he
officially made that change. There is little doubt, however, that Scott's political
world was changing, as were his playgrounds and his business affairs in Cairo.
His alliance with John Bird had ended in acrimony during the 1883 Springfield
convention, with Bird as firmly attached to the camp of the Republican Party's
Stalwarts as Scott was to that of its most rebellious Independents, although that
change did not keep the Republican governor of Illinois from appointing Scott,
as one of the state's more successful black entrepreneurs, to represent the state
of Illinois at the New Orleans Cotton Exposition in 1884.[1] Personal attacks
against him at the 1885 Springfield convention, however, removed any lingering
doubt that Scott might still be an Independent Republican.

Scott's economic world also was changing, but in a direction that was detrimental to his financial standing. The temperance movement, which had arrived
as a part of suffrage reform in the 1860s, had taken on new vigor in the 1880s. If
saloons and dance halls could not be legally closed, it was still possible to increase

saloon license fees and create a financial disincentive that encouraged less-successful owners to abandon the trade. These changes in Cairo and Illinois were occurring at a time when Scott's political base among black voters in Cairo had nearly disappeared with his move to the Democratic camp and when his primary attention was shifting to the state and national levels. It was a time when Scott needed to reinvent, to market himself as the editor of a black newspaper rather than someone dependent upon liquor, gambling, and vice for his livelihood. Many of his mugwump friends who opposed party bosses also were reformers who equated political graft and corruption with payoffs from saloons, brothels, and gambling halls.

The years 1883 and 1884 had been particularly difficult for Scott. Leaving the party of Lincoln was a monumental change. For many blacks, it was still an impossible option, because most blacks considered abandoning the Republican Party as nothing less than an act of treason. Peter Clark, a prominent educator, editor, and political activist in Cincinnati, for example, had left the Republican Party for the Socialist Workingmen's Party in 1877 but had rejoined the Republicans in 1879, only to leave it again in 1882 to become a Democrat.[2] Changing party membership twice in less than a decade came at a cost that involved issues of trust and commitment, and Clark never recaptured the status in the black community that he held in the early 1870s.[3]

With the retreat of the Republicans from civil rights issues and the cooling in northern states of Democratic rhetoric that had universally opposed giving blacks the vote, it was possible for some blacks to consider economic issues contained in the platforms of both parties.[4] By 1883 Scott and Bird had allied themselves to opposing camps of black Republicans, and Aleck Leonard had replaced Bird as head editor of the *Cairo Gazette*.[5] By 1885 Scott had added Joseph Houser to his newspaper staff as associate editor when the *Gazette* changed from a weekly to a daily sheet.[6] Scott's conversion to Democracy also placed him within a small cadre of editors who either had already made that break or had announced their unhappiness with Republican Party leadership and the direction that politicians in federal and state governments were taking the nation. As the owner and editor of what was then believed to be the nation's first black daily newspaper, Scott had obtained special recognition among black editors, and his move away from the Republican Party was duly noted and pondered. When Scott or Leonard traveled to cities in the Midwest or the East, they visited the offices of black newspapers and met their editors, and those meetings were reported in the local press.[7]

By 1884 the black press was becoming a vibrant and influential part of black politics and black society. Newspapers survived financially only if revenues

William Thomas Scott, editor of the *Cairo Gazette* (Penn, *Afro-American Press*)

were sufficient to cover costs. One of their sources was readers' subscriptions, which encouraged editors to print information for a particular audience that was primarily linked to the Republican Party. Advertisers comprised a second source. Many businessmen were Republicans, although they advertised in papers of all parties to reach the maximum number of customers. Third was a political party that relied on a committed press to carry its message to a particular population, in this case, a group with historic loyalty to the party that had liberated it. And fourth was the presence of someone with sufficient outside income who was willing to gamble on a different publication model and expand its audience in a different way. In Cairo's case, that investor was W. T. Scott, who continued in the hotel/tavern/gambling business, which his son, William E. Scott, managed after 1887. Scott also expanded into a detective agency and property management. He claimed he owned twenty-nine rental properties in the black town of Hodges Park (Unity ward) near Cairo and admitted that he had made his fortune "very rapidly." Additionally, he diversified his holdings by investing in a "wood and coal yard" and in a "stock farm."[8] By the early 1890s he was considered the wealthiest black in Cairo and one of the wealthiest in the state.[9]

No copies of Scott's newspaper have survived to indicate how Scott and his editors shaped the *Gazette* for both a local and a national audience, nor have any papers been found to describe his financial holdings. Other editors mentioned that newspapers operating in small communities needed a run of 700 copies to remain economically viable, a number that Cairo's black population alone could have supported, assuming that it was reading Scott's paper. In 1888 Scott reported his circulation at 952 copies, in comparison with the 1,200 to 1,400 claimed by the major Cairo newspapers.[10] Scott maintained that four-fifths of his readers were whites, a likely characterization, since by that date nearly all of his readers were Democrats.[11] There was one other black paper that was competing for Cairo black readership in the early 1880s, but the *Three Rivers* ceased publication in 1883, soon after its editor, Aleck Leonard, left and helped to form the *Gazette* and before Scott declared his paper Democrat.[12]

Between 1884 and 1894 blacks living in Cairo continued to struggle with white leadership within the Republican Party for public service jobs, such as janitor, fireman, postman, clerk, or policeman, or for jobs as workmen in railroad and river commerce or in numerous industrial plants that had taken root in the city and whose owners were beholden to Republican policies. In 1886 a group of dissatisfied black voters called a convention that was to meet on 19 August to discuss "the feasibility of placing a colored county ticket" on the ballot in the next election cycle and elect blacks to positions with authority to make those appointments.[13] While nothing came from that convention, it signaled to the editor of Decatur's *Review* that blacks, who outnumbered whites in several of Cairo's wards and were able to decide election outcomes, were becoming more insistent and needed to be brought more directly into the political and patronage process. If that did not occur, they might withhold their votes as a cost for inaction. Changes came, but they came slowly. In 1895 voters had elected only four blacks as aldermen, but by 1897, with the continuing flight of white voters from the city center, ten blacks held elected offices, all as Republicans.[14]

With his political base in Cairo essentially lost, except for those voters the *Cairo Citizen* claimed he "owned," Scott carried the lessons learned to other areas of interest, among which were fraternal or social organizations that played nearly as important a role in black social organization as did the black church.[15]

Most of these had elaborate secret rituals and an array of offices and rankings through which members advanced. Many societies had their origins as voluntary associations, which provided safety nets in the form of financial assistance in case of misfortune, illness, or death.[16] Many insurance companies had their beginnings as benevolent societies or assistance groups whose members paid small monthly dues, expecting to collect benefits when times were difficult.[17] Fraternal organizations also acted as networks where members groomed leadership skills and built relationships useful for exchanging information or simply prospects for alternative employment.

Those secular societies were every bit as elaborate and complicated as those found in white society. In black communities that dotted the Ohio River, the most common of these were the lodges of Prince Hall Freemasons, United Brothers of Friendship, Knights of Tabor, Independent Sons of Honor, Grand United Order of Odd Fellows, Knights of Pythias, and Colored Grand Army of the Republic. In 1893 alone Cairo's city directory listed four lodges of the Prince Hall Freemasons, one of the Grand United Order of Odd Fellows, two posts of the Colored Grand Army of the Republic, seven temples of the Knights of Tabor, six of the United Brothers of Friendship, and one of the Free Benevolent Sons of America.[18] It was common for men to belong to more than one of these. The society with the largest membership was the United Brothers of Friendship, which sought to "visit the sick, relieve the distressed, watch over and bury the dead, comfort the widow, and guard the orphans."[19] Most societies sponsored parades, festivals, sports events, and picnics, and they competed against each other with showy brass bands and dress. They served as important bridges between congregations of black churches and encouraged an exchange of ideas and opportunities. And they helped to produce a racial solidarity and masculine identity among men, many of whom had been born slaves and lacked adequate male models or ideas of community.[20] And they were intensely secret.

There were two midsummer celebrations when the societies were most active. The annual Emancipation Day picnic, held in August to commemorate the end of slavery in the British West Indies, largely substituted for the Fourth of July festivities, because whites generally wanted the latter to be reserved for whites.[21] It was a time of parading, baseball playing, speech making, politicking, and, of course, beer drinking and dancing. Crowds of blacks arrived in Cairo by train and boat to attend these events. Scott had a particular interest in baseball. He sponsored teams in Cairo and then in 1902 was an organizer of an eight-club league that included Jacksonville, East Saint Louis, Murphysboro and Danville in Illinois; Vincennes and Evansville in Indiana; Jackson in Tennessee; and Saint Louis in Missouri.[22] For young people, Emancipation Day also was an opportunity for matchmaking, especially for those from small communities where choices of likely spouses were limited. The other festival occurred on 24 June, Saint John's Day, which was the last day of the summer solstice and longest day of the year.[23] In many areas, this celebration was called Juneteenth Day, after the date when the Emancipation Proclamation was first proclaimed in Galveston, Texas, on 19 June 1865.

The earliest of these black societies to emerge in Cairo were Lincoln Lodge No. 5 of the Prince Hall Masons and the Free Benevolent Sons of America (FBSA). Scott was a founding member of the Lincoln Lodge, which was organized in 1867, and it is likely that he also belonged to the FBSA. By the time of his death, Scott claimed to belong to many such societies and to know "three hundred grips and four hundred pass words," an exaggerated number but still an indication that Scott recognized the importance of these kinds of associations within black society.[24] In May 1878 Scott attended the national convention of Prince Hall Masons in Wilmington, Delaware, where he was the only delegate from Illinois and where he was selected as a vice president to serve as Illinois's voice on the society's national board.[25] Scott was elected grand master of the Illinois District of the Grand United Order of Odd Fellows in 1880, the highest office within that society in the state.[26]

John Bird, who also was one of the founders of the parent Prince Hall Grand Lodge of Illinois in 1867, was the first grand master of Lincoln Lodge No. 5, an office he held until 1873, when Scott succeeded him for one year.[27] Bird's accomplishments within Prince Hall Freemasonry were extraordinary and enhanced Scott's statewide status through their Cairo association. Though only twenty-three years old in 1867, Bird had moved rapidly through the grades of right worshipful grand junior warden, right worshipful grand senior warden, and deputy grand master before obtaining the rank of grand master of the Grand Lodge of Illinois in 1878, a position he held for only one year.[28] Scott enjoyed Bird's success nearly as much as Bird did. Both traveled the state, visiting lodges in Illinois and Wisconsin as a part of Bird's office, and both he and Scott became "major factors in the region."[29]

A second arena was journalism, although, as a financial investment in Cairo, that may not have been a resounding success. Nevertheless, most of the nation's black press recognized the *Cairo Gazette* as the first black daily, and that special status gave Scott an introduction to journalistic circles as a consequence of the notice the newspaper received.[30] The *Indianapolis Freeman* obviously was impressed, calling Scott "the fire-eating editor of *The Cairo Gazette*," "the plucky editor," and "the Egyptian self-made orator."[31] But Scott and his *Gazette* also had critics. T. Thomas Fortune of the *New York Globe* and the *New York Freeman* dismissed Scott as a "hebetudinous [mediocre] crank" who "makes us smile way down in our boots" and positioned Scott as "very near the thing that

Balaam rode."[32] The *Cleveland Gazette*, a Stalwart paper whose editor, Harry C. Smith, consistently opposed the Independents and who intensely disliked Scott, described Scott as "blindly" stupid and the *Cairo Gazette* as "a little, dingy mercenary sheet, published by W. T. Scott, whose political faith is guided only by the hope of the spoils of office" and as a paper that "should find its way into the waste basket where it justly belongs."[33]

No copies of Scott's weekly or daily have survived to reveal his stated reasons for abandoning the party of Lincoln and joining a party in which he would need to rebuild his support base. Other black edited papers occasionally reprinted articles and notices from the *Gazette*, which the *Decatur Review* (Democrat) described in October 1888 as a "redhot democratic paper."[34] The *Western Appeal* (Independent) mentioned in July 1887 that someone from the *Gazette* was scheduled to participate in a panel titled "Journalism and Journalistic Ethics" at the forthcoming National Colored Press Convention in Louisville, Kentucky.[35] Scott's name in the state and national press generally appeared in connection with the *Gazette*, thus connecting him with editors who were considered leaders in their communities.[36]

Scott made the most of his claim as editor of the nation's first black daily.[37] He presented papers and met with persons who were important players in black journalism. That exposure introduced him to some of the race's most outspoken and yet impressive voices who were questioning the motives of Republican leaders and who were providing solutions other than a thoughtless attachment to the Republican Party. A fire at his printing shop in June 1889 ended the *Gazette*'s publication, but newspapers continued to refer to him as the editor of the *Cairo Gazette*.[38] In November 1889 Scott remodeled his Congress Saloon and billiard room "in the highest style" and announced his return to the hotel business—Scott's Race Parlors—which would be open to a man of any race, "provided always that he is quiet and orderly, and has money to pay his bills."[39]

The stage Scott enjoyed most, however, was politics, where he could best apply his considerable talents. His break in 1882 with John Bird, who decided to remain within the Republican Party, and the increasing polarization of Cairo's political climate led him to focus on politics outside of Cairo. His immediate dilemma centered on the fact that few blacks were Democrats, and even fewer of those with whom he had worked successfully as an Independent Republican were interested in making that change and losing whatever status they claimed as Independents. In 1886 Scott attempted to organize "among the Negroes of Illinois, a new party to be known as the Administration Independents," but that idea never found statewide support.[40] In effect, his list of power players had changed, requiring him to build new alliances outside of Cairo.

Saint Louis was an ideal place to build a network of new friends who either were Democrats or were Independents who had voted for Cleveland in the 1884 election and who were preparing for his reelection in 1888. The prominent leaders of that Saint Louis–based group included Professor James N. Vena and J. Milton Turner, the latter having served during President Grant's terms as minister to the Republic of Liberia (1871–78) when Edward Roye, originally from Newark, was president of that republic. Upon his return to America in 1878, Turner settled in Saint Louis. From that central location, Turner traveled the country to deliver rousing lectures in support of immigration to Liberia. In January 1879 he gave a lecture in Cairo that "was rich in information concerning the dark and mysterious continent" and of the advantages of migrating to Liberia.[41] Scott was his host. Between 1880 and 1888, however, Turner had grown steadily disenchanted with the Republican Party but had not yet declared his independence from it. That changed in 1888. By that date, "colored" Democratic clubs were already functioning in the larger cities of Illinois, especially in Chicago and in East Saint Louis, where Democrats were numerous enough to control city or ward governance and hand out patronage positions. In April 1888 black clubs in New England states formed a National League of Democratic Clubs and invited all Democrat clubs in the United States to send delegates to a national convention that would be held in Baltimore, Maryland, on the Fourth of July to inaugurate a new organization and prepare for the reelection campaign of President Grover Cleveland.[42]

Rather than abdicate leadership to New Englanders, with their focus mainly upon local patronage positions, a group of Independents and Democrats gathered in Saint Louis in June to establish an alternative organization that would change the focus from the local to the national level and offer that organization to the Baltimore convention as an option.[43] Nearly one hundred delegates from twelve midwestern states attended the Saint Louis meeting to select delegates to the Baltimore conference.[44] Charles Vena of Saint Louis was elected temporary chair of the proposed league, and Herbert A. Clark of Chicago was elected chairman of the group's executive committee. Clark issued "An Address to the Colored People," which read in part:

> Fellow Democrats:
>
> ... The members of this league are negroes whose democracy is pronounced and unquestioned. Many of them have never affiliated with any party other than the democratic, others have been advocates of democracy since 1872 and others cast their lot with the party of progress and reform in 1884. In espousing the cause of democracy the members of the National Negro Democratic League have been actuated alone by their belief and faith in the time enduring principles of democracy.

They believe that the welfare of the negro race in America will be best promoted by a division of the negro vote between the great parties of the country.

They believe that the failure of federal legislation to affect favorably the condition of the negro in the states, and the repeated decisions of the supreme court, admonish colored men to seek an improvement of their condition through state action.

They believe that the negroes of the country being mostly agriculturists and laborers, their interests will be promoted by a reform of the tariff, thus reducing the cost of living to those who most sorely used such relief.

They believe that the administration of President [Grover] Cleveland, so clean and so just toward all classes, should commend itself to all men and cause them to labor for its continuance.

Thus thinking they invite their fellow citizens of negro lineage to unite with them next November in voting for the candidates of the democratic party—Cleveland and [Allen] Thurman. . . .

The league proposes to extend its organization throughout the states, and to have in each state an executive committee pledged to the defense and dissemination of democratic principles.[45]

Scott's selection as the league's second vice president and as one of its delegates to the Baltimore meeting was a testament to his acceptance as a coequal and also as someone ready and able to carry the new league's message to a national audience.[46]

Within a month of that initial meeting, the wire services carried a report that blacks in the Midwest were increasingly dissatisfied with promises from the Republican Party and that "men distinguished among their race as men of high character and mental superiority" were leading a "revolt" against the party. That report listed five rebel leaders: J. Milton Turner of Saint Louis, minister to Liberia under President Grant; Peter H. Clark of Cincinnati, noted educator and a former Socialist; T. McCants Steward, a successful lawyer in New York; T. Thomas Fortune, "the leading journalist in the United States" and editor of the *New York Evening Sun*; and William T. Scott, "editor of the *Cairo Gazette*."[47] Essentially, others had placed Scott within an elite group of black activists.

Only five delegates from the Saint Louis group attended the meeting in Baltimore, where the National League of Democratic Clubs was formalized. Turner and Scott were among that group.[48] The Baltimore convention, however, recognized the National Negro Democratic League as little more than one of many clubs that made up the National League of Democratic Clubs, not quite what the Saint Louis group had expected to accomplish. In anticipation of that outcome, however, the Saint Louis group had broadened its strong regional and midwestern base to include James M. Trotter of Boston (but at that time recorder of deeds in the District of Columbia) and had issued a call for a national convention for black Democrats and Independents (Independent Republicans) that would meet in Indianapolis on 26 July, less than three weeks after the Baltimore convention. This one, however, was to be a nonpartisan meeting, and in J. Milton Turner's words: "Let it be distinctly understood that the proposed conference is not called in the interest of any particular party or individual, but purely of the negro."[49]

Calvin Chase, the editor of the *Washington Bee*, was not so convinced, for he reported that a rumor was circulating in Washington to the effect that President Cleveland had suggested this convention to Trotter and that Trotter, a Democrat, "has been selected to divide the negro vote."[50] A paragraph contained in a circular letter that accompanied that call had suggested otherwise: "What part are we going to act in the great political drama of 1888? Are we to stand 'up and be counted by this party or that,' like so many dumb driven cattle, or, on the other hand, are we going to act as men, each in accordance with his own uncoerced conviction, and vote with that party which he may deem most likely to promote the interest of himself and race?"[51]

While attending the Baltimore meeting of Democratic clubs, Scott delivered a talk in which he explained that Illinois's Twentieth Congressional District contained four thousand "colored voters," yet the victor in the last election had won in a tight race, receiving only seven hundred votes more than his Democratic opponent, essentially repeating the substance of the Cairo convention's resolution presented in Springfield in 1883. For Scott and the convention's delegates, the implications were unambiguous: if 351 black voters had switched from Republican to Democrat, that district would have sent a Democrat to Congress.[52] On his return to Cairo, Scott stopped in Newark, Ohio, to visit relatives and while there met with the editor of the *Newark Daily Advocate*, a Democrat newspaper, who described Scott as "bright, intelligent, and influential." The *Advocate* also indicated that Scott had claimed that the recently launched "National Colored Democratic League" had already obtained a membership of twenty-five thousand men.[53] Scott was prone to exaggeration. And he expressed optimism about participating in the upcoming Indianapolis conference:

> Yes, by all means, for the reason that the best brains of the race will be there and take part in the deliberations for delivering our people from political slavery. They recognize the fact that the [Civil] war is over, and that we, as a race, cannot live in the memory of the past. We must meet the living issues in the same way as our white fellow-citizens do. The issue is the tariff question in this campaign.

We believe every negro in this country should favor a low tariff, for the reason that there are not 100 negroes employed in all the manufactories of the United States. Trades-union men employed in them refuse to work with the negroes. All talk about the capture of the convention by Fred Douglass and other colored Republican leaders is nonsense. There will be men at Indianapolis that were born since the rebellion who have forgotten more political wisdom than Fred Douglass ever possessed. Tickets of admission will be issued under the super- vision of the executive committee of the colored league, of which I am a member, and no man will be admitted unless he is vouched for by some man in sympathy with the movement, which means Cleveland and Thurman, reform, low tariff and no more Chinese immigration.[54]

When Scott arrived in Indianapolis later in July as a loyal member in Turner's camp, the announced conference of "independents and Democrats" turned out to be anything but "independent." When the committee on organiza- tion met at the English Hotel the night before the conference's opening session, committee members had already split into factions. One group, led by J. Milton Turner, whom Chase of the *Washington Bee* described as "a man of brains and a first class orator," wanted delegates to debate without party identification and emphatically declared that the Democratic Party had neither sponsored nor sanctioned the conference.[55] Charles H. J. Taylor, editor of the *Public Educator* of Kansas City, with firm credentials as a Democrat, wanted it to be a "straight- out" Democratic meeting.[56] Both Turner and Taylor had served as minister to Liberia, but they disagreed significantly in their views about immigration and the prospects of American blacks on the African coast.[57] Turner considered Taylor a party "boss" and publicly called him "a national buffoon and a national ass . . . an empty barrel rolling down a rocky hill. I have no words to waste upon him."[58] Taylor, in turn, warned the convention that "new converts to democracy [Turner and Scott] should not be put in charge of the ship."[59] Taylor and his more numerous allies outvoted Turner's group at every contentious step, with one delegate even threatening to assault another with a chair.[60]

The disharmony that had characterized the preliminary and organizational meeting of 24 July continued when the convention officially began the next morning. All, however, were now avowed Democrats, except for Republicans and Independents who refused to attend or who left not long after it convened. The convention declared its support for the reelection of Grover Cleveland, and it elected officers for the coming two years. After long debate, delegates chose Peter H. Clark, who had been a Socialist and who was the candidate of Taylor's camp, as the organization's first elected president, and they selected a national committee with a single representative from every state. That committee also elected its chair, William T. Scott of Cairo, Illinois, who represented a balance between the two camps and a new voice unencumbered by a history of long membership in any of the factions that then divided black Democrats.[61]

Chase, editor of the *Washington Bee*, wrote a scathing and sarcastic review of the conference. He called it a "boodle" conference that was interested only in obtaining graft and appointed positions for a few black Democrats: "They represented no one, but were there [in Indianapolis] simply to bid for boodle, at the expense of the negro race which they did not represent. . . . We could see that the fight was to cast aside such men as [Blanche K.] Bruce, [John R.] Lynch and others. It was bo[l]dly asserted that these men were in the way of the rising young negro. It was self interest and not that of the race. . . . The conference was a conspiracy and a scheme of a few ambitious men to sell out and deceive the colored people."[62] Moreover, Chase personalized his attack, naming names and listing the appointed positions each sought. He was convinced that Trotter had arrived from Washington, DC, with all the conference's resolutions already in hand. Scott's name appeared only twice in Chase's tirade. The first was in connection with a telegram from Scott to J. Milton Turner that stated that a representative from the national Democratic Party would soon arrive in Indianapolis "with money" to distribute to deserving delegates. He did, and it was.[63] Chase later offered his opinion that had the Republicans offered a similar or greater amount, the conference would have ended with different results. Chase had kind words, however, for Scott: "W. T. Scott is the leader of these men from Ill. He is very influential among the negroes. He edits the *Cairo Gazette* and is worth some property. He is supported handsomely by the democrats of Illinois."[64]

Scott's selection as chair of the new group's national committee was understandable although unexpected. His was an untested voice in Democratic circles, yet he spoke the language of Democracy. He was an editor and gifted organizer and was part of a new class of blacks with wealth. The speech that he gave at the Hendricks Club on 24 July convinced enough delegates that he could be a neutral choice to unite their warring factions. Or perhaps it was his spirit that recommended him to the convention. He had arrived as a soldier within the Turner camp, but he had demonstrated his ability to adjust when the convention turned in Taylor's favor. He was the delegate who made the national news when he called Charles Oglesby of Ohio a liar, and Oglesby struck him in the face.[65] Scott and Oglesby had been appointed vote counters, and they disagreed on the tally for permanent chair of the convention. Both Scott and Oglesby drew weapons, as did another "half-dozen" delegates.[66] It was a lively convention.

Scott returned to Cairo energized by the Indianapolis meeting and by his rapid rise and apparent success among the nation's black Democrats. Neither his two-year term as chair of the newly formed Negro Democratic League's executive committee nor that of Peter H. Clark as the league's president were rewarding following the defeat of Cleveland for reelection in 1888, however. Leadership in the National Negro Democratic League was hardly an attractive and sought-after post during those years. In contrast to city politics, where patronage depended upon local elections and the activities of local clubs, the national league had little influence on national party policy, and it had no spoils to distribute among black loyalists. Still, Scott traveled widely as a part of his post's responsibility and increased his influence among America's black political leaders. Many of these men were located in the cities of the Midwest where Democratic machines regularly won elections and where political rewards continued to flow to party loyalists skilled at bringing black voters to the precinct polls. The *Indianapolis Freeman* described him in 1889 as "the happiest man in the country."[67]

Scott's move from chair of the National Negro Democratic League's executive committee to league president two years later should have been celebrated as a major accomplishment, but that did not occur. Instead, Scott's term as the league's president from 1890 to 1892 covered the years when Democrats remained out of power at the national level, and the league was still too young to have developed a set of objectives to carry it through to the next election. Essentially, Scott was president of an empty and still inoperative league whose nominal members were prepared to collaborate only in national election years.

Scott continued to live in Cairo during those years. The *Cairo Gazette* had ended publication in 1889 following the fire that destroyed Scott's print shop, but he still had his hotel and saloon business, and he was involved in other business enterprises. At the local level, he continued his interest in and his activities with the Prince Hall Freemasons, the Odd Fellows, the Knights of Pythias, and the Knights of Tabor lodges.[68] But the games he enjoyed most were baseball and politics. In October 1892, after he had relinquished the office of president of the National Negro Democratic League to Charles H. J. Taylor of Kansas City, Kansas, Scott hosted a campaign visit in Cairo by T. V. J. Hill, an Indianapolis lawyer, and George Edwin Taylor, editor of the *Negro Solicitor* of Oskaloosa, Iowa. Hill and Scott had met each other at the Indianapolis meeting in 1888.

George Taylor, in contrast to Charles Taylor and most black editors, was a newcomer to Democratic politics who had been an Independent Republican but also had roots in Populist and labor politics. For a brief period, Taylor had been the secretary of Wisconsin's Union Labor Party. Just a few months before his visit to Cairo, Taylor had been a member of a three-man committee composed of himself, Frederick Douglass, and Charles Ferguson that had carried recommendations to the platform committee of the national Republican Party, then meeting in Minneapolis, only to have all of their proposed planks rejected. Taylor bolted from the party even before the national party had completed its business and published a document titled "A National Appeal," which criticized the Republican Party for having abandoned its loyal black voters.[69] Within a few months Taylor was campaigning for the Democratic candidate, Grover Cleveland. Taylor, like Scott, was an energetic speaker. He had edited the *Wisconsin Labor Advocate* in La Crosse, Wisconsin, before moving to Iowa in 1891. He too was convinced that blacks would make progress only by exercising their leverage in close elections.

Scott and Taylor had much in common. Both were born in the Midwest, and neither had attended one of the universities or training schools established during and after the Civil War to create a black leadership class. Both had grown up in northern communities in which blacks were less than 5 percent of the total population. Both had been editors of small-town newspapers read by a predominantly white clientele, and both were political activists who had obtained success quickly. Both used their identities as editors, dynamic speakers, and "fancy dresser[s]" to gain them entry and acceptance with a national group whose members were respected and better educated than they were. Both men were excellent networkers. But there was a nearly twenty-year difference in their ages, which likely meant that Scott, already fifty-three years old in 1892, was a potential role model for Taylor, who was positioning himself to assume a leadership role in the Democratic Party and in nonpartisan groups that formed almost annually during this period.

Neither Scott nor Taylor was of the same caliber as T. Thomas Fortune, editor of the *New York Age*, who was developing a nonpartisan group of his own.[70] Considered one of the most influential black journalists of the nineteenth century, Fortune had been concerned, since the Supreme Court ruling against the constitutionality of the Civil Rights Act in 1883, that the Republican Party was abandoning its civil rights agenda. It would be prudent, Fortune argued, for blacks to look elsewhere for allies and for reform. But blacks had little leverage other than votes, and most blacks were still solidly attached to the party that had liberated them from slavery. In 1887 Fortune had attempted to form a blacks-only association that would be linked to none of the major parties and that would provide venues where blacks of all political persuasions and of both sexes could meet in nonconfrontational settings to discuss issues important to the race. That idea had failed to take root in 1887 because Fortune had not planned it carefully and, according to some women, because the men simply were unable to sustain it.[71] Scott also had opposed Fortune's league because—so he wrote—"there is a white man at Editor Fortune's back [likely Albion W. Tourgee of Ohio] who will sally forth, if this League is organized, as the Negro's

Ivanhoe. This white man has political aspirations and wants the Negro's vote. We are not prophets but can see beyond our noses."[72]

Fortune tried a new approach in 1889 when he issued a convention call for a meeting to be held in Chicago in January 1890. Membership in a redesigned National Afro-American League (NAAL) would be open only to blacks, and the league would avoid affiliation with any political party. Local conventions would select delegates in each state, and delegates would come to conferences unallied to any party. The Afro-American League was to be nonconfrontational, and its members would discuss only issues of importance to the race, including the problems of disenfranchisement spreading then in the South; mob rule, which came with an increase in lynching; unequal distribution of school funds; the convict-lease system, which used prison labor; Jim Crow laws, which were being enacted in the South; and voting rights for the District of Columbia. Discussions regarding patronage and government jobs were to be forbidden, and no person holding a political office or patronage position would be eligible to hold any office in the Afro-American League. The league would act as a bridge between blacks from the North and the South who had different experiences both before and after the Civil War and those who advocated industrial education and self-help against those proponents of litigation and solutions within the legal system.[73]

Fortune's vision of the Afro-American League also suggested a model of organization that was different from clubs and associations at that time. National associations generally took the form of umbrella organizations, under which existing like-minded local, state, and regional organizations collected for a common purpose. Fortune's league, against that confederate model, was that of a national organ that would take the initiative to form subordinate leagues at the state level. In effect, all state affiliates would share the parent organization's objectives and would be answerable to it in all matters. In July 1891 Scott attended a meeting in Joliet to form a state affiliate to Fortune's national league. While Scott apparently did not seek an office in this league, his friend and colleague from Quincy, the Reverend Jordan Chavis, was elected its vice president, and Scott was selected as one of seven delegates from that league to attend the national meeting scheduled for Knoxville, Tennessee, on 14 July.[74] Fortune's plan also called for the formation of national committees that would focus on the parent organ's identified issues. In all cases, the preferred approach was to be nonpartisan and collegial.

Collegiality, whether Republican or Democrat, was still a rare commodity in 1890 and 1891. Republicans considered black Democrats as traitors, and they could not understand how blacks could ally themselves to a national party that—at least in the South—was systematically depriving its black citizens of the right to vote or offering them separate accommodations, transportation, waiting rooms, and even drinking fountains and toilets. Most meetings of the Afro-American League ended in boisterous arguments and accusations, and little was accomplished. The lack of order and courtesy in the league so discouraged many women that they, in protest, formed their own associations, the National League of Colored Women and the National Federation of Afro-American Women, which merged as the National Association of Colored Women.[75]

Scott called the next national meeting of the National Negro Democratic League to meet in Chicago in June 1892, coinciding in time with the Democratic National Convention, which would select its candidates for president and vice president of the United States. Three hundred delegates representing fourteen states were expected to attend that meeting.[76] That convention, however, accomplished little more than declare its support for the candidacy of Grover Cleveland and issue a statement. It read in part: "The Republican Party of to-day, which we turn away from in sorrow, stands as a sectional party, as a political necessity. It is dictatorial, overbearing, autocratic."[77] In testimony to Scott's tenacity, the African American *Appeal* of Saint Paul described him as a "wide-awake man."[78]

The convention also selected Charles H. J. Taylor of Kansas City, Kansas, as its president for the next term. Scott became the chair of the league's executive committee, and Alexander Manning, the editor of the *Indianapolis World*, was chosen as the league's vice president. Encouraged to move the league forward as a vital part of the national Democratic Party and to expand its influence from a midwestern to a national association, Taylor initiated a plan to organize affiliates in all states. He also proposed to seek patronage for Democrats who had supported Cleveland's campaign in 1888. Taylor wrote of his concerns and vision; only a few phrases from that letter appeared in the *Atlanta Constitution*:

> The league stood with the democratic party when it was routed in 1888, and those who had received recognition were promptly chastised and summarily dismissed by the successful republicans. In the last campaign the negro democrat in "the face of insults and injuries of every kind," with his voice, his pen and his best energies proclaimed for Grover Cleveland and reform. "Negro democracy then became a positive factor in the body politic of the nation."
>
> The letter recites that the league is placed in a false light before the country because of the failure of the party to recognize them in the distribution of patronage, and asks the president if the places held by colored republicans who have been and are now hostile to the league, are to remain longer in the hands of political enemies.
>
> To correct this abuse and to prove to the country that the democratic party is true to the negro, as well as to redeem pledges made during this campaign,

the league asks that speedy recognition be given by the president to negro democrats and the places now held by negro republicans be given to the league.[79]

Essentially, Taylor argued that Democrats had won in the 1892 election and that black Democrats should replace black Republicans in all appointed positions, a stand that Scott also had supported while in Cairo.[80]

At the state level, Scott became an important player in two of nineteen or more regional protective leagues that formed in Illinois in the 1890s. One league was led by the Reverend Jordan Chavis of Quincy and became known as the Jordan Chavis League.[81] The statewide league, the Afro-American State Protective League of Illinois, was led by John G. Jones and was more popular in the Chicago region.[82] Of the two, the league led by Chavis was more militant, because its support came from a part of the state where whites were more likely to challenge black manhood and to lynch.[83] In 1896 Scott became a member of the Jordan Chavis League's executive committee and its first vice president.[84] Scott also was a member of the statewide league and was elected its third vice president.[85]

Both leagues had associated with Fortune's Afro-American League and likely with the National Colored Men's Protective Association, which had launched itself as a national organ during the Columbian Exposition, hosted by Chicago in 1893.[86] That organization had emerged in the early 1890s as an alternative to T. Thomas Fortune's Afro-American League, which had already obtained a reputation for disorder and lack of progress. George E. Taylor of Oskaloosa, Iowa, had become president of the Colored Men's Protective Association in 1892, and he brought to it a top-down administrative model that was similar to that of the Afro-American League but without the political baggage and disadvantage of a leader who was both controversial and well known. In Taylor's model, the national association would commission state associations or leagues that then would organize local units. Membership would be open to persons of all political parties and to women as well as men. It would not be concerned about patronage, for that would certainly result in conflict rather than harmony and progress. Its focus would be on the race and only on those issues related to the race. The Colored Men's Protective Association's most successful meeting occurred in Chicago in 1893, when Frederick Douglass, who was the titular head of black society, gave it his blessing.[87]

Without question, Scott thrived on his state and national activities. They freed him from traumatic events in Cairo and from the daily necessity of watching his business interests in southern Illinois. His tavern business still thrived.[88] Unless reports of his net worth were wrong, he had accumulated enough assets by 1893 to be able to do whatever he wanted. That gave him access to people and position and the ability to move about without having to make a living at the same time. Whether those assets were the result of his investments in Cairo or payments received as president of numerous organizations is unknown. He even had toyed with supporting the establishment of a separate political party in 1886 that would attract black Independents from the Republican Party and would use voter leverage to secure concessions from any party. But clearly, he was a Democratic operative by 1893 and presumably also received financial support for services delivered to the Democratic Party.

In the meantime, however, temperance was becoming a major problem for Scott and his business interests. Annie Sneed and Alice Peterson had raised the temperance issue at the National Negro Press Association meeting in Saint Louis in 1883, "urging that [black] children be instructed regarding the evils of alcohol."[89] Maud Rittenhouse of Cairo, who had described Scott in 1882 as "the keeper of a gambling-hell," wrote often in her diary about meetings of Cairo's Young People's Temperance Association (YPTA), which met in Cairo's Temperance Hall to discuss the excesses of drinking and its effect on Cairo.[90] Maud's father was a prominent leader within Cairo's Republican Party, and her mother was president of the local Woman's Christian Temperance Union (WCTU). A National Prohibition Party had been founded in 1869 with basically two goals: prohibition and universal suffrage. If black males were to have the right to vote, why could that right not also be given to females? Even Cairo's black population had passed a resolution "in favor of female suffrage" in August 1871.[91] Democrats strongly opposed both objectives, while Republicans, in general, stood mute on the topic. When a prohibition plank was rejected by the platform committee at the 1884 Republican National Convention, John P. St. John, the Republican governor of Kansas, switched to the Prohibition Party and became that party's standard-bearer for the office of president of the United States. In the 1884 presidential election, he obtained more than 150,000 votes nationwide. That number, while relatively small, was sufficient to attract the attention of leaders in both major parties, especially Republicans in states where candidates in nominally Republican districts had lost in an election that had sent Grover Cleveland to the White House and where Republican wives were most involved in the WCTU.[92]

Prohibitionists recognized that they could never win a national election as a third party, and they devised a stratagem to accomplish their agenda by capturing control of the Republican Party. The large Methodist Church nationwide had already pledged to support prohibition, and a significant majority of prohibitionists were already Republicans. Since few of them would desert the Republican Party in an election that was expected to be close, their plan called for prohibition activists to seize control of Republican precincts where delegates were selected for regional conventions and upward through the party structure. If enough precincts were led by prohibitionists, the party would have little choice but to add a strong prohibition plank in its national platform.[93] At that point, the Republican Party effectively would have become a Republican/Prohibitionist Party.[94] By 1893 that strategy was working.

Scott's Frenetic Decade,
1893 to 1904

Great excitement and almost a panic prevailed on the stock exchange
this morning . . . a stampede to sell set in . . . prices went down as if on a
toboggan slide.

Daily Illinois State Journal, 5 May 1893

The president's [Cleveland's] order closing the white house to office
seekers formed the chief topic among the politicians today.

Daily Illinois State Journal, 9 May 1893

Between 1893 and 1904 Scott involved himself in many projects but seemed
to lack purpose. He had encountered significant challenges before, but
perhaps only the war and its immediate aftermath trumped the problems and
the changing mood of the country that he faced at the end of the century. The
enormous growth in America's industry in the 1880s had led to an overproduc-
tion of goods, an aggressive speculation in railroad construction, currency, and
stocks, and a stock exchange collapse that brought with it one of the worst
and longest depressions in the nation's history. The reform movement, which
had focused on slavery before and during the war and on civil rights in the
two decades that followed it, had changed into forms that endangered his
livelihood—antipatronage, antialcohol, antigambling, and antivice. The country
was looking for scapegoats to blame for the nation's ills, and it mattered little
whether they were in the business and political sectors or in race. And finally,
the old guard of black activists who had emerged from slave roots and who had
fought battles to obtain civil rights as preachers and newspaper editors was
being overtaken by activists consisting of university graduates and lawyers who
saw themselves as a vanguard of talented and privileged leaders. Living the life
of a gambler, Scott could take a chance and change his game. Rather than a
time of despair, this was a time to redesign and increase his wager, even if that
needed to be along a path that was anything but clear.

The turn of the century was not a time of progress for blacks in America, whether they were located in the old South or in the Midwest and North. The Civil War had ended slavery, but it had not ended the issue of states' rights or the overwhelming belief among whites that they were superior to all other races. Nor had it ended an economic system that allocated nearly all wealth and property to whites. The Fifteenth Amendment to the Constitution had given blacks enormous voting power in states and districts where they either out-numbered white voters or were numerous enough to determine election out-comes. Republicans in the South and in several states in the North relied upon black votes for election success, and for a time it seemed possible in several sections of the country that blacks and whites who were collaborating in third-party movements might change the nation's party structure, as had occurred with the emergence of the Republican Party in the 1850s. That ended, however, with the convincing argument of Lily-White Republicans and resurgent white Democrats in the 1880s that success for any third-party movement would in-evitably bring with it a "Second Reconstruction," a prospect unacceptable to nearly all southern whites.

When Democrats regained control of state legislatures in the South, they focused their attentions on constitutions that had been rewritten during Re-construction and on issues that were reserved for states in the U.S. Constitu-tion. These were, in large part, the same enduring problems that had divided the nation and its political parties since the country's inception. The Fifteenth Amendment guaranteed the right to vote for all males, but neither the Constitu-tion nor its amendments specified how elections were to be held in states. Nor did the Constitution stipulate anything about interactions between peoples, except that they needed to be treated equally before the law, as required in the Fourteenth Amendment. Essentially, the civil rights laws passed in the post–Civil War period attempted to remedy that void by defining the rights of blacks in American society. Those laws were found unconstitutional by the U.S. Supreme Court in 1883. In 1890 the state of Mississippi was the first to adopt a constitution that included a poll tax and provisions for a literary test that effectively removed blacks from its voting roll, and state after state in the South followed Mississippi's example.

What was equally disturbing to black activists, however, was a growing racism that was manifesting itself in violence against black males and was spreading from the South into northern and midwestern states. Some of the random violence against blacks dated to the Reconstruction period and was part of a strategy to intimidate and keep black males away from voting places. But there also was an underlying belief that black males were sex-crazed and violent and that they needed to be controlled. That belief was reinforced at the end of the century in scientific and theoretical studies that sought to prove that races were fundamentally different and that social deviances were traceable to race, ethnicity, and specific physiological traits. Black males and black manhood were not the only targets of this type of study. Native Americans, eastern and southern Europeans, and Asians were assigned particular labels, all of which were solemnly accepted by scholars and the general public. All of those trends impacted Scott.

For most of this period, Scott lived in Cairo, with the possible exception of 1893, when he claimed to have been the "managing editor" of an obscure Chicago-based newspaper known as the *Chicago Gazette*. No copies of the *Gazette* have survived to indicate its political affiliation or the dates of its publication. Scott did not indicate whether he moved to Chicago or whether he had simply loaned his name to the sheet.[1] Brief items from the *Gazette* appeared in other papers as early as 1881, but it is uncertain that these came from the same *Gazette* managed by Scott. Others identified the *Gazette* as a "race paper" in 1891 and as "Democrat" in 1893, but little more remains to reveal its editorial policy or Scott's attachment to it.[2]

Whether Scott was living in Cairo or in Chicago, however, he certainly would have had an opinion about the stock market crash that began on 4 May 1893.[3] Brokers and investors at first believed that the market was simply going through one of its regular corrections. Europeans were buying American stocks at cheapened prices, at least until news broke that banks were failing and that companies were declaring themselves insolvent and closing their doors. Within days financial institutions were refusing to make new loans and were adopting a wait-and-see policy. Money became scarce and then dried up, and the nation's economy faltered. Nationwide unemployment reached a high of 18.5 percent in 1894 and remained higher than 12.4 percent until 1899, when the economy began to recover.[4] Most scholars agree that this was a defining period in American history that included massive outbursts from the unemployed, violent strikes, political disruptions, changes in national policy, and far-reaching social and intellectual developments, all issues that directly affected Scott and his black-focused world. It also was a time when a section within the Democratic Party led a crusade to cheapen the value of money by adding silver to the monetary standard, an action that would increase the amount of money available for investment.[5]

The Panic of 1893 had ended a long period of economic growth and prosperity and quickly brought with it an expected contraction in Cairo, with many workers of both races either losing their jobs or being forced to accept significant wage cuts. That produced "bitterness, poverty, [and] uncertainty" within both groups and a violent workers' strike against the Illinois Central Railroad in 1894. The nationwide Pullman strike had begun early in that year, but Cairo's white railroad workers joined it late in June, and only after city officials refused to permit an "industrial army" of workers, led by Charles T. Kelly of California, to cross through Cairo or to pass Cairo "even on the river."[6] Kelly's Army was a western branch of Jacob Coxey's Army, which was marching on Washington, DC, to demonstrate the impact of massive unemployment on American workers and their families. Kelly's group of "Commonwealers" had ridden railroad boxcars from California and had gotten as far as Council Bluffs, Iowa, where the railroad's guards and security force ejected them. In Iowa they obtained 140 small boats, intending to follow the Mississippi to Cairo and then the Ohio River into Pennsylvania, where they would join forces with Coxey.[7] Cairo's workers rallied to support Kelly with nine wagonloads of provisions, and a Captain Beatty of nearby Paducah, Kentucky, sent his steamship, the *A. S. Willis*, and barges to transport Kelly's Army past Cairo.[8] Cairo's workers were in a belligerent mood. They shut down all trains with Pullman cars leading into and out of Cairo. The Cairo-based strike lasted twenty-four days, and by the time it ended in the railroad's favor, there had been "heavy rioting in Cairo," and rails had been removed from railway tracks leading into the city.[9] Strikers also had stood their ground against "thirty or forty armed Pinkerton detectives" and "two to three hundred Illinois National Guardsmen" that Illinois's Democratic governor, J. P. Altgeld, had sent to settle the strike.[10] Falling wages and job losses reduced the status of white workers and placed them closer to that of blacks who held menial jobs as janitors, watchmen, and day laborers, all tasks that seemed appealing to whites who were unemployed.[11]

At the same time, advantage did come to some blacks during a period of layoffs and strikes. Strikes were generally the result of worker dissatisfaction with wages or with working conditions and were attempts to force employers to make changes that met worker demands. In good times, most skilled jobs were reserved for organized white workers, who refused to work alongside blacks because whites and their unions believed that black workers demeaned labor and reduced whites' status as workers. During periods when workers called strikes, however, employers replaced whites with strikebreakers, most of whom were blacks. Strikebreakers were always considered the enemy of organized labor and scapegoats who could be easily attacked without the likelihood of legal repercussions.

Worker discontent, however, did have an immediate impact on Cairo's political landscape. Neither Democrats nor Republicans seemed responsive to the root causes of worker unrest. The governor of Illinois, who was a Democrat, had ended the Pullman Strike in Cairo, and, believing themselves betrayed, many white workers who had voted Democratic were looking for an alternative party to support. At the same time, the black press was openly discussing the issue of "manly self-defense," the right to defend oneself against violence and against lynching, which was becoming far too common within the black community.[12] In September 1894 many of Cairo's blacks and whites ignored their differences and attended a Populist Party's convention that had convened to select candidates for county offices. Scott attended that meeting and nominated S. A. Turner, a black schoolteacher, for the office of Alexander County clerk. Of the forty-three candidates running for county offices in the 1894 election, twenty were listed as Populists. Turner lost that election by a vote of 741 to 2,303 for the Republican candidate (there was no Democratic candidate for that office, and no Populist won in that election).[13] In 1896 Scott supported Populist as well as Democratic candidates in Cairo's city election for ward aldermen. In that election, however, Scott ran as a Democrat but lost by a resounding vote of 13 to 309 votes cast in his ward. The editor of the *Cairo Citizen* (Republican) credited Scott's defeat to his reputation as a "notorious" gambler and as a person who had "probably done more dirty work for the Democratic party than any other negro in the state."[14] Scott claimed to be popular at the state and national levels and to have a significant following within Cairo, but that certainly was not the case in his own ward, which included his residence and was located away from his principal constituency.

Significant challenges faced Scott in 1898. Lizzy, Scott's wife of twenty-six years and "an old and highly respected resident of Cairo," was gravely ill and, "in search of health," had gone to a resort in Hot Springs, Arkansas, where she died in early August.[15] A month later, the coalition of white and black voters that had dominated Republican politics in Cairo after 1870 collapsed. By that time, Cairo's black voters approached or exceeded 50 percent of voters in several of the city's wards. At the Alexander County Republican Convention, held to produce a ticket for the 1898 election, delegates were evenly divided by race, with neither group trusting the other to vote at election time for the candidates the other had nominated. By Scott's estimates, 1,700 of the 2,400 Republican votes in the previous election had been cast by black voters.[16] Both sides reached an early agreement, however, that whites would support a black candidate for county commissioner if blacks promised their support to a white candidate for county sheriff. Despite that agreement, when final votes within the convention were tallied, only seven of the seventy white delegates had voted for the black candidate for commissioner during the nominating processes. The convention ended abruptly with the exchange of angry accusations and without having selected a ticket agreeable to both sides.[17]

The immediate impact of that convention and its failure to develop a united party ticket was the creation of a Cairo branch of the Negro Protective Party, an Ohio-based party that had fused with Populists, Liberty Party members, Free

Silver Republicans, and Social Labor advocates to form the Union Reform Party, which obtained 14,104 votes in the 1897 Ohio election.[18] William Jennings Bryan, the candidate of the Democratic Party for president of the United States in 1897, had written a letter to organizers of the Ohio party, applauding them for their stand on bimetallism.[19] In Cairo, the Negro Protection Party fielded its own list of candidates for the 1898 election, but most of its sympathizers voted for the Democratic ticket. While the Republican ticket likely still received a majority of black votes in Cairo's 1898 election, the numbers were insufficient to carry it or the Republican Party to success, and the Democrats won the county offices of sheriff, treasurer, superintendent of schools, and commissioner. The *Cairo Citizen* reported that "the republican vote in Cairo fell off 37 per cent."[20] Interestingly, Scott accepted full credit for the Democratic victory, reporting to the *Illinois State Register* that "1,200 voted with me."[21] John Lansden, whom black Republican voters had elected mayor of Cairo in 1871, was outraged that blacks in 1898 had turned against the party that had liberated them from slavery, and he observed in print: "The elective franchise in their hands seems to be a travesty. . . . They seem to be without any real leaders to conduct them on to a better state of things."[22]

At the same time that Scott was engaged in Populism and Democracy in Cairo, he remained active within the National Negro Democratic League, which he had led as president from 1890 to 1892. He served as chair of its national executive committee from 1896 to 1898 and chair of the committee on credentials at its biannual meeting in 1896 in Chicago.[23] That meeting had been particularly acrimonious, indicating a serious divide between those blacks supporting free silver and bimetallism and those still championing the gold standard.[24] The divide also involved the issues of Cleveland's run for a third term and his support of the gold standard. The convention's call indicated that its committee on resolutions intended to submit a resolution that would "censure the present administration for issuing gold bonds in a time of peace."[25] Cleveland's decision in 1893 to support a professional civil service by closing the door of the White House to office seekers also had not generated enthusiasm among those within the league and particularly with Scott, who continued to champion patronage for loyal party members. In September 1896 Scott and the league's executive committee met with William Jennings Bryan, the party's newly selected standard-bearer, and expressed the league's support for bimetallism and unlimited coinage of silver at a ratio of 16 to 1.[26] Scott also attended the league's 1898 meeting in the clubhouse of Tammany Hall in New York City, where the league finally received recognition as a national organization that would remove barriers between those clubs that sought patronage at the state and local levels and those that sought appointment only at the national level. At that meeting, Edward E. Lee, who was chair of the United Colored Democracy of New York, was elected the league's president, with A. E. Manning, editor of the *Indianapolis World*, stepping down to become chair of its executive committee and George Taylor of Iowa, editor of the *Negro Solicitor*, becoming its secretary.[27]

By 1897 Scott was president of the Negro Free Silver League of Illinois.[28] In August 1897 he attended the inaugural conference of the newly formed Negro Inter-State Free Silver League in Quincy, Illinois, where he read a paper titled "The Power of Organization."[29] In a letter of support written to George E. Taylor of Oskaloosa, Iowa, who was president of the interstate league, Scott claimed that there were twenty-six subordinate free silver leagues in Illinois with a total membership of nearly three thousand black males.[30] At that time, Scott also remained active in Cairo, where he operated a real estate agency.[31]

At the state level, Scott was elected first vice president of the nonpartisan Afro-American State Protective League of Illinois, led in 1896 by Jordon Chavis of Quincy.[32] In well-chosen words, Scott described the league as "organized for the protection and upbuilding of the negro morally, intellectually, socially and politically, and it is the duty of the league to condemn all men, corporations, trusts and individuals that acts, speaks or renders decisions detrimental to the interests of the race."[33] The Republican *Cairo Citizen* noted that Scott was "well known all over the state."[34] In 1898 he was chosen one of thirty-seven delegates to represent that league and the state of Illinois at the Omaha Congress of Representative White and Colored Americans, which was to convene on 17 August 1898 in conjunction with the Trans-Mississippi and International Exposition the state of Nebraska was hosting. John J. Bird, Scott's former partner in Cairo's political battles between 1867 and 1882 and still a staunch Republican, also was selected to represent Illinois at the Omaha meeting.[35] It is doubtful that Scott attended this congress, which intended to provide a nonconfrontational and biracial forum.[36] By that date, Scott was convinced, like Fortune, that whites would dominate in any biracial forum established to resolve the nation's racial problems. The predictable outcome of the congress was to form yet another association, the Representative White and Colored American Association of the United States.[37]

As if that were not enough to keep him busy, Scott took time to continue his interest in fraternal societies.[38] He was grand master of the Illinois Knights of Tabor in 1893.[39] He was a "moving spirit" in the Grand Army of the Republic (Colored) in 1897.[40] He attended the national camp of the United Brothers of Friendship in 1898.[41] He also kept in touch with events in Ohio. In September 1899 he wrote a long letter to James Russel in Columbus, Ohio, as founder and president of yet another organization, the National Negro Anti-Expansion,

Anti-Imperialist, Anti-Trust and Anti-Lynch League (also known as the Anti-Expansion League).[42] That league was structured on the same model as the Colored Men's Protective Association and the National Negro Democratic League, with a parent organization over state and local branches. It supported free silver, and it opposed territorial expansion on the premise that Americans should first take care of problems at home before attempting to solve problems elsewhere. It also opposed imperialism, because the federal government was suggesting that nonwhite peoples, whether in Hawaii, Cuba, the Philippines, or Chicago, were unable to rule themselves and that it was the "white man's burden" and his destiny to rule over nonwhites. The league opposed trusts, because trusts controlled much of the American economy and were large enough to force their will on consumers and those outside of trusts. And it opposed lynching and supported federal enforcement of existing laws, even if states refused to do so. In Illinois there was no statewide equivalent of the Anti-Expansion League, although the Negro Democratic State League sent representatives to its national meetings.[43] There was a local branch of the Anti-Expansion League in Cairo, because Scott was still living there in 1900.[44] In 1899 Scott also was proprietor and manager of Cairo's Maceo Social Club, which took its name from Antonio Maceo, whom the Chicago-based *Inter Ocean* had described in 1896 as the greatest hero of the Cuban nation.[45] And Scott still had time to found the Negro Democrats of Illinois in 1895 and to deliver Emancipation Day addresses in Pana, Illinois, on 16 August 1900 and 23 July 1901.[46]

When the National Negro Democratic League met in Kansas City, Kansas, in July 1900, Scott's ability to deal with factions among black Democrats received its greatest test. Until the 1898 meeting, the league's leaders had come from the Midwest, where the group had its origins. While one of its principal objectives was to support patronage appointments for loyal Democrats, that goal, following Charles Taylor's model, referred mostly to the highest levels within the federal government. Lee, the league's president between 1898 and 1900, in contrast, came from another tradition, that of a big city's political machine. While he may have been concerned about patronage at the federal level, Lee's primary interest lay in what positions were available to loyal black Democrats within cities and states. Lee's term as the league's president opened a divide between these two traditions. It isolated those with midwestern backgrounds whose interests seemed more attuned to political changes occurring in the nation's midlands, where the impact of franchise changes for blacks in the South and the reemergence of virulent racism was greater. That divide also separated activists with Populist and rural and small-town backgrounds from those who emphasized litigation and court solutions to black problems. Both had some success in the nineteenth century, but Populism had waned by 1900, and those with urban and upper midwestern or eastern solutions were asserting their leadership.

Divisions became most evident when Lee refused to issue the call for the National Negro Democratic League's biannual meeting for 1900, partly because the meeting would convene in Kansas City, which also was the designated location for the Democratic National Convention. Another likely reason was a decision already made by several leaders in the league: either Lee would remain as president for a second term, or Frederick McGhee rather than George E. Taylor, the league's secretary and its presumptive president, would be elected as Lee's successor. Manning of Indianapolis, James A. Ross of Buffalo, J. Milton Turner of Saint Louis, Frederick McGhee of Minneapolis, John G. Jones of Chicago, and others advised Taylor not to call a new election of officers, but Taylor ignored that advice, citing the league's constitutional requirement as his authority and thereby precipitating the league's first major crisis.[47] What was at stake was the league's presidency, the financial assistance it received from the national party, and the direction that it might follow in coming years. Those issues loomed at a time when black society nationwide was struggling to retain civil rights gained during and following Reconstruction and when polite white society and even sympathetic white leaders seemed intent to view the "Negro problem" as a scientific problem that some formula could solve.

The Kansas City meeting proved anything but harmonious. Three hundred delegates from thirty states participated in its sessions, but the largest number came from states located close to Kansas City. Delegates selected Scott as chairman of the convention, and in his opening address, he spoke both to the nation's blacks and to delegates that he would temporarily command:

> There are men who are political cowards, who have not the manhood and courage of their convictions. They still fear their political masters. My advice to you is to be governed by the great issues now confronting the American people and divide your vote, as other nationalities [do] and vote for the best interests of all concerned.
>
> The Constitution is broad and strong enough to protect the humblest citizen when properly enforced as it will be by the party of the people. I make the statement here to-day, without fear of successful contradiction that ninety five per cent of the intelligent Negroes of the country are against Wm. McKinley and his administration, for the manner in which they have been treated by said Imperialistic administration. This league with its thorough organization in each state as it will be headed by an acknowledged leader and organizer, will cast seven hundred thousand votes for that matchless statesman and advocate of the common people, Wm. Jennings Bryan our next President.[48]

During conference debate, however, it was evident that those supporting Bryan and bimetallism and allied with George Taylor constituted the majority of delegates. Still, those who opposed Bryan and bimetallism and who represented the old guard, city-based clubs, and the preference to litigate, vigorously argued their positions. Taylor was the candidate of one camp, while Frederick McGhee, the lawyer from Minneapolis, was the candidate of the other. Lee did not attend the convention. Scott sought to mediate these camps and to a degree was successful. As expected, Taylor was elected the league's president, but James A. Ross of Buffalo, New York, one of those who had originally opposed the convention, was elected secretary of the league, a position that normally identified the convention's choice to succeed that person elevated to the league's presidency. Scott became its vice president.[49] Delegates selected Manning as chair of the league's executive committee, a position normally reserved for the outgoing president. Frederick McGhee was elected chair of the committee on resolutions. On the surface, it appeared that a split in the league had been averted. In a grand street parade of Democratic clubs, the league's 310 marching delegates were led by a twenty-two-piece "colored band" and followed by an open carriage that contained Scott, Taylor, "two friends," and a large picture of William Jennings Bryan, the party's nominee for president.[50]

Had that ended the struggle for control of the league, all might have been forgiven and forgotten. Even before the Democratic National Convention concluded, however, J. Milton Turner of Saint Louis was erroneously introduced before delegates of the national party convention as the league's new president, and he claimed that he alone was capable of conducting the campaign for Bryan.[51] Taylor responded quickly and forcefully. He hand-carried an order to desist to John G. Jones of Chicago, who was a member of Turner's group, and Turner discontinued his campaign.[52] The nation's mainly Republican black press interpreted these maneuvers as evidence that black Democrats were irreconcilably divided and represented no threat to continued Republican control.[53] In fact, they were correct. Taylor and McGhee never reconciled, and the National Negro Democratic League receded from its promise of becoming an effective advocate of black rights.

The reasons for Scott's move from Cairo to East Saint Louis in January 1901 may never be known for certain.[54] One account suggested that he had moved first to Saint Louis and had lived there for a brief time before moving across the Mississippi River to East Saint Louis, near the intersection of Fourteenth and Poplar Streets.[55] John Q. Adams, editor of the African American *Saint Paul Appeal*, reasoned that George Chavis, who had followed Joseph Houser as editor of the *Negro World* in Saint Louis, had enticed Scott initially to leave Cairo and that Scott moved back to Illinois when Chavis moved his publishing office from Saint Louis to East Saint Louis.[56] Houser had worked for Scott as an editor of the *Cairo Gazette* in the mid-1880s.

There also were other enticements. The ranges of opportunities or activities available to Scott in Cairo were not nearly as exciting or as personally rewarding as were those at the state and national levels. He had run for a seat on Cairo's board of aldermen in 1896, and he failed that time too.[57] By 1901, however, he was the acting president of several national and statewide organizations with headquarters centered in the upper Midwest that required him to travel long distances. Immediacy and availability were important for a person holding those offices, and he could have neither of those as long as he lived in Cairo, located at the southern tip of the state.

There also exists a report from April 1901, only three months after his arrival in East Saint Louis, that Scott had organized a "mass meeting" at Saint Louis's Forum Club to encourage those planning the Louisiana Purchase Exposition scheduled in Saint Louis for the summer of 1904 to have a separate and thoughtful "negro" exhibit that would show black accomplishments in America.[58] Until that date, exhibits about America's blacks had generally consisted of minstrel bands or scenes of blacks going about their daily lives in stereotypical plantations, singing and picking cotton. The exception was the 1893 Columbian Exposition in Chicago. Exposition planners had re-created an African village with one hundred tribesmen brought from West Africa, but they also hosted an impressive Congress on Africa that brought the best minds in the Pan-African movement to Chicago. Ida Wells, who questioned whether the exposition's planners could deliver a dignified exhibit, had boycotted the exposition.[59] Scott was not interested in boycotting the 1904 exposition. What he wanted was for it to be even better than Chicago's exposition. In typical Scott style, he appointed a committee to investigate the plan, with himself as its chair.[60] The editor of the *Broad Ax* was especially critical of those listed as committee members, noting that nearly all of them were persons who were constantly seeking federal appointments.[61]

But equally important as reasons for Scott's move to East Saint Louis were the lack of success by Populist candidates for aldermen in Cairo's 1896 election and the collapse in 1898 of the coalition that had governed Cairo since blacks obtained the right to vote in 1870. As a Democrat, Scott had welcomed and had even taken credit for that change, but it also signaled a resurgence of racial separation that increased the city's stress and its inability to produce a harmonious community. And it redefined what the Republican Party represented. Cairo would again become a Republican city, but that would be accomplished without the overwhelming support of black voters.[62] Cairo, after all, was still a southern city in a northern state, and notions of racial separation spreading rapidly through the South became more firmly rooted in Cairo than in any other Illinois city.

By 1901 the sister cities of Saint Louis in Missouri and East Saint Louis in Illinois had become major transportation and industrial centers, and services available to black residents, while effectively segregated, far exceeded anything available in Cairo. In both of these cities, blacks were sufficiently numerous to be able to engage in ward politics and still be expected to cooperate with political machines at the city level. In 1894 P. J. Pauley had formed the Liberal Thought Club in Saint Louis as a nonpartisan discussion group, but that group had declared itself Democrat in 1895 when it hosted a Democratic convention. Three years later Joseph Houser moved the *Negro World* from Minneapolis to Saint Louis and joined forces with George Vashon, who was a Democrat. By 1900 black Democrats in Saint Louis were divided by wards, with separate clubs in each ward, and there also was a citywide club, the Greeley Negro Democratic Club of Saint Louis, which had several hundred members. The "Greeleys" were particularly responsible for maintaining order in an area of the city called the "Badlands," where saloons, gambling halls, dance halls, and brothels were located. Blacks who were club members in Saint Louis, and likely those in East Saint Louis, also tended to be in their twenties or thirties. They had no memory of the Civil War or of the civil rights struggles that followed it, and few had ever voted for the Republican Party.[63] Party machines took care of loyal lieutenants, and with that came patronage, contracts, and respect. Those were attributes that Scott had envisioned for Cairo rather than what actually had evolved there by 1900.

East Saint Louis also had particular attractions for someone with Scott's history.[64] It was an Illinois city governed by Illinois laws that he understood. Blacks made up only 6.1 percent of the voting population in 1900, but that was still large enough for political parties to consider blacks important but non-threatening.[65] Rather than a political party, an "independent" political machine that included a group involved with real estate, business, and industry governed this "wide-open town," where sufficient opportunities and patronage provided rewards in exchange for loyalty.[66] Within that paradigm existed another layer, however, a black political machine that was composed of several "independent colored clubs."[67] That machine distributed patronage and acted, according to historian Charles Lumpkins, as a vehicle for "African American attainment of political power independent of white control."[68] That model was not unique, and it took a relatively large population of patronage and service receivers for it to operate smoothly. As long as those in command of the controlling machine received their benefits, they were willing to permit the subordinate black machine to have its share of "boodle." With a population of eighteen hundred blacks and nearly thirty thousand whites, whites were not frightened that blacks would seize control of the system.

But there also were other attractions. In a sense, East Saint Louis gave Scott an opportunity to begin anew, and at nearly the top of a black political ladder. People knew him and his reputation. In contrast to Cairo, East Saint Louis's blacks tended to vote the Democratic or Independent ticket and seemed willing and able to play parties against each other. And they often punished parties and politicians who failed to deliver on promises made at election time.[69] Leaders in the community also were members of state and national associations, such as the Afro-American League and its Illinois equivalent, and were able to win concession that often came in the form of patronage and school improvements. And black East Saint Louisians were association joiners, not unlike those in other cities of the upper Midwest. The largest number belonged to the Prince Hall Masons, but the Grand United Order of Odd Fellows, the Knights of Pythias, and the Knights of Tabor were attracting members by the end of the century. And the prospects of population growth were great, because industrialization was occurring rapidly in meatpacking and piecework manufacturing, all of which provided menial jobs for black workers.[70]

But there was also another attraction. Scott in 1901 was not yet ready to abandon the revenue maker that had brought him wealth since he entered the liquor/vice business at the end of the Civil War. Scott established his base in East Saint Louis in February 1901 in his European Hotel, Spa, and Café, which was located at the intersection of Walnut and Champa Streets, and his tavern and beer garden at 430 South Fourteenth Street.[71] This was a part of the city known as Denver Side, located near the "Denver-side yard" of the Southern Railroad Company in the southeastern part of East Saint Louis, roughly between Tenth and Twenty-First Streets. This section after 1900 evolved into the city's "black belt" or Badlands, where residences, businesses, and factories intermingled.[72] The rules of engagement between a tavern owner and the police and courts in Denver Side were similar to those operating in Cairo. The laws called for rigid enforcement of drinking curfews and opposition to gambling and prostitution, but most offenses were forgiven and forgotten if fines were paid in municipal courts and if police received gifts to ignore infractions. As in Cairo, Scott petitioned East Saint Louis's mayor to increase the number of blacks in the police force and fire department.[73] And, like Saint Louis, if blacks maintained order within East Saint Louis's Badlands, the city would not aggressively interfere. Like Cairo, East Saint Louis obtained revenue from license fees and fines and was not yet ready to forgo those practices for fear of losing those sources of income.

Scott also opened a "resort," "saloon," and "vaudeville pavilion" outside the East Saint Louis city limits in a part of Saint Clair County called Fireworks Station. The area contained a large number of such taverns, which attracted customers from East Saint Louis. Saint Clair County authorities were not as forgiving as were officials in either Cairo or East Saint Louis, and they were applying rules unfamiliar to Scott. They seemed determined to discourage these taverns and "resorts" either through large license fees or through frequent raids for legal infractions. His resort at Fireworks Station became immediately known for its rowdiness and for its large crowds. The *Belleville News Democrat* reported that "various gambling devices are run wide open at any hour of the day or night."[74] Slot machines were becoming commonplace, and Scott was adjusting as technological improvements came on line. He was also, at least in appearance, moving toward the trend of gentlemen's clubs. Within a few days of opening his "resort" on 11 May 1901, county officials charged him with keeping a disreputable resort and "a certain lewd house for the practice of fornication." Rather than refer him to a municipal court, as had been the practice in Cairo, officials instead sent his case to the circuit court, where he would be tried for a criminal offense. He was found guilty on those charges by a jury on 21 June 1901.[75] Six days after his initial arrest, he was arrested for selling liquor without a valid license, and Saint Clair officials again referred his case to circuit court, where he was found guilty and paid a fine.[76] He also was charged with operating an illegal gambling establishment, but the evidence for that case was insufficient to obtain a conviction.[77] On 3 August officials charged him with "running a disreputable resort," at which time he posted a two-hundred-dollar bond and was bound over for later trial.[78] At his trial in August, the jury found him guilty and assessed him $50 and costs of $146. He could not pay the fine and "was locked up."[79] In that instance, however, he professed his innocence, explaining that he should not be held responsible for the morals of his customers. In December 1901 he was charged with permitting the sale of alcohol after closing time, and he lost his saloon license, likely for a few days.[80]

There is little doubt, however, that Scott's arrival in East Saint Louis was, once again, a time of transformation. He began publishing a weekly newspaper called the *East Saint Louis Leader*.[81] He had been elected vice president of the National Negro Democratic League in 1900 when that association was obtaining recognition as an official and funded bureau of the national Democratic Party. But he had become increasingly disillusioned by the seeming inability or un-interest by national Democratic leaders to control their southern affiliates, which were systematically disenfranchising their black citizens. Nor was either party willing to enact meaningful laws to force an end to lynching, which seemed to be becoming increasingly frequent.

The National Negro Liberty
Party and the Debacle
of the 1904 Election

It is an insult to the Negro of the state of Illinois and of the United States by placing such an objectionable Negro at the head of such a movement. It is now time for the Negro papers to speak out, and show that Scott is put up for sale. God save us from them.

Saint Louis Palladium, 16 July 1904

The promptness with which the negro candidate for the presidency was landed in the East St. Louis jail would indicate that the "national liberty" party is to have severe fighting from the first.

Cedar Rapids Weekly Gazette, 20 July 1904

Objectionable Negro"? T. Thomas Fortune at the *New York Globe* had called Scott a "hebetudinous crank" twenty years earlier, but that paled in comparison to calling someone objectionable.[1] In the heat of an argument in 1872, Reverend Shores had labeled him a "fiend" and had questioned his moral character.[2] When Maud Rittenhouse described him as "the meanest man in town" in 1882, she was a teenager, and her comments were contained in a diary that she likely thought would remain forever private.[3] Sufficient others, however, had considered Scott a reasonable and likeable person; otherwise, they would not have selected him to so many high offices. Nor would they have invited him repeatedly to give addresses at Emancipation Day celebrations. Others may have considered him vile, but no one had yet said that in print. Black newspapers and their editors apparently had been willing to overlook a life of peccadilloes so long as it stayed hidden and personal and did little damage to the party. In 1904, however, it was a different time; personal histories really mattered. There was also a struggle between "good" and a mysterious and devious "them," the ultimate antagonists.

The year 1904 should have been Scott's most satisfying year and July his most gratifying month. Living in Saint Louis's sister city of East Saint Louis, Scott was a tram ride's distance from the center of the American universe in 1904. The eyes of the nation, especially those in the Midwest, were trained on Saint Louis, which was hosting a spectacular world's fair and international exhibition. The fair, named the Louisiana Purchase Exposition, was to commemorate the hundredth anniversary of "Jefferson's Folly," the purchase of the Louisiana Territory from France, which doubled the nation's size with the stroke of a pen. The fair was to be open for visitors between 30 April and 1 December. Railroads that crisscrossed the country offered discount fares to travelers heading toward Saint Louis and its fair. Even a song, "Meet Me in Saint Louis, Louis," was written to stir the imagination and draw the crowds.[4] Saint Louis was a major hub of railroad communication and was large enough to feed and accommodate the thousands of outsiders who would attend the fair's scheduled events. The national Democratic Party would hold its convention in Saint Louis, as would scores of other associations that would convene and visit the fair at the same time. Fair organizers also planned the "Games," which they billed as the Third Olympiad, to run between 20 August and 7 September. And the fair scheduled separate Anthropology Days, when costumed members of the world's "uncivilized tribes" would compete against each other because they were believed to be racially inferior and unfit to compete with whites.[5] The marathon was a "farce," and the Anthropology Days were "ridiculous."[6] Pierre de Coubertin, who was the founder of the modern Olympics, was embarrassed: "In no place but America would one have dared to place such events on a program."[7]

Scott in 1904 was not willing to tolerate such nonsense. If there was anything "objectionable" that surrounded the fair and its activities, it was the malignancy of racism, which seemed to permeate everything. Fair planners had ignored Scott's offer to assist them in designing an exhibit that reflected the realities of black life and instead had re-created a mythological ideal of planter life. This ideal reinforced an emerging southern school of historical thought that was then convincing the nation that the Civil War had destroyed a system that worked well before the war and in its wake had created a "Negro problem." That view also taught that the Civil War had been fought to subject the South to a form of economic colonialism and that slavery and black subservience were parts of nature's order. White workers who were building the fair's exhibits closed their work sites to black workers and effectively kept them from profiting from the construction boom attached to the fair or to hotels and restaurants being built or remodeled to serve the fair's thousands of visitors. Planners of the games also borrowed liberally from the U.S. Supreme Court's decision in *Plessy v. Ferguson* by creating two sets of games and even separate grandstands, those for the "civilized tribes" and those for the "uncivilized" ones. This inserted Jim Crow into the fair and into the nation's fabric as the new norm. It would be separate, but it certainly would not be equal.

Whites in the country also were in full recovery from the economic downturn of the 1890s, but such a severe and lengthy depression had left scars. Thomas Dixon's novel *The Leopard's Spots* was being read nationwide and was encouraging "white rage" against black males, whom Dixon portrayed as sexual predators and a danger to white society and the sanctity of white females. At the heart of the debate were the issues of race, manhood, and civilization. The observation of man in his "savage state," clearly visible in the exhibits and the games, was to become a mirror of what he could become again. Scientific racism, for some, had also obtained a gender perspective that identified men as irresponsible and women as enablers or persons with the power to guarantee change, capable of stopping the slide of man back to his original savage state.[8] White women, like Maud Rittenhouse, had been discussing this issue from the 1880s, but reforms to limit access to alcohol consumption, gambling and dance halls, and disorderly houses had largely been confined to "white light districts." This was the contradiction that likely had brought Scott a spate of arrests and convictions in 1901.

There also is little doubt that Scott was becoming disillusioned by the inability of the nation's Democratic leaders to control the party's southern strongholds where black voters were being systematically disenfranchised. Nor was either major party willing to exert sufficient will to force an end to lynching, which was gaining in frequency and spreading northward. In 1902 Scott stepped down as vice president of the National Negro Democratic League, leaving his friend George Taylor to lead the struggling league another two years without his help.[9] Scott was an avid joiner and was looking for a change. Surely he could juggle another league or association.

Scott found that alternative in an association that had been formed in 1897 by the Reverend Isaac L. Walton of Little Rock, Arkansas. Its roots traced back to early schemes to obtain pensions for slaves who had received no wages before the Civil War and to Judge Albion W. Tourgee of Ohio, a frequent contributor of articles to the Chicago *Inter Ocean* who in 1891 had proposed the establishment of the Citizens' Equal Rights Association to assist "Afro-Americans in the legal assertion of their rights."[10] Partly in response to Tourgee's initiative, the Colored National Personal Liberty League was established in 1895 with headquarters in Washington, DC, and for several years it drew its membership primarily from black lawyers, journalists, and political figures in and around the District of Columbia.[11] By 1900 personal liberty leagues had been formed in most states.[12] The Illinois league was less involved in litigation and more in providing a nonpartisan forum, and it associated itself with personal liberty leagues at the regional and national levels only at convention times.

Civil and personal leagues in the South had become popular among blacks either who had been slaves before the war or who were focused on the special needs of former slaves in a changed postwar economic and social environment. When the Civil War ended, federal administrators had faced an enormous problem of injured and disabled soldiers and sailors who asked for and received government pensions. For a time, it seemed that it was only necessary to request a pension for it to be awarded. Numerous bills to compensate ex-slaves for wages not received in slavery times were introduced in Congress, but none passed both houses.[13] When the United States Supreme Court in 1883 ruled the Civil Rights Act of 1875 to be unconstitutional, many thought that the issue of reparations and pensions for ex-slaves had been settled. But that was not the case.

Bills that addressed the problems of an aging population of former slaves continued to be submitted and stalled in Congress, and bogus societies or leagues sprung up across the South that claimed that individual membership in specific ex-slave pension leagues was necessary if former slaves expected to meet requirements and sustain eligibility for receiving an initial bounty or lump sum, followed by a monthly pension based on age when the war and slavery ended. A local community could set up a subsidiary branch of a supposedly qualifying league for a fee ($2.50), and members would receive a certificate of registration (25¢ each) and would pay monthly fees (10¢ per potential recipient) to maintain memberships and remain qualified for the pension when and if Congress passed such a bill.[14] The federal government tried unsuccessfully to stop the proliferation and activities of these bogus leagues by charging their leaders with mail fraud, but that maneuver failed to stop their popularity.[15]

One of the most successful of these pension leagues, and the one to which Scott linked himself in 1904, was one that Walton established in 1897.[16] This league, which Walton initially named the Ex-Slave Petitioners' Assembly, followed the pattern others already had adopted, and federal prosecutors charged Walton with mail fraud. Walton reorganized the assembly in 1900 as the National Industrial Council of Ex-Slaves (also called the National Independent Council), but that group and its leaders also failed to escape federal charges of illegal use of the postal service.[17] In 1901 the council met at a national meeting in Washington, DC, when Walton handed the national council's reins to Stanley P. Mitchell, a young and promising Kentuckian who had been the editor of the *Southern Sentinel* in Memphis, Tennessee, and who was then living in Lexington, Kentucky.[18]

Mitchell in 1901 was not a newcomer to the ex-slave pension movement sweeping the South, nor was he unaware of significant Jim Crow changes then unraveling the progress of Reconstruction. He was in 1900, at age thirty, a practicing evangelist and president of the National Education Council, which emphasized industrial education and self-help, similar to the formula Booker T. Washington from Tuskegee Institute in Alabama also supported. He also was a proclaimed Democrat with enormous ambition.[19] A turning point came for him, so he reported, in January 1903, when he and a group from the National Industrial Council traveled to Washington, DC, to appeal for legitimate pensions for blacks who had served the Union during the Civil War as engineers, bridge builders, and iron forgers. President Theodore Roosevelt had met with them, but he, according to Mitchell, had dismissed them and their petition so abruptly, completely, and impolitely that Mitchell threatened to deliver three hundred thousand black votes against Roosevelt in the coming 1904 presidential election.[20]

At a second council conference held in Memphis, Tennessee, in July 1903, Mitchell transformed the council by reducing its emphasis on pensions for ex-slaves and collection of dues from possible pension recipients and by adding disfranchisement, lynching, scientific racism, Jim Crow, and mob rule to the council's agenda. Those changes broadened its appeal among black midwesterners who had little sympathy for ex-slaves and problems associated with aging without the safety net of the previous plantation system. But more importantly, Mitchell suggested that the council be dissolved, that it be reconstituted as the National Negro Civil Liberty Party with its headquarters in Chicago, Illinois, and that it field candidates in the upcoming presidential election.[21]

At some point, Scott became aware of Mitchell and his movement. The *Washington Bee*, the *New York Times*, the *Colored American*, and the *Appeal* regularly carried coverage of Mitchell and his activities, all newspapers that would have been readily available to Scott. Scott in 1903 also was president of Illinois's Negro Personal Liberty League.[22] Perhaps it was Mitchell's proposal for a headquarters based in Chicago that drew Scott's initial attention. Or perhaps he was attracted to the notion that a separate political party could have an impact on a federal election or the platforms of either party. In any case, the Louisiana Purchase Exposition would begin in Saint Louis on 30 April 1904, and numerous associations, leagues, and societies were scheduling their annual meetings for that city. The national Democratic Party would hold its meeting there in July, as would the National Negro Democratic League.[23] Even the Negro Lincoln League, a society of "independent Republicans" with headquarters in Minneapolis, Minnesota, and strong ties to Albion Tourgee, would meet there. Saint Louis was the preferred destination of many travelers in the summer of 1904.

By March 1904 Scott and Mitchell had met and had reached an agreement. Scott advanced to membership in the National Civil Liberty Party's executive committee and chair of its convention committee, the latter a logical appointment, since East Saint Louis was then his hometown and nearby Saint Louis was the nation's preferred location for conventions.[24] On 31 March Scott announced that preparations for a convention of the new party had been completed and that it would occur in Saint Louis on 6 July at the same time as the Democratic National Convention. Scott also indicated that the convention would call for government ownership of the nation's transportation system and a pension list for ex-slaves.[25] A similar announcement from 6 May indicated that the party intended to focus its statewide efforts for local candidates in New York, Pennsylvania, West Virginia, Indiana, Illinois, and Missouri, all states where the black vote was large enough to affect election outcomes.[26] The convention was to convene at the newly opened Douglass Hotel, where it would formalize the beginnings of a new political party. In the meantime, other committees would develop a constitution and agenda and select a list of potential candidates for the office of president and vice president of the United States.[27] Conference planners hoped for a conference of twenty-five hundred delegates and unrealistically predicted that the party might receive five hundred thousand votes in the upcoming election.[28]

The national press was amused, puzzled, and perplexed by these announcements. The *Palestine Daily Herald*, a Democrat paper in Palestine, Texas, wondered whether this was merely a scheme to set off alarms within the Republican Party and to remind its leaders that the black vote in New York, New Jersey, and Indiana was large enough to swing those states into the Democratic column. It suggested that Republican Party leaders would surely "buy off" the new party's leadership to keep the party from competing for votes.[29] The editor of the African American and Republican *Wichita Searchlight* was less polite:

> It is to be regretted that a few of our [black] men are inclined to use their political
> privileges in a way that is not all credited to the principles of manhood. They
> bob up in every campaign, whether it be national or municipal, and an [sic]
> interested in selfish aggrandizement, tha [sic] assume to be leaders and lay in
> wait for some one out of whom tha [sic] may fleece a few paltry dollars and for
> some reason their game is easily caught, as a result the entire Negro family is
> besmirched by the narrow-minded who declare that the entire Negro vote can
> be bought for a song, and for that reason the entire Negro population should be
> disfranchised.[30]

Even the editor of the *Freeman* of Indianapolis was willing to describe the new party as little more than "Stanley Mitchell's Civil Liberty Democratic-annex scheme."[31] J. Q. Adams of the *Appeal*, while describing Scott as "always a disturbing element in 'Egypt,'" dismissed the party as "nothing but the thinnest sort of a Democratic scheme to capture the Afro-American votes in southern Illinois and Indiana. The trick won't work."[32]

Even before the convention began, however, Scott announced a convention of the Illinois branch of the new party. It would meet in Springfield, where delegates would select congressional candidates for Illinois's Seventeenth, Twenty-Second, Twenty-Fourth, and Twenty-Fifth Congressional Districts.[33] Rumors meanwhile circulated in the black press that the new party intended only to proclaim its platform and to nominate Booker T. Washington to lead its national ticket.[34] And some delegates wanted to select Calvin Chase, editor of the *Washington Bee*, or perhaps Bishop Alexander Walters of New Jersey, or J. Milton Turner of Saint Louis, who had served as minister to Liberia.[35] Stanley Mitchell also wanted the nomination, but he was too young, constitutionally, to serve as president.[36] There also were the Independent Republicans, the "Negrowumps," who opposed many of the Republican Party's platform planks and wanted only to declare their objections in a dramatic fashion by placing acceptable planks in a separate party platform. They expected the new party to join with the national Republican Party, however, by selecting Theodore Roosevelt as the party's standard-bearer. Finally, there was that group that was thoroughly disillusioned with both political parties. Like Scott, they wanted only to show, through a complete separation of votes, that blacks comprised a constituency that needed to be considered and whose issues needed to be addressed. That could only be done, so they thought, by a dramatic demonstration to catch the attention of existing leaders of both parties.[37]

Scott was new to this group and to its objectives. He had participated in the founding of several such leagues, but as a newcomer, he knew little about those soon to attend the convention, and they knew little about him. He was a mature and imposing person of sixty-five years of age, was then president of several national associations, and had been a founder of the National Negro Democratic League. He was an excellent organizer and a dynamic speaker. From his experience, he knew that he would likely play an important role in conference deliberations as its convener and that he would be operating on his home playing field. He also knew that a sizeable number of the convention's delegates would come from Illinois and Missouri and that conventions tended to vote for hometown favorites.

When approximately three hundred delegates from thirty-five states were confirmed and seated on 6 July, Scott opened the convention, and W. L. Smith of Maryville, Missouri, delivered a rousing and welcoming speech. Smith reminded delegates that "nearly every door of industry . . . [was] closed against him" and that since there were two million offices in the country, and since black voters accounted for one-eighth of the voting population, blacks "should have 250,000 of those offices."[38] After normal conference procedures were followed, a committee on resolutions presented a platform that was a wish list of wants.[39] The convention then turned to the process of nominating its candidates for the offices of president and vice president. Delegates first offered the nomination to Bishop Alexander Walters, who declined, as did J. Milton Turner of Saint Louis. Republican papers reported that both Walters and Turner, although Democrats by that date, had recommended that the convention unite with the Republicans at the top and accept Roosevelt as the party's standard-bearer. The convention followed that advice and selected Roosevelt to lead the ticket.[40]

The night of 6 July was filled with politicking and, at least for some, including Scott, lamenting that the convention had not given adequate time to the nomination process. When they reconvened on 7 July, the number of delegates had swelled to nearly 550 persons. The first order of business was to reconsider the vote of 6 July.[41] After lengthy debate, and after a significant number of dismayed Independent Republicans had left the convention, delegates reversed the vote for Roosevelt and reopened the floor for new nominations. Symbolically, they offered the head of the ticket to Mitchell, who everyone knew was too young to serve in that office, and he declined.[42] One account reported that what followed was "a spirited contest, lasting for over an hour," which, in comparison to other conventions of that time, was extraordinarily brief.[43] The convention had selected Col. William T. Scott of East Saint Louis for president and Capt. W. C. Payne of Warrenton, West Virginia, for vice president of the United States.[44] Nice Chiles, reporter for the *Plaindealer* of Topeka, Kansas (black and Republican), was neither amused nor impressed. He bluntly dismissed the convention as a "Democratic party for boodle" and labeled it as "the Greatest Farce in the History of American Politics" and its participants as "a gang of grafters."[45]

Reporters from across the nation who were already in Saint Louis to cover the Democratic National Convention were fascinated, however, and they scurried to inform readers of these relative unknowns in the general black population. The African American *Palladium* of Saint Louis described Scott as an "old man" and an "objectionable Negro," and the African American *Daily Miami Metropolis* reviewed his move to East Saint Louis, noting that Scott was known for "his diamonds and gold-filled teeth" and regionally as "the only Democratic negro in the State of Illinois."[46] Captain Payne, in contrast, they described as "a new issue negro" and as "only 37 years old."[47] Payne had served on board the transport ship *Dixie*, which had taken troops to Puerto Rico during the Spanish-American War.[48] He had attended Wayland Seminary in Washington, DC, and had obtained patronage that was for a "long time connected with the Naval Observatory."[49] Born in Virginia in 1867, Payne was still considered an Independent Republican and was expected to provide regional and party balance to the ticket and draw significant votes from those blacks in the South who could still vote.[50]

The party's platform reflected a coalition of dissatisfied voters that comprised the new party. The plank regarding "unrestricted suffrage for all American citizens, without distinction or qualification" deserved universal concern, for black males in the South were reeling from a barrage of state-based laws designed precisely to deprive them of the right to vote, and to do it without violating the Fifteenth Amendment to the nation's Constitution. A second plank dealt with the army and the often-cited complaint that there were not enough black officers nor sufficient black regiments for those blacks who might choose a manly career in the military. It requested promotions and pensions for blacks who had served in the Spanish-American War. Imperialism and American involvement in the Philippines were major issues for the Anti-Imperialism League and for Scott, who had been a founder of that league in 1899. Essentially, that plank called for the United States to adopt a policy of "non-interference in the affairs of the Far East until the government is able to protect its citizens at home." Another plank focused on a topic dear to the hearts of all Populists, and there were still many within the rural black population. It stipulated that the government should assert ownership of "all common carriers"—railroads. It also asked for "self-government for the District of Columbia." The platform asked that all religious denominations assist in the suppression of mob rule and support a lynch law that would enable the federal government to use its full might against those persons' intent to lynch.[51] And finally, it supported a pension bill for ex-slaves.[52]

Still convinced that the National Negro Liberty Party served as an arm of the Democratic Party, Republican newspapers and their editors insisted that the new party was involved in a Democratic-paid conspiracy to split the Republican vote, especially in the southern parts of Illinois, Indiana, and Ohio, where black votes were crucial to Republican victory. The *Appeal* of Saint Paul concluded that it was "a good scheme [for Scott, Payne, and Mitchell] to hold out their plates while the soup [money] is being passed around."[53] The *Saint Louis Republic* believed that the party might actually deprive the Republicans of victory.[54]

Within days of the convention's end and once delegates had left the Douglass Hotel, circumstances changed quickly and dramatically. Scott later explained that his Independent Republican "friends" in East Saint Louis, who believed that the only purpose of the new party was to split the black vote and who were jealous of his success, arranged that he be arrested for failure to pay the full fine that had been imposed on him earlier for "conducting a disorderly house."[55] At the time of his initial arrest in 1901, Scott had professed his innocence of the charge, but, following the practice of that day, he had agreed to pay $50.00 of the $149.80 costs and fine the court imposed. He believed that he "was given time to pay the balance," which everyone knew to mean that it might never be paid and that he had reached an agreement or plea bargain with the court to the effect that he had paid a portion and the remainder "was to be remitted pending no other charges."[56] Even the *Decatur Review* agreed, suggesting that "if Scott had been an ordinary negro the authorities would have been content with a fine of $3 and costs, but a candidate for the presidency had to be treated with more distinction, so they pushed him up close to the $100 [$2,600 in 2010 dollars] mark."[57] Upon his rearrest on 13 July, however, he was taken to Belleville, Saint Clair County, where he was sentenced to spend twenty days in jail.[58] The *Washington Post* ridiculed both the party and Scott, describing him and his campaign as being "a little handicapped by reason of being in jail."[59]

Scott should have been able to pay his full fine when it was levied, but perhaps he interpreted the fine itself as part of a game he had played with the police and the courts from his earliest days in Cairo. As a seasoned gambler, he was a risk taker. He had accumulated significant wealth that way. Even Chase of the *Washington Bee* noted that "at the time of his nomination, Scott was wealthy."[60] But surely, as a risk taker, Scott had lost assets during the panics that had gripped the nation in the 1890s. In 1889 he claimed that he owned rental property in the black town of Hodges Park (Unity Ward) near Cairo and admitted that he had made his fortune "very rapidly." Additionally, he had diversified his holdings, even investing in a "wood and coal yard" and in a "stock farm."[61] But wealth in property or business ownership did not mean that he had ready access to liquid capital.[62]

Mitchell, surprised by this turn of events, summoned the party's executive committee to an emergency meeting to be held on 20 July and, against Scott's objection and while he was still in Belleville's jail, removed him as the party's standard-bearer.[63] Rather than advance Payne to the top of the party's ticket, Mitchell and his committee turned to George Edwin Taylor, the past president of the National Negro Democratic League. Taylor, at age forty-seven, had not attended Mitchell's convention, but he had met with party leaders twice while in Saint Louis and likely had expressed his interest in their objectives, especially since the nation and the Democratic Party had regressed significantly in civil rights issues during his four years as president of the league.[64] When James Ross of Buffalo, New York, replaced him as the league's president in 1904, Taylor knew that Ross would return the league to its earlier focus of finding state and city offices for black Democrats. Taylor's term also had coincided with the growth of a virulent form of racism based on scientific theory and on the premise that blacks were inherently different from and inferior to the white race.

Taylor's background was different from that of the leaders of this new party.[65] He was born a free black in the slaveholding state of Arkansas in 1857, had left Arkansas in 1860, and was orphaned in Alton, Illinois, at the height of the Civil War. He ended up at age eight in La Crosse, Wisconsin, where the courts fostered him to a black farmer until he reached the age of twenty. Taylor was fortunate. His foster parents sent him to the private Wayland University in Beaver Dam, Wisconsin.[66] From there he returned to La Crosse, where he developed superb organizational skills and engaged in local and state politics, never seeking public office for himself. He became secretary to the Wisconsin Union Labor Party in 1886. He was an engaging and humorous speaker. Taylor also owned and edited his own newspaper in La Crosse before he moved to Oskaloosa, Iowa, where he fine-tuned his administrative abilities. In quick order he transitioned from Republican to Democrat and within a decade climbed steadily within the ranks of politically active midwestern blacks. He was president of the National Colored Men's Protective Association in 1892, president of the Tri-State Free Silver League in 1897, member of the executive board of the Anti-Imperialist League when Scott was its president, and president of the National Negro Democratic League in 1900 when Scott was its vice president. But like Scott, Taylor was ready to leave the Democrats, who seemed increasingly willing if not eager to jettison any resolve to protect black civil rights after 1900.

Scott believed himself betrayed when he learned that Taylor had replaced him on the ticket. Yet he remained loyal to the party. He campaigned for the Liberty Party's congressional candidates in Illinois in 1904, despite the fact that the party failed to obtain a place on the Illinois presidential ballot.[67] Whatever initial enthusiasm that had existed for the party and its candidates had evaporated, however, with the debacle of Scott's arrest. The regular press dismissed the party as led by "fools, cranks, and would-be-democrats."[68] The three hundred stump speakers and six thousand candidates promised nationwide as a way to rally black voters to the party failed to materialize, although W. L. Smith, who had given the party's inaugural address, continued to make that claim as late as 31 October 1904, only a week before the election.[69] Taylor wasn't even in charge of his own campaign, which Mitchell directed from Chicago. Not a single black newspaper championed the party.[70]

When the 1904 election ended, Taylor, whose enthusiasm waned during the campaign, had had enough of the party and black politics, and he retreated to his farm in Iowa, where he secluded himself at a time when the country seemed to be jumping into an abyss. The Republican landslide of 1904 had also been large enough to demonstrate that Republicans no longer needed black votes to win elections. For Scott, however, the 1904 election had only strengthened his resolve to make a difference. He even hedged his options during that election cycle. He campaigned for the Liberty Party's congressional candidate in Illinois's Twenty-Second Congressional District, thereby pulling black voters from the Republican column, although that was not enough to defeat the Republican candidate in a landslide election year.[71] That gesture, however, reconnected him to his links with Illinois's Democratic leaders, who rewarded him on 2 January 1905 with a patronage appointment as custodian of the Democratic cloakroom at the Illinois state legislature.[72] Scott had sought such an appointment in 1893 and had then been offered "a job cleaning spittoons," which he had declined.[73] Scott accepted the cloakroom appointment and moved to Springfield, Illinois's capital and the seat of state government. Unlike Taylor, Scott was not interested in leaving his field fallow in 1905.

Hard Landing and
Slow Recovery in Springfield

[Scott:] I still had principles left and I did what I could for the party, which sooner or later would have a black man in the white house without waiting for some white man to ask him in to supper.[1] With all the troubles we had, the liberty party got 65,000 votes in the election and four or five hundred right around East St. Louis.

I ain't very mad now, though, because I am here at Springfield, where I can find out about national affairs, and when the time comes they had better look out for me. There is going to be a rattling of the dry bones among some of those East St. Louis niggers when I get back to them.

Marshfield Times, 19 February 1905

In 1905 Scott was hardly at an age to embrace an opportunity to start over. Nor was he particularly concerned about being accurate in his assessment of the failed 1904 campaign. The Negro Liberty Party and Taylor's name were on no officially sanctioned ballot, and it is doubtful that Taylor obtained sixty-five thousand write-in votes. Nor were there four hundred or five hundred votes cast for the party's congressional candidate near East Saint Louis. Scott's salary of $3 per day (approximately $75 in 2010 dollars) as custodian at the state legislature's Democratic cloakroom was adequate for the times but not enough to satisfy his ambition or keep him in his accustomed style. That appointment, to last only for that legislative session, gave him recognition within Springfield's black community and reentry into local Democratic politics, but any chance that he might recapture a leadership role among black Democrats at the national level had vanished as a result of his erratic behavior in 1904, as had any opportunity for obtaining revenge.

Captive in a small place with limited ideas, Scott seemed oblivious to changes in black leadership flowing to the Niagara Group after 1905, the National Association for the Advancement of Colored People after 1909, and finally to the National League on Urban Conditions among Negroes after 1910. Though white Democrats in Springfield had thrown him a meager lifeline and an opportunity to change, he seemed satisfied to follow paths that led back to his old habits of alienation, independence, confrontation, and exaggeration. Unable and unwilling to evaluate and lower his expectations of what could be achieved, he could not resist joining or forming yet another league. He complained that he was "property poor ... without sufficient cash to keep up his rented houses."[2] Scott needed to focus on new circumstances, because the political, economic, and social worlds he knew had changed. Scott already was a news item and had been arrested more than once for maintaining a disorderly house. Within a single year he had gone from presidential candidate to custodian of a cloakroom. Springfield's newspapers followed him because he was newsworthy; their readers were interested in his audacious activities.

Once settled in Springfield, Scott temporarily abandoned his ties with Democrats at the national level and turned to businesses he knew best. Perhaps he had little choice. Within a few months of his move from East Saint Louis, he was operating a successful saloon and dance club known as Maceo's Palm Garden and Social Club at 1901 East Cook Street in Springfield.[3] He followed the model dominating the saloon business in 1905. Scott was owner-operator of the saloon, but the Reisch Brewing Company owned the building and all of the equipment that stored beer and channeled it to the beer tap at the bar counter. The company even owned the "stock." Scott brought to the enterprise forty years of experience as a tavern owner and his reputation as an efficient manager. He had ample financial resources to cover essential costs or, at the least, knew how to obtain those resources. He also was following another trend within the business. He labeled the saloon a men's social club, but his customers tended to be the same noisy crowd. The *Daily Illinois State Journal* characterized it as a "colored amusement resort."[4] Neighbors complained that "shouts of laughter" and "the thumping of a piano were audible for blocks around" his club.[5] Those complaints also attracted the police, who arrested forty-two of Scott's customers on or about 1 August 1905. On the morning of 29 August, police arrested another "forty-odd" of Scott's customers on charges of disorderly conduct. While Springfield's courts eventually dismissed charges against those arrested, these raids were only the first of numerous police harassments that plagued Scott and his customers for the coming decade.[6] Essentially, his reputation (and practice) of operating rowdy nightclubs also followed him to Springfield, where police watched him attentively.

Naming his first business in Springfield after the Cuban independence fighter Antonio Maceo Grajales signaled that Scott had changed little from his behavior in Cairo. Rather, he returned to patterns that had brought him financial success and political fulfillment in the past. He identified with warrior-heroes whose combination of physical strength and intellectual prowess won battles against those exercising power, whether outright opponents or supposed allies. Maceo, known as the "Bronze Titan" because of his skin color and his reputation as a fearless opponent of Spanish rule in Cuba, was a rebel opposed to the ruling classes, and so was Scott. Prominent in Cuba's Freemasonry movement, Maceo opposed slavery and servitude in any form. He had joined the Cuban independence movement before 1870, and, despite the racial prejudice against him among his fellow rebels, he became a leading guerrilla warfare strategist before his death at the battle of Punta Brava near Havana in 1896.[7] George E. Taylor, Scott's replacement on the National Negro Liberty Party's ticket in 1904, described Maceo as "the greatest Negro soldier and general of modern times," and the *Colored American* identified him as "the greatest hero of the nineteenth century."[8]

Scott had operated the Maceo Social Club in Cairo in 1899, following examples set in Saint Paul, Minnesota, Richmond, Virginia, and elsewhere.[9] These clubs maintained halls where large groups could meet to discuss political issues, and they sponsored baseball teams.[10] Both of those activities interested Scott. What most linked Scott to Maceo, however, was a growing attitude among white Americans—even among some who supported civil rights—that while nonwhites might excel as great warriors, they were incapable of becoming effective rulers. Maceo served as more than just a heroic symbol of black manhood, however. He personified the principle of blacks' capacity to manage their own affairs, whether in Cuba or in Saint Paul, Richmond, or Springfield. He symbolized the notion that blacks could conduct themselves on their own terms without white assistance, an approach that put Scott at odds with new trends developing on the East Coast and in upper midwestern urban centers.

Nor was Scott particularly humbled by his rearrest after being named to the National Negro Liberty Party's ticket. In 1905 he gave two interviews in which he claimed that he had been jailed for political reasons, the victim of a "double-cross down in that East St. Louis town." He said that the charge of operating a "lewd house for the practice of fornication" was insignificant, "a matter of minor importance."[11] Although he freely admitted that he often had operated on the edge of the law and that he "used to run up the river a little way," he claimed that he had campaigned in 1904 for L. E. Dudley, Liberty Party candidate for Congress from Illinois's Twenty-Second Congressional District.[12] His efforts to reduce the number of blacks voting Republican were unlikely considerations when Democrats in the Illinois legislature appointed him as their cloakroom custodian in 1905. They obviously considered him a loyal Democrat, despite his independent rhetoric and his consistent claims to support "the best man and measure irrespective of party name."[13]

Scott's dance hall and saloon on East Cook also attracted attention. Others could observe his success by the numbers of his customers, and success brought him at least one potential investor, Henry Rhodes, who, for a single payment of $200, had become Scott's partner. Scott, however, apparently failed to explain to Rhodes that the club's building and all of its equipment belonged to the Reisch Brewing Company. Rhodes complained to authorities, who arrested Scott and charged him with fraud for "obtaining money under false pretenses."[14] Justice Connelly dismissed charges against Scott on 20 December 1905; it is likely that Scott's reputation as a "sly" businessman had followed him to Springfield and that Rhodes was merely attempting to recapture a bad investment.[15]

Scott's status as a political activist and community "organizer" also followed him, although it took him nearly four years to regain the momentum he had lost in 1904. In September 1905 Scott and his club were enough established to host the city's Labor Day celebrations, which included music, dancing, and, according to the *Illinois State Journal*, "a watermelon barbecue."[16] In November 1906 he served on a Springfield committee raising funds to support a school-related lawsuit in Alton, Illinois, and by November 1907 he was president of a new society that he founded to focus on local issues and to advance himself politically within Springfield's black community. By that date, Scott also had opened a print shop at 706½ East Washington Street, where he published a new weekly newspaper, the *Springfield Leader*, which he continued to print as a Democrat and insurgent newspaper until 1916.[17] And he was active in Springfield's Colored Personal Liberty League. The league opposed the state's local option law, which was passed by the state legislature on 16 May 1907 and permitted wards to outlaw saloons and the sale of alcohol within their territories, thereby compressing saloons into ever smaller zones within the city and affecting his livelihood.[18] By 1908 he had become the secretary of the Frederick Douglass Lodge of the United Brothers of Friendship and was a member of the Ambidexter Institute's auxiliary board of directors, which had been given the task of purchasing a home for dependent orphaned black children.[19]

Nor had Scott divorced himself completely from what remained of the dysfunctional National Negro Liberty Party or removed himself from national politics. In 1905 he told a reporter that "if the colored race will demonstrate its power by showing how many votes it can pool[,] then its people will command respect and consideration."[20] Most of all, Scott wanted blacks to vote for their own political and economic interests.[21] And he continued to insist, even in a time when the nation was moving away from patronage to a regularized civil service, that parties "give the negro his pro rata of representation in some representative positions."[22] He believed—and was willing to state even while accepting Democratic patronage—that blacks would rally to the Liberty Party once they understood that neither of the established, white-dominated parties would give adequate attention to issues important to black Americans, especially as long as there were black leaders such as Booker T. Washington, whom he accused of flattering whites for personal gain.[23] He was not a team player and certainly not interested in collaborating with whites to secure advancement for his race.

Scott was sufficiently grounded by 1908, however, to champion another attempt to secure illusive collaboration among black-only political organizations. On 19 June Scott met in Chicago with a large and enthusiastic group of blacks who had joined forces locally to campaign against the presumptive Republican candidate for the presidency, William H. Taft of Ohio.[24] That anti-Taft group appointed a committee, chaired by Scott, to convene a joint convention of the National Negro Democratic League, the National Negro American Political League, the National Negro Anti-Expansion League, the national Niagara Movement, and the remnants of the National Negro Liberty Party to be held in Denver, Colorado, at the same time and place as the Democratic National Convention. Organizers directed the convention committee to develop a statement and a list of suggested platform planks and to issue the conference announcement. One major question in 1908 was whether delegates to such a joint convention would support the nominee of the Democrats or chose to field a separate "colored man's ticket."[25] Scott indicated that delegates would "consider their affiliations, and conditions, and develop plans to change the political complexion of states wherein the negro vote is the balance of power" and could exercise the most leverage.[26] Essentially, Scott's focus shifted from making a statement through votes at the national level, as he and others had attempted in 1904; instead, he turned his attention, as with the Pittsburgh convention in 1884, to states, districts, and cities where the number of black voters might have a direct impact upon local election outcomes. Another question to discuss and possibly resolve concerned a continuing debate within the black community regarding President Roosevelt's abrupt dismissal of 167 black soldiers attached to the Twenty-Fifth Regiment in Brownsville, Texas, in 1906.

The Denver convention, held on 8 July, was a strange affair. The conference call had indicated that delegates from thirty-seven states had requested the joint meeting and that its conference committee was comprised of major voices within the black community and leaders from all sponsoring leagues. The conference call also indicated that Scott then chaired the national committee of the National Negro Liberty Party. It listed Bishop Alexander Walters of New Jersey, Monroe Trotter of Boston, W. E. B. Du Bois of Ohio, J. Milton Waldron of Washington, E. L. Gilliam of Ohio, W. C. Payne of Virginia, and Fredrick L.

McGhee of Minnesota as possible candidates for president of the United States should the convention decide to select a separate ticket.[27] Delegates elected Scott temporary chair of the convention. George Taylor, National Negro Liberty Party candidate in 1904, delivered a "forceful speech" in which he condemned President Roosevelt for ordering the dishonorable discharge of black soldiers in the Brownsville Affair and also called for the formation of yet another league, the National Negro Anti-Taft League, that would "merge all negro political organizations into one party," a plan that had little chance of securing the 250,000 to 400,000 votes promised by convention delegates.[28]

The convention accomplished its principal purpose, electing officers and appointing committees for the new league. Selected as the new league's second vice president, Scott served on the committee on resolutions along with George Taylor.[29] On 14 July a delegation consisting of Scott, Taylor of Iowa, and P. C. Thomas of Kansas "called on" William Jennings Bryan, the Democratic candidate for the presidency, at his home in Lincoln, Nebraska. They pledged the league's support for the "Great Commoner" and indicated that the league would concentrate its efforts in Indiana and New York, where the number of black voters was large enough to swing those states into the Democratic column.[30] Scott's activities in Chicago, Denver, and Lincoln signaled his reentry and acceptance into black Democratic politics, at least at the regional level. But they also indicated that Scott chased a chimera. He was attempting to revive a plan that had earlier failed to bring success, and he was linking himself to a presidential candidate whose time had passed and who had little chance of winning. In the meantime, America's black leadership in the upper Midwest and along the East Coast was moving in another direction.

It is unclear that Scott had returned to Springfield by 14 August when a small group of "drunken and reeling [white] men" began a period of three days of looting, burning, and lynching that left two blacks and four whites dead.[31] At that time, Scott's printing business was located on the riot zone's edge, which included nearly every black-owned building along East Washington Street between Eighth and Twelfth Streets. White owners flew white flags and handkerchiefs to indicate which buildings to leave untouched. When the rioting ended, large sections of black Springfield were in ruins. Nearly all blacks had fled the city or to the protection of the National Guard Armory. The governor of Illinois had summoned twenty-five hundred members of the National Guard from surrounding towns to maintain order, but he refused to give troops orders to fire upon crowds of rioters, looters, and onlookers. When fire engine crews attempted to control the spread of fires, people cut their water hoses.[32]

As the hometown of the president most responsible for liberating the slaves, Springfield was not a place America expected a race riot. Many viewed Springfield symbolically and reverently as a center of antislavery and as a memorial to

Abraham Lincoln's legacy. Of its forty-seven thousand residents in 1908, approximately twenty-five hundred (a little more than 5 percent) were blacks.[33] Culturally, however, Springfield was "a Northern city by only the barest of margins."[34] Whites held nearly all the skilled jobs, leaving blacks with menial posts as janitors, servants, cooks, waiters, domestics, and day workers. Blacks lived in two compressed sections of town. In the Badlands, located near the city center, city authorities permitted cheap saloons, billiard and gambling rooms, and bawdy houses to flourish, if for no better reason than to keep those businesses from spreading into the city's business and government sectors. Approximately 90 percent of Springfield's blacks lived in the Badlands.[35] So long as blacks remained quarantined within that zone, most of Springfield's white population ignored them, unless whites used blacks' services.[36] Once blacks began to spread into Springfield's government and business districts, however, attitudes began to change.

Other undercurrents in Springfield's racial setting involved blacks in the workforce and the continuing growth of reform-minded societies. In economic downturns, large numbers of Springfield's underemployed blacks became "scab" recruits for employers seeking to break attempts by white labor to hold the line on the number of hours worked and on wages. White workers viewed blacks as competitors for unskilled jobs and always as enemies of organized labor.[37] Reformers also sought to rid Springfield of liquor "dens," around which they believed prostitutes, pickpockets, and bad sorts collected. Many within these reformist groups fed upon pseudoscientific eugenic theories that identified "criminal types" and racial behavioral traits, all of which supposedly explained society's ills, which somehow could be fixed. Most white Americans believed that whites were superior to all races and that they alone had the wisdom and ability to solve the "Negro problem."[38] The psychological theories popular at the time also emphasized that certain people, aggressive by nature, were destined to become rulers. White heroes were insistent, and they always won in the cosmic struggle between good and bad. Two immensely popular novels, *The Leopard's Spots* (1902) and *The Clansman* (1905), portrayed black males as lazy and racially inferior, and these novels were as important for fueling white rage in the early twentieth century as was *Uncle Tom's Cabin* for freeing the slaves in the antebellum period.[39]

Although not the first of its kind in the North, the Springfield riot became the catalyst for significant changes. Six persons had died, but of the 107 indictments brought against eighty persons identified as rioters, only one person spent any time in jail—for thirty days.[40] The conclusion of the jury was simple and startling: "We believe no innocent man met his death at the hands of the mob."[41] Most national newspapers covered the riot because of its violence and because it had occurred in Springfield. Some blamed the victims and identified the saloon and vice trades as causes. But most editors and social activists pondered the problem and its solution. They also noted that blacks had taken up arms to defend themselves in Springfield.[42] By that date, "manly self-defense" had become a necessity rather than an option. Blacks proved not as docile as the general population had thought.

Perhaps the most lasting positive outcome from the Springfield riot was a conference that met in the city six months later on 12 February 1909. A distinguished group of national educators, jurists, social workers, religious leaders, and publicists attended this meeting to focus on the root causes of rioting and lynching, which seemed endemic in American society. This group differed from the Niagara Group, which formed in 1905 under the leadership of W. E. B. Du Bois. That group had consisted of black professionals mainly from the New England states or graduates of universities who were intent upon producing an educated elite and who believed that black voters lacked leadership and "creative consciousness." Those qualities, they suggested, would come from a self-appointed "Talented Tenth," a group of "exceptional men" who would act as a vanguard of the race, as an "aristocracy of talent."[43] The attendees at the 1909 conference, in contrast, consisted of intellectuals of both races, and they laid the foundations for a new organization, the National Association for the Advancement of Colored People (NAACP). At its inception, the executive board of the new association contained only one African American—W. E. B. Du Bois. Educated at Harvard University and the University of Berlin, Du Bois viewed the "Negro problem" from a distance, from "outside of the American world, looking in."[44] The NAACP would not elect a black president until 1975. Of the early association's leaders, only two were blacks.[45]

Whether the horrific events of 1908 had chastened Scott or the creation of a new association controlled by whites had changed his mind or influenced his behavior is unclear. Both had occurred in his hometown. He apparently had escaped the riot's destruction. He certainly did not fit well in an association dominated by whites. Scott, instead, seemed willing, if not eager, to remain close to his base during his remaining years. At seventy years of age in 1909, he chose to reduce traveling and speaking in public. Conversely, perhaps others dismissed him because of his age and his infamous 1904 fiasco. He could not claim to be a member of the new intellectual elite that was emerging on the East Coast and was proclaiming its own brand of black independence.[46] The divide between white and black America had probably never been greater. And the distance between black midwesterners from small cities and those from large urban centers in the upper Midwest and East Coast had widened, rapidly leaving Scott and others of his generation and small-town social class behind.

While the riot and the activities of reformers and prohibitionists had not changed Scott's attitude about the rights of saloon owners, he had changed the nature of his business. On the second floor of the building at 706½ East Washington, where he printed the *Springfield Leader*, Scott in 1909 opened a cafe-restaurant-resort called the Pekin Red Moon Club, named after the black-operated and famously successful Pekin Theater on "the Stroll" on Chicago's State Street and the popular musical comedy *The Red Moon*.[47] Scott described his cafe as an exclusive and private men's social club, a refuge for black men no longer secure in an environment that openly assigned them to second-class citizenship. His club was not licensed to sell alcohol, and women could be invited as guests but could not become members, characteristics similar to those of a fraternal society whose membership was known only to members. Scott held the club's presidency.

Understandably, Scott's association with the club and its claim of privacy brought the attention of Springfield's police, newspaper editors, and public. In October 1909 a fire at the neighboring Dunbar Theatre, located at 710 East Washington, forced an evacuation of the Red Moon Club's occupants: "Kimona clad women visitors at the Red Moon club tumbled over male members in a mad fright [*sic*] down the narrow stairway and joined the scared Blacks emerging from the theatre." A month later, a police raid on "rooms" at the Red Moon Club resulted in the arrest of Scott, eight other men, and thirteen women on charges of disorderly conduct, sale of liquor without a license, and sale of liquor to a minor. When police asked Scott for a list of club officers and members, he claimed that he could not remember or disclose their names. Scott explained that the club met twice a week, that its seventy-five members brought their own liquor, and that no liquor was sold within the club.[48] In that instance, and to avoid a police investigation of the club and its activities, Scott pled guilty and paid a fine of $10 and costs, but he also claimed consistently that his club was a social and private organization and was not required to purchase a liquor license.[49] Police arrested Scott at least fourteen times between 1909 and 1916 on charges of selling liquor without a license and permitting illegal gambling.[50] The police chief explained that raids were conducted only "to improve moral conditions in Springfield."[51] A raid on the Red Moon in February 1912 resulted in charges against four persons for "being inmates of a house of ill-fame."[52] The reading public and newspaper editors were fascinated. Those published accounts did not, however, convince Scott to remove himself from that sort of business.

That Scott was able to hold fast to a matter of principle that, while perhaps laudable from a libertarian perspective, was questionable nevertheless and at the same time to involve himself in political action at the state and national levels was a tribute to his ability to focus and not concern himself with contradictions—which were many. Unfortunately, no copies of the *Springfield Leader* have survived to enable an in-depth analysis of his reasoning during this period. The *Daily Illinois State Journal* and the *Broad Ax* of Chicago, however, followed his activities because they provided readers with a view of black politics at the state and community levels and tawdry tidbits of vice and more than a bit of audacity from a black person at the turn of the century. But their reports also were incomplete and focused on Scott's more problematic activities. Scott was living with his newspaper's stenographer, Helen "Lizzy" Shelby, thirty-three years his junior.[53] He was president of a men's club that—if its arrest record and convictions were correct—provided its members with female companionship, but not, according to the *Illinois State Journal*, of the "high-toned" quality of that supplied at the Grill, "another negro club said to exist in a building near Eleventh and Washington" in Springfield.[54]

After 1909 Scott spent his efforts, aside from his role as president of the men's club and editor of his newspaper, in three fields. He remained active in Illinois's Colored Personal Liberty League, not to be confused with the Civil Liberty Party of 1904, of which Scott also was president. The latter had transformed into the National Negro Liberty Party, which had nominated him for the presidency. This league was less involved in litigation and more concerned with providing a neutral but progressive forum outside the political party structure. It associated itself with the national group only at convention times. Newspapers seldom reported their activities, and when they did, they often confused them with civil and personal liberty leagues, which were opposed to reformist movements attempting to enforce Sunday drinking laws and curb alcohol consumption and vice.[55] Scott involved himself in both of these types of personal liberty leagues. He served as president of the nonpartisan Colored Personal Liberty League from 1913 to 1916; its state headquarters were at the same address as Scott's print shop.[56]

In addition, he was president of the Negro Independent State League of Illinois when he issued a call for a conference of "Negro Progressives, Insurgents and Democrats" to meet in Springfield on 5 October 1911 "for the purpose of discussing the feasibility of entering onto [*sic*] a coalition for the purpose of organizing a state league for their [own] protection."[57] More specifically, Scott wrote: "They [black men] do not propose to stand pat in the coming [presidential] campaign of 1912 and get left [behind], but will go with the tidal wave—as there is not an intelligent progressive or insurgent Negro in the country who but believes the time has come when we should cast our votes independently, regardless of politics, as party affiliates in the past have proven to be detrimental to the best interest of the race. They will therefore agitate, educate and organize under the banner of manhood rights."[58] He added: "Any Colored voter who is interested in the advancement of his people . . . will be entitled to a seat, privileges of the floor and participate in the discussions." The call did not mention white people. The *Broad Ax*, which was prone to hyperbole, announced the conference as "the largest and most prominent that has ever been held in this state among our people in a political movement,—as much dissatisfaction exists."[59] That group met as scheduled and passed resolutions to the effect that it was "opposed to all political parties" and that it urged its members "to vote for men and measures rather than party affiliations."[60] The new organization elected officers, among them Scott, who became chair of the league's executive committee and assumed the title of league "grand organizer," which he held until at least 1916.[61]

At the state level, Scott also remained active within the state branch of the National Negro Democratic League, which he had abandoned in 1904 when he became one of the founders of the National Negro Liberty Party. He regained status with that league in 1908, when he was the convener of the union conference of Democratic leagues that met together in Denver. He emerged from that conference as the second vice president of the new National Negro Anti-Taft League, which lasted only through that election cycle. He attended the Democratic National Convention in Baltimore, Maryland, in June and July 1912 and was especially proud that a "Colored" troop of two hundred men, led by a musical unit, had marched through the streets of Baltimore before arriving at the convention site and "entered it on tickets furnished them by prominent Democrats."[62] The National Negro Democratic League, which met and elected new officials in 1912, selected Bishop Alexander Walters as its president and W. T. Scott as Illinois's representative and member of its executive committee.[63]

Against that success, Scott's most humiliating experience while in Springfield came in July 1912, when Rufus A. Lackland, a wealthy cattleman and land speculator from Tarrant, Texas, parked a railcar on the tracks at the Wabash Railroad station, advertising his products and inviting the public to come in and visit his exhibition. Lackland had posted a sign at the railcar's door indicating that only whites would be admitted. That was a challenge that Scott could not resist. He entered the car, and Lackland's men removed him "forcibly." Scott swore out an arrest warrant, charging Lackland with violating his civil rights and with assault and battery. Lackland claimed that his car was personal property and therefore was immune from proscriptions outlined in civil rights laws. Springfield's blacks crowded the courtroom when the case came before Justice James Reilly. Reilly ruled that the exhibition car indeed was private property, and he dismissed Scott's charges.[64] "Jim Crow" was alive and thriving in the Wabash Railroad Company yard and in Springfield.

It is uncertain that Scott was among the large assembly of black leaders who attended Woodrow Wilson's inaugural ceremonies in March 1913, although the

Illinois State Register reported that Scott had been "head of the negro reception committee" at Wilson's inauguration.[65] The *Alaska Citizen*, a Republican press, in its own demeaning way, announced that the National Negro Democratic League would host a separate inaugural ball and that "all the fancy dances to which the colored race is prone will be shown, cake-walking, turkey trotting, ragging, Texas Tommy and every gyroscopic movement that the mind can conceive."[66] Wilson's inaugural, however, was a grand affair for African Americans. Julius Taylor, editor of Chicago's *Broad Ax*, described black participation in different terms: "It was the first time in the history of this country that the best and the most distinguished Afro-American men and women dressed in the height of fashion."[67] The inaugural parade contained a unit of fifty members of the National Negro Democratic League, each "wearing high silk hats," but Scott was not listed among the marchers. George Edwin Taylor, who had been president of the league from 1900 to 1904 and candidate of the National Liberty Party in 1904, and James A. Ross, president of the league from 1904 to 1908, marched, even though Taylor, like Scott, had abandoned the party during the 1904 election cycle. Bishop Alexander Walters, a respected confidant of Wilson and one of those who had declined to be the standard-bearer of the National Negro Liberty Party in 1904, sat near the newly elected president during his inaugural address.[68] Taylor's participation in both the Denver Convention in 1908 and the inauguration of Wilson four years later certainly raises the question of how independent the National Negro Liberty Party had been of the National Democratic Party in 1904.

At age seventy-four, however, Scott received at least the dubious honor of having his name considered in 1913 as a candidate for the post of minister to the Republic of Haiti, a patronage appointment that had been held by blacks since the Civil War.[69] Scott had attempted to secure the nomination and appointment in 1892, and Cairo's newspapers had then supported his application more as a potential banishment from Cairo than a reward for service rendered.[70] In 1913 every state nominated a favorite son, with Indiana and New York State nominating three each.[71] Scott's age, health, and arrest record, however, were not the only reasons for denying him that post. President Woodrow Wilson appointed Madison R. Smith, a white southern Democrat and former congressman from Missouri. Calvin Chase of the *Washington Bee* suggested simply that it "was too big a plum for the Bourbon South to give to one outside their [white] ranks."[72] According to the *Cleveland Daily Plain Dealer*, the Haitians also had objected to another black holding that post.[73] The State Department argued that no black within the diplomatic service was prepared to serve in that capacity. The actual reasons likely related to Wilson's reluctance to reappoint blacks to patronage positions held over from the Taft administration. The

Oregonian noted only that "southern Senators had been antagonizing the nominations of negroes to important offices," and, with southern Democrats in control of the Senate's agenda, Wilson had chosen instead to avoid controversy within the party by appointing only whites to positions requiring Senate approval.[74] It had become another "Jim Crow" issue.

But Scott's nomination, in spite of his lack of qualifications, also demonstrated Scott's resourcefulness and his exaggerated regard for his own achievements. During the preceding session of the Illinois legislature, Scott had been the unpaid "janitor of the speaker's offices," and he had quietly carried his application papers to support his nomination around to members within the legislature.[75] His activities in the National Liberty Party were overlooked, as were his activities with other leagues and associations that seemed to be asking black voters to select alternatives to both established parties. And apparently no one was concerned about the past activities of his Red Moon Club nor had knowledge of his legal infractions and convictions in Cairo, East Saint Louis, or Springfield. At the same time, party officials again placed his name on the payroll of the Illinois legislature as custodian of the Democratic cloakroom.[76]

Nor would he retire from politics. In May 1914, then president of Illinois's Negro State Democratic League, which claimed a membership of twenty thousand men, and clearly a dedicated Democrat, Scott summoned a conference of like-minded Democrats to be held in Chicago to prepare for the primary election in September. At that time, Scott also was a member of the executive committee of the National Negro Democratic League, of which Bishop Alexander Walters was then president.[77] The Illinois league met in August and selected Lawrence B. Stringer as its choice for U.S. senator from Illinois.[78] In October, however, and before the November election, Scott met with blacks in Decatur, where they established a branch of the Illinois State Coalition League, of which Scott claimed to be president and "organizer." Scott maintained that the coalition league's aim was to support "the best man and measure irrespective of party name."[79] Scott apparently saw no contradiction in being an executive committee member of a national Democratic league and the president of a state-based league that was willing to support a candidate from other than the Democratic Party and that claimed that "the negro has no party" and "has been deserted in the house of his friends."[80]

By June 1915 editors Julius Taylor of the *Broad Ax* and Scott of the *Springfield Leader* had joined forces to question the expenditures of a biracial state commission that the Illinois legislature had established in 1913 to organize and stage a state-funded celebration of ratification of the Thirteenth Amendment to the U.S. Constitution, which ended slavery in 1865. Taylor of the *Broad Ax* was the principal investigator in this enquiry, having learned that only $2,000 of the initial allocation of $25,000 ($568,000 in 2010 dollars) remained, with no one knowing precisely how the commission had spent the missing $23,000. The commission had asked for an additional $25,000, but Taylor had objected, requesting instead that the legislature establish a strict accounting system. Taylor, Scott, and several other black editors met with the state Appropriation Committee on 9 June 1915 and requested that only $5,000 additional be allocated, but only if there were "apparent results" forthcoming.[81]

Nor was Scott entirely ready to abandon the Illinois Liberty League, which dated to 1900 and of which he remained the perpetual president. In early July 1915 he hosted a league convention at the Masonic Hall in Chicago, although only one report of that meeting appeared in the press.[82] He also attended the Thirty-Seventh Annual Session of the United Brothers of Friendship, held in Chicago in August 1915.[83] He remained in 1915 the president of the Negro State Democratic League, and he continued to be active in the National Negro Democratic League, submitting, as chairman of the league's committee on resolutions, a proposed plank during the 1916 Democratic National Convention to the party's platform committee. The plank read in part:

> We solemnly affirm the civil equality of all elements of our American citizenship and we emphasize our advocacy of proportionate, dignified representation of each such distinct element in official service under this government of the people without any restricting consideration of race, color or other invidious distinction; and we truthfully aver that any appearing departure from these principles in the acts of any Democratic administration has resulted from extraneous exigencies and not at all from disregard of the just axioms here enunciated, to which we unequivocally commit the nominees of this convention with the respectful counsel that any appearing violation thereof be made clear by pronounced illuminating action. We recognize, without favorable or unfavorable criticism, the existence of race likings and race aversions, but we can not find place for them in the laws or governmental processes of our republic.[84]

That statement, assuming that Scott agreed with it, signaled that Scott was willing to compromise. It reaffirmed his fifty-year-old commitment to "proportionate representation," but he seemed willing to accept "dignified representation" as a near substitute. More importantly, it suggested that he was ready to excuse President Wilson's failure to reappoint blacks to service posts and his use of racially charged words to "extraneous exigencies," a position Scott had rejected for his entire political career. He finally had become a team player and a politician.

Essentially, Scott remained attached to leagues that he had joined late in the nineteenth century or to successor leagues linked to them. None of Scott's friends belonged to the Niagara Group, which had formed in July 1905 in response to disorder within the Afro-American Council and the seeming ineffectiveness of the National Negro Democratic League. Nor were his friends leaders in the NAACP. Scott simply lacked the credentials, which required that members of the new leadership be well educated, urbane, and sophisticated.

Unfortunately, the few scattered newspaper accounts of Scott's declining years in Springfield tell us little about his activities outside of politics or his Red Moon Club. When his newspaper ceased publication and how he earned a living are uncertain. The fate of the fortune he had accumulated while in Cairo is unknown, for there was no estate probate in either Sangamon or Alexander Counties following his death.[85] How he spent his last year is a mystery. The contradictions in his words and actions during his last decade are unexplained. His death came on 23 January 1917 in Springfield, less than four months after the death of his partner, Lizzy Shelby.[86] He was interred in Cairo near the body of his first wife, Nellie Scott.[87] His death notice appeared in at least ten newspapers, five of which were major black newspapers in Chicago, Saint Louis, Savannah, and Washington, DC. Not many of us can expect to have death notices posted in ten newspapers.

Conclusion

More Complicated Than That

Born a free black in Newark, Ohio, Scott spent his youth in a part of the nation where racism existed, but of a stripe different from that found in America's South. Ohio's laws forbade slavery and indentures, but they did not guarantee equal treatment, equal opportunity, or even civility for its black residents. While Ohio established public schools, it did not include equal access for black children. Instead, Ohio treated blacks as residents within the state, rather than as citizens with all the rights and responsibilities that citizenship implied. This was an environment, however, that encouraged blacks to think for themselves, even if it required them to do it secretly.

Newark made Scott aware of his color, his race, and the prejudice that came from whites who believed themselves superior to all other races. His relatives and his mentors in the barbering trade produced in him a determination to shape his own future, even if that meant that he would need to do it in a distant place. They encouraged him to keep secrets and to keep his worlds separate. And they gave him a trade, one that provided him a ticket to escape his small-town origins and use his talents upon a larger stage.

He sought that adventure first on board riverboats that plied the Ohio and Mississippi Rivers. He worked on these boats for several years before the Union closed the rivers to riverboat traffic at the beginning of the Civil War. Scott's riverboat experience introduced him to trades that were legal as well as illegal, with riverboat captains and crew members acting as coconspirators in a game they played with civil authorities at each port. Riverboat captains operated in two worlds. They were hoteliers, saloon keepers, cruise leaders, and captains of the table, servicing the rich and famous and catering to their needs and wants. As long as their boats were docked, they adhered to land and town laws, but once in motion, another more relaxed set of rules applied. They made the rules and permitted what their customers demanded.

Those were powerful lessons for Scott, as they would be for anyone of similar circumstances who reached the age of majority during the Civil War years. Corruption on the river and in river towns was endemic and tolerated. Some openly flouted the laws, only to be forgiven by a fine or by graft paid to the right person. Filled with military personnel and the flotsam that followed river commerce, Cairo tolerated a culture of self-indulgence, bordering on the illegal and immoral. Scott joined that world by choice and, in a sense, by necessity. Few well-paying occupations were open to young blacks, and few were able to own and operate businesses that required substantial financial outlay and that whites permitted. Scott had learned, however, that there always were investors for profitable enterprises, regardless of their legal status. Riverboat captains, waiters, stewards, bartenders, and even barbers participated in a game to fleece customers of their wealth, and others tolerated these disreputable enterprises because they viewed them as entertaining.

To survive and become successful in that world required nerves of steel and a willingness to ignore risk. A gambler obtained success either because he was a very good player or because he was lucky. Scott was a careful player. But he also had a secret partner who allowed him soon after the Civil War to separate himself from the black masses, and he kept that person's identity unknown for nearly forty years before revealing it in a 1905 interview. He diversified his commercial interests, investing in land, rental property, and businesses that withstood public scrutiny and where risks were low relative to cards or craps. He considered a modicum of risk part of his overhead. He was willing to break the rules and find himself occasionally in court, so long as authorities imposed low fines and permitted his businesses to continue. He was a practical man and not interested in litigation. He believed himself not responsible for the morals of his customers or for the trouble that his businesses attracted. He carried a revolver, and he used it. He seemed unconcerned that his business model was connected to liquor and vice, activities that preachers, politicians, and mainstream society universally condemned.

Against that record of accomplishment, however, were several areas in which Scott misjudged changes coming with reform movements and the impact of those changes upon his businesses. He failed to recognize, even after the serious downturn that followed the Panic of 1893, that the temperance movement was linked to woman suffrage and that their memberships were nearly the same. Temperance advocates viewed saloons, gambling halls, and brothels as antifamily and antiwomen, as debasing to women's status in American society and exploitative of their labor. In the 1870s reformers essentially had assisted his businesses by creating "red light districts" as a way to regulate and isolate his "unsavory constituents" from the good people of "white light districts." Criminal behavior, as long as it was confined to specific districts, was to be endured, at least until businesses from those areas began to spread into neighboring districts, often the centers of government. Legislation in the 1880s and 1890s drove some of these businesses underground and had the unexpected result of increasing rather than decreasing payoffs to police and political officials. Even Scott had opposed political bosses, but he saw graft and payoffs as one of the inevitable costs of doing business.

John Bird, the lawyer and judge, and Scott, the gambler, saloon operator, and bail bondsman, had fought for reform in Cairo, and their expectations were similar enough in the 1860s and 1870s that they were able to collaborate for limited objectives. By the early 1880s, however, their primary goals had spread beyond Cairo and progressed along increasingly separate paths. Both wanted more appointive positions for loyal blacks—patronage—but Bird believed it possible to reach that goal through persuasion and through working with whites within the system. Bird steadily improved his status among the black Stalwarts within the Republican Party. Scott, in contrast, operated within a black-only world and was guided by his commercial experiences. He wanted more fundamental change that included removing those in power and using votes and intrigue to do so. He tried that frequently, and while it worked in the short term, it failed to bring lasting advance for himself or his race. His collaboration with Bird ended once he identified Bird as a member of the party's leadership. He gambled by attaching himself to the Chicago group led by Lloyd Wheeler and Ferdinand Barnett, but that led nowhere, except to introduce him to a national crowd that exploited him for the management skills he possessed but denied him a meaningful leadership role.

The national stage was crowded and already established when he joined it at age forty-four in 1883, and the nation was awash with leagues, associations, and committees to which he might attach himself. There was always, apparently, room for yet another league that he might found or join. Most of these groups accomplished little more than meet, elect officers for the coming year, appoint committees, and debate resolutions. That was especially true for Democratic or Democrat-leaning leagues during periods when national Democrats were both out of power and without patronage positions to distribute. Scott's membership on boards of directors of leagues reflected less his skills than his reported wealth and a requirement that someone from Illinois be a member.

The puzzle in Scott's story is how he was able to continue through his life in businesses that others considered undignified, yet still play an active role in a world of politics. With the exception of his arrest in 1904 after becoming the presidential candidate of the National Negro Liberty Party, there appears to have been no one at the national level who accused him publicly of impropriety regarding his businesses. Cairo's newspaper editors regularly reported his arrests and the activities that characterized his businesses, but those reports reached only a local readership. Few of those items were reproduced in Springfield or Chicago papers, and none made it into the national press, unless they dealt with his wealth. After 1905 Springfield's editors included items about him because he was already a national figure, and Springfield's readers were fascinated by reports of his Red Moon Club. None of those items were reproduced in the national press, likely because Scott after 1905 was no longer a newsworthy person at the national level. A few editors identified him as a nasty person, but that was relatively mild and expected from editors who delighted in being sarcastic and nasty themselves. Readers expected it. Yet no one wrote an exposé, attempting to destroy his credibility and his character.

His absence from the national press, however, likely was a measure of his popularity and the importance of the leagues he joined and led. Editors were willing to criticize Fortune, Douglass, Chase, and Washington, but Scott clearly was not within that class. Fortune had labeled him a "crank," and the African American *Palladium* of Saint Louis had described him as "objectionable," but others ignored him and his leagues because they had little impact upon their lives or national politics. Scott was an anomaly and of little interest to readers, unless his activities were nonpolitical.

As a politician, Scott was unique. He lacked formal education, and what he learned of politics he obtained through experience and association with others better trained than him. He failed in his attempts to win elective public offices. He was convinced that white voters would always vote for white candidates, regardless of party affiliation. As a superb manager within black society, on the other hand, he was able to secure influence and respect, because others needed him. Scott seemed willing to settle for that.

But Scott also was able to play politics on an entirely different level. He learned quickly that it was important to attend conventions, for his presence improved his ability to play a role within black organizations. Scott obviously enjoyed attending conventions, and he had the financial resources and freedom to make that happen. He was an orator, and he recognized the importance of the speaker's platform for influencing a convention's outcome. He possessed organizational skills that others appreciated, and he had the time and willingness to share those abilities, especially if there were rewards and positions as a consequence.

Although tied to no particular party nor to any political philosophy, Scott did maintain a mantra consistently through his adult life. As a successful businessman, he knew that one used assets to obtain other assets. He believed that the only asset his race had after the Civil War was a mass of newly franchised voters with the potential to determine election outcomes in specific regions. A businessman always expects an investment to pay a dividend, preferably one that could be planned and expected in advance. Scott believed that blacks should cast their votes only for persons who championed issues important to their race. Their willingness to withhold or deliver votes was their leverage. And he believed that patronage positions—which in his pre–civil service day were many—should be a part of a grand bargain that should be promised to voters as payment for loyalty and votes. Essentially, party affiliation mattered little to Scott, although he certainly allied himself to the Democrats after 1883 and even flirted with Populism briefly in 1894 and 1896. Whether a Republican, a Democrat, or a Populist, however, Scott tended always to identify himself as an Independent in the sense that he could opt to challenge party bosses and lead insurrections, even if only to draw attention to issues important to his group and to himself.

Perhaps others at the state and national levels considered him an interesting anomaly, but they were willing to excuse his excesses because he was a "wide-awake" person. To be sure, he was that. Known as a fancy dresser who flashed his gold-filled teeth and diamonds, Scott constantly set himself apart from the regular crowd attending conventions. He carried a gun. People believed him to be a wealthy man, reputedly the third wealthiest black person in Illinois. Moreover, people knew him because he attended so many conferences. An accomplished orator, he made speeches at conventions because those in charge knew that he could attend and deliver a rousing address.

But he also was a troublemaker. Whether in Cairo or at the state level, he often led dissidents who championed proposals that challenged the status quo, particularly bosses who controlled patronage or an agenda. As a political strategist, he was willing to threaten a timely revolt or an exit. In a sense, he took a gambler's bluffing skills to the political table. But he also knew when to "fold" and accept defeat without losing face and status at the same time. For him, politics became his passion, his habit, and his game, and he played it reasonably well throughout his adult life.

At the same time, Scott's is a personal journey into the world of politics as it was played in a northern medium-sized town with a black population large enough to swing elections. It evolved into an attempt to become a prominent player at the state and national levels, primarily because he had become financially secure and had the time and inclination to become deeply involved at those levels. Locally, Scott became an adept manager and manipulator because the nature of his businesses kept him from becoming anything better. His vision, even at that level, however, was always focused upon jobs for his race and not for himself, although he attempted several times to win elections and lost every time.

Once he moved to the state and national levels, however, Scott thought on an entirely different scale. He spoke always in terms of proportionality—so many votes in exchange for so many jobs. This was not "boodle" or graft, just simple mathematics. If party bosses refused to accept that argument, Scott was willing to fight them, because he believed his equation only fair and because, being financially independent, he could afford it. This put him at odds with those in the professional party apparatus, for they were willing to accept token patronage assignments while disavowing the threat of voter rebellion if change did not occur. That was not a bargain Scott was willing to make or accept.

For Scott, the principal obstacle to reform and progress for the race was a mass of black voters that remained unquestioningly loyal to the Republican Party, the party that had liberated them from slavery. Frederick Douglass had coined a phrase that every black person knew and almost everyone believed: "The Republican Party is the deck; all else is the sea." But even Douglass questioned the wisdom of that expression in the mid-1880s, advising his audiences to be aggressive in their demands and to question the agenda of parties, for "parties are made for men and not men for parties." That was an ideal and a degree of mistrust that Scott understood.

Scott, moreover, was a product of a time and a place that separated him from a generation of black leaders emerging at the beginning of the twentieth century. He was a midwesterner with a memory of the Civil War and the excitement and promise that came with passage of the Thirteenth, Fourteenth, and Fifteenth Amendments to the Constitution and civil rights laws at both the state and national levels. He had lived through those momentous changes as a participant. While he was building his businesses and acquiring wealth in a part of the nation where racism was virulent and growing, a new generation of leaders was attending cloistered universities and preparing to become lawyers and business leaders. This new self-appointed group rejected the notion that leaders could emerge from the masses, and they accepted the premise that they alone had been chosen to lead as a vanguard.

Scott lacked the credentials of the emerging black elite, and his vision was too narrow, too midwestern, too old-fashioned, and too inconsistent to capture and hold their attention. But Scott also found reasons not to work well within this group. They were too focused on urban problems and not enough on improvements that were still possible at the grassroots level. And they were not particularly interested in jobs for blacks. For Scott, that was fundamental.

And finally, there is the conundrum that this biography has avoided thus far. Scott's critics almost universally accused Independent Republicans, black insurgents, and Independents of being nothing less than dupes who were creating dissension and confusion within the ranks of black Republicans by convening disingenuous conventions and creating bogus nonpartisan leagues outside the framework of the Republican Party. They had failed as traditional Republicans but had remained attached to the party because there were few acceptable options, because the Republican Party was where blacks cast their votes, and because the Democratic Party wanted them to remain where they could create the most mischief. They were most active at election time, when corrupt politicians of both major parties handed out rewards to those who brought success for their candidates. They were eager to replace blacks who had obtained government appointments soon after the Civil War without giving them credit for their considerable accomplishments. They were a menace that was looking out for their own personal welfare and not for the success and welfare of the race.

These critics also considered any criticism of the Republican Party to be part of a conspiracy—initiated within and financially supported by the Democratic Party—to reduce the number of votes cast for Republican candidates, no matter whether those lost votes were given to Democrats, Populists, or candidates of any other party. Loyalty to the Republican Party was paramount and universally required. They believed that any vote cast outside the Republican ticket was actually a vote supporting Democrats, for it reduced the number of votes cast for Republicans. That was not a small issue for loyal black Republicans who lived in districts or states where their overwhelming support for Republican candidates effectively determined election winners and losers.

A convincing argument could be made that Scott was precisely such a devious person. He failed to obtain either an elective office or a political appointment, except for that of janitor after 1904. He readily admitted that party loyalty mattered little to him. He was willing to be a member of the executive committee of a national Democratic league and at the same time to be "grand organizer" of a league that advocated that all political parties were corrupt and that blacks should vote for policies rather than parties. He either was naive in seeing no contradiction in those positions or was cynical or disingenuous in his disregard for that inconsistency. He was not shy to manipulate a conference and its rules to guarantee the success of his own agenda. Scott was not a dependable person. Likeable, perhaps, but not dependable.

Those critics may have been correct in their assessment. But I doubt it. He was much more complicated than that.

Notes

Introduction

1. In most cases, attempts to reconstruct family history at the local level involve careful review of documents found in the courthouse of the respective county. In this case, however, Licking County's courthouse was destroyed in a fire in 1875, and nearly all official documents dealing with births, marriages, and deaths were lost. Some records were reconstructed from census records, church and cemetery records, and newspaper accounts, but there remain significant gaps. That is especially true for black Americans living in Newark before 1875. Much of that reconstruction was done by the Licking County Genealogical Society and is most complete for prominent white families. None of the records from the pre-1875 period are found in the Ohio State Archives. There were no periodic state censuses taken in Ohio. The 1840 census lists only head of household and numbers of persons within that household. In that instance, only Samuel Scott's name was listed. William T. Scott's father's name was not.

2. For a brief discussion of Ohio's Black Laws, see Taylor, *Frontiers of Freedom*, 32–35. For a description of the debate on issues of civil rights for blacks as held at the 1802 convention, see Quillin, *Color Line*, 11–20. See also Woodson, "Negro in Cincinnati," 2–3, for a precise description of these laws.

3. An Act, to Regulate Black and Mulatto Persons, chap. 21, 5 January 1804, 1804 Ohio Laws 356, as cited in Finkelman, "John Bingham," 672. A letter from Tyler Ridella to Bruce Mouser dated 10 June 2011 indicated that the clerk of courts of Licking County, Ohio, had searched their records and found none that related to required registration of blacks in compliance with this or subsequent laws.

4. Quillin, *Color Line*, 21–22; Sheller, "Struggle of the Negro," 210. See Love, "Registration of Free Blacks," 39, for details from the 1804 and 1807 bills.

5. An Act Regulating Black and Mulatto Persons, chap. 8, 25 January 1807, 1807 Ohio Laws 53, as cited in Finkelman, "Strange Career," 377, 384–85.

6. Copies of the 1804 and 1807 acts are appended to Taylor, *Frontiers of Freedom*, 203–5. For laws respecting the militia and juries, see Quillin, *Color Line*, 22–23, 33. For testimony against a white person, see Baily, "From Cincinnati, Ohio," 427.

7. Moody, "Too Many Questions," 18.

8. Middleton, *Black Laws*, 5, 55. See also Finkelman, *Imperfect Union*, 156.

9. Howard, "Changing the Law," 30. See also Middleton, *Black Laws*, 5. See the *Zainesville (OH) Courier*, 4 January 1849, 3, for a list of resolutions being considered in Ohio's legislature that were attempting to define the word "white."

10. Sheller, "Struggle of the Negro," 217; Finkelman, "Strange Career," 291–93.

11. For a discussion of differences between northern, southern, and central Ohio, see Gerber, *Black Ohio*, 9–14.

12. Graham, *History of Licking County*, 436.

13. Finkelman, "Strange Career," 385, 387–88.

14. Woodson, "Negro in Cincinnati," 6–7; Middleton, *Black Laws*, 71–72; Sheller, "Struggle of the Negro," 213.

15. *Newark (OH) Advocate*, 22 April 1984.

16. King, "Abolitionists in Granville," 1–2.

17. See Price, "Further Notes," 367, for a set of resolutions adopted by the group that formed Licking County's chapter of the American Colonization Society.

18. Price, "Ohio Anti-slavery Convention," 176–78.

19. Shimansky, "The Granville Riot." For the standard description, see Howe, *Historical Collections*, 2:80–81. See also King, "Abolitionists in Granville," 6–7, for a reproduction of the proclamation of November 1835 issued by Mayor Elias Fasset opposing the 1836 scheduled meeting of the Anti-Slavery Society "and sustaining the Colonization Society."

20. Price, "Ohio Anti-slavery Convention," 185. See also Gilje, *Rioting in America*, 81–82; "The Granville Riot."

21. Bennett, "Granville's Big Historical Moment," 3–4.

22. The full texts of these resolutions are reproduced in Lovett, "Black Laws," 15–17.

23. Bushnell, *History of Granville*, 1:291. For the 1841 incident, see also Middleton, *Black Laws*, 175–76.

24. Bushnell, *History of Granville*, 307–8.

25. Quillin, *Color Line*, 75, 81. B. G. Smythe, writing for the *Newark (OH) Advocate* on 20 May 1924, wrote: "During the crusade and notwithstanding it, Newark and Licking county were pro-slavery, — not in the sense that the people of Licking county favored the institution of slavery. They were pro-slavery in the sense that they opposed the methods and purposes of the abolitionist. In this sense Licking county was so strongly pro-slavery that there was not one avowed Abolitionist in the county with the exception, perhaps, of Sam White, whom the Granville people rode on a rail for attempting to preach abolition" ("Recollections of Newark," 14).

26. Steinglass and Scarselli, *Ohio State Constitution*, 29. See also Terzian, "Ohio's Constitutions," 371–75, for additional discussion of these votes. Quillin, *Color Line*, 86, reported different voting figures.

27. Quillin, *Color Line*, 72, 74.

28. *Palladium of Liberty* (AA, Columbus, OH), 12 June 1844, 2.

29. U.S. Census of 1830, Ohio, Licking County, Newark, series M19, roll 134, p. 397, National Archives and Records Administration (NARA), http://www.heritagequestonline .com, accessed 26 February 2014.

30. Blyden, "Fifth President," 121. See also Holsoe, "Portrait of a Black Midwestern Family," 41–52; Graham, *History of Licking County*, 540. See also Howe, *Historical Collections*, 1:140–44, for a discussion of the nature of early common schools.

31. The *Newark (OH) Advocate*, 22 April 1984, reported that Roye decided to migrate to Africa, perhaps inspired by "the scene around the Square that day in his youth." See also a series of articles on Newark education written by Minnie Hite Moody that appeared in the *Newark (OH) Advocate* on 7, 8, and 9 December 1970.

32. U.S. Census of 1850, Ohio, Licking County, Newark, series M432, roll 702, p. 29B, NARA. Moderates elected to the new board of education included Gibson Atherton, president of the board for fifteen years and Democratic mayor of Newark from 1860 to 1864. Atherton also was a congressman for the Twelfth Congressional District between 1879 and 1883. For a detailed view of Newark's schools during this period, see Ohio State Centennial Educational Committee, "History of the Schools." This report indicated that Israel Dille, a moderate Republican, also was elected to the first board. By 1850 Newark operated twelve graded schools, mainly in private residences. During the winter quarter 722 students attended, and 524 were enrolled in summer school. A "central school building" was built in 1850, and all upper grades were consolidated to that one location. By 1855 1,400 students were attending schools. See Brister, *Centennial History*, 410–19, for the 1847 to 1855 phase of school development in Newark.

33. Graham, *History of Licking County*, 373. Johnson, "Educational Work," 392, noted that it was a "duty" of the church to establish common schools and Sunday schools.

34. Middleton, *Black Laws*, 5, 55.

35. See U.S. Census of 1850.

36. See U.S. Census of 1860, Ohio, Licking County, series 653, roll 998, p. 94, NARA. Finkelman, "Strange Career," 394, noted that "by 1850 more than 25% of Ohio's black children between six and twenty were attending schools."

37. Graham, *History of Licking County*, 543.

38. U.S. Census of 1860; *Cleveland (OH) Herald*, 22 January 1853. Arnold had published *Memoir of Hannah More* (1834), *The Life of George Washington* (1840), *Biographical Sketches of Distinguished Jerseymen* (1845), and *The Life of Patrick Henry of Virginia* (1854).

39. Article in the *Newark North American*, n.d., as reproduced in the *Coshocton (OH) County Democrat*, 29 August 1860, 2.

40. *Coshocton (OH) County Democrat*, 3 April 1860, 2. The *Coshocton County Democrat* had published on 11 January 1860 a resolution of the state Democratic Party, which had met in Columbus: "Resolved. That the provisions for the suppression of the African Slave Trade after the year 1808, and the rendition of fugitive slaves, are two of the

compromises on which the Constitution was adopted and our Union of slaveholding and non-slaveholding States established, and the laws of Congress enacted in accordance therewith but define duties which are clearly imposed by the terms of the federal compact, and ought to be promptly and faithfully executed. The Democracy of Ohio have proved their fidelity to the Union by repealing all laws passed by a sectional opposition to embarrass and defeat the operation of the fugitive slave law, and they will not cease to employ every lawful means to avert from their State the opprobrium and disgrace, that would be indicted by the reenactment of such laws." See U.S. Census of 1860, p. 87, for William Henry and John Clark.

41. "Death of the Slave's Friend," *New York Times*, 24 April 1895, 16.

42. Irwin, "Willard Warner," *Encyclopedia of Alabama*, online at http://www.encyclopediaofalabama.org, accessed 1 April 2011.

43. For Wilson's political maneuvers in Alabama, see Fitzgerald, "Republican Factionalism."

44. Moody, "Too Many Questions"; Moody, "Both Men Were Teachers." Barber, "Report on the Condition," described teaching in black schools as a "most *contemptible business*" and noted that a black school in nearby Chillicothe had been burned in 1840 (5, 11). Barber also described "Sabbath schools" as a common aspect of black education in Ohio (ibid., 13).

45. *Indianapolis (IN) Freeman* (AA), 19 October 1889, 1.

46. U.S. Census of 1860, p. 109. See http://www.measuringworth.com/ppowerus/?redirurl=calculators/ppowerus/, accessed 16 September 2012, for a formula in measuring "purchasing power of money in the United States from 1774 to present."

47. *Lincoln (NE) Evening News*, 30 January 1905, 2. For the history of secondary education in Cincinnati, see Matthews, "John Isom Gaines," 41–48; Trotter, *River Jordan*, 46–51; Taylor, *Frontiers of Freedom*, 162–74; Bigham, *On Jordan's Banks*, 39–40. For a recent and complete biography of Clark, see Taylor, *America's First Black Socialist*.

48. Hartshorn, *Era of Progress*, 472.

49. *Cairo (IL) Daily Bulletin*, 16 July 1876.

50. *Indianapolis (IN) Freeman* (AA), 19 October 1889, 1. For black barbers, stewards, cooks, and waiters onboard riverboats before the war, see Buchanan, "Rascals," 807–8.

51. Childs, *Mighty Mississippi*, 61; Swanson, *Riverboat Gamblers*, 9–10. Buchanan, "Slave Mississippi," wrote that most barbershops were entrepreneurial in the sense that barbers were not on the boat payroll and that they earned their wage by setting prices and through tips, which could be considerable (104–5, 121–25). He also noted that Cincinnati was a major port on the Ohio where riverboats took on crew (ibid., 77–79).

52. Devol, *Forty Years a Gambler*, 284–85.

53. Buchanan, "Slave Mississippi," listed jobs available to blacks: barber, steward, skilled cook, deckhand, fireman, cabin crew, porter (94–95, 97–103). He described the "steward" as "the most prestigious position that African Americans could hope to obtain on board"—"the captain of the cabin" (ibid., 102).

54. Chafetz, *Play the Devil*, 72–73; Swanson, *Riverboat Gamblers*, 10–11. Findlay, *People of Chance*, 75, described riverboat gambling as operating with high expectations,

opportunism, risk taking, and movement. See also http://www.library.ca.gov/crb/97/03/Chapt2.html, accessed 12 July 2011, for a history of gambling in the United States.

55. Findlay, *People of Chance*, 68–71. Chafetz, *Play the Devil*, described an elaborate scheme used by three professional gamblers to confuse and fleece victims (76–78). For a similar system used in the upper Mississippi, see Merrick, *Old Times*, 140.

56. Childs, *Mighty Mississippi*, 63; Swanson, *Riverboat Gamblers*, 13.

57. Merrick, *Old Times*, 138–39. According to Childs, *Mighty Mississippi*, riverboat gamblers "were unashamed rapscallions who pretended to only the lesser of the chivalric virtues; they would never, well hardly ever, gamble for a lady's diamonds, even when the gentleman claimed to have got them without undue violence. A successful gambler on the Mississippi had of necessity to be adroit, tactful, a preeminent judge of human nature, a fighter who could defend himself with bare fists, teeth, feet, swords, whips, pistols, or whatever other weapon the exigencies of the moment might demand." He made "thousands and hundreds of thousands of dollars" (63). Childs also noted that "the river front [where boats landed] was lined with bagnios in which harlotry ran the color scale from midnight black to purest white. The price went by color, too. Deckhands enjoyed a black woman for fifty or even twenty-five cents. Other whores, the aristocracy of their profession, did an excellent trade on the fine packets. Virtuous captain-owners, jealous of the reputations of their 'family boats,' found it difficult or impossible to suppress this traffic" (ibid., 65).

58. Chafetz, *Play the Devil*, 78.

59. Sandlin, *Wicked River*, 102.

60. Chafetz, *Play the Devil*, 79; Swanson, *Riverboat Gamblers*, 11–13, 15; Merrick, *Old Times*, 140–41.

61. Swanson, *Riverboat Gamblers*, 14.

62. *Indianapolis (IN) Freeman* (AA), 19 October 1889, 1.

63. Buchanan, "Slave Mississippi," 141–42.

64. Findlay, *People of Chance*, 76–77.

65. *Indianapolis (IN) Freeman* (AA), 19 October 1889, 1; Buchanan, "Slave Mississippi," 275–76.

66. Woodson, "Negro in Cincinnati," 21–22.

67. Taylor, *Frontiers of Freedom*, 162–64.

68. T. J. Shores, letter to the editor, *Cairo (IL) Bulletin*, 2 August 1872. Shores was a minister at Cairo's First Missionary Baptist Church, a black politician, and a rival of Scott.

69. See U.S. Census of 1900, Illinois, Alexander County, series T623, roll 236, p. 69, NARA.

70. Bureau of Naval Personnel, *Register* ranked a wardroom steward as below cabin steward and steward to the commander but ahead of steerage steward (5). He was responsible for the officers' mess. Scott reported variously that he had served on the USS *Victoria* and the USS *Clara Dolsen*. The *Victoria* was a side-wheel steamer that was commissioned in 1858 and purchased by the Confederate government to use as a troop transport on the Mississippi. Union forces captured it in June 1862 and renamed it the *Abraham*. It was

used as a storeship and inspection vessel. In May 1864 it was moved to Mound City, Illinois, where it remained for the rest of the war. For the *Victoria/Abraham*, see http://www.history.navy.mil/danfs/a2/abraham.htm, accessed March 2011. According to http://www.hazegray.org/danfs/steamers/c_dolsen.htm and www.hazegray.org/danbs /csn/c.txt, accessed 1 July 2011, the *Clara Dolsen* was a side-wheel steamer of 939 tons that the Union navy captured in July 1862 and used as a receiving vessel at Cairo until April 1864, when it was returned to its owners. The *Daily Times-Picayune* (AA, New Orleans), 27 April 1861, described it as a "regular passenger steamer" (4) and the *New Orleans (LA) Times*, 9 April 1865, as a "large and superb passenger packet" (8). The *New Orleans Daily True Delta*, 2 February 1861, described it as "one of the largest and best adapted business steamers ever constructed for the trade. . . . The cabin is finished in a very neat style, and will accommodate from 75 to 80 passengers comfortably. . . . Her cabin accommodations are of the first order" (8). It is possible that Scott served on both vessels. See also Kemp, "Civil War Reminiscences," for an account of a landsman from Buffalo, New York, who served as a guard on board the *Clara Dolsen* while it was moored at Cairo in 1862.

71. Wegner, "Little Egypt's Naval Station," 75.

72. The most complete description of urban transformation and the impact of the Civil War on Cairo's society and economy is found in Hays, "Way Down in Egypt Land," chaps. 3 and 4. Smith, "Negro Lore," 159n2, identifies "Egypt" as that part of Illinois located south of an imaginary line drawn between Vincennes, Indiana, and East Saint Louis, Illinois. For a detailed discussion of "secret meetings" held in Pope and Alexander Counties relative to possible secession of Illinois's southern counties to the Confederacy, see Cole, *Era of the Civil War*, 258–61. See Kionka, *Key Command*, 35–39; Wheeler, "Together in Egypt," 106; and Hicken, *Illinois in the Civil War*, 12–13, for discussions of secessionist sentiments within Cairo. See the *Southern Illinoisan* (Carbondale), 27 April 1861, for a letter to the editor printed in the *Cairo (IL) Gazette* on 14 April 1861 that read: "We cannot consent to remain a part of the Northern Confederacy. Our fortunes are with our Southern brethren. We must divide" (5). For sentiment from northern Illinois, see the *Chicago Daily Tribune*, 14 May 1861.

73. Merrill, "Cairo, Illinois," 243. For similar analysis, see Pitkin, "When Cairo Was Saved," 284–85, 296–97. VanderCreek, "Economic Development," wrote that the early war nearly shut down Cairo's economy, and it transformed Cairo into "a huge Union military camp and supply depot" (n.p.). Lansden, *History of the City of Cairo*, called this the "Cairo Expedition" (130). Kionka, *Key Command*, noted that the "Cairo Guard" had essentially decided to remain neutral in the war, but that decision was made only when troops from Chicago were about to occupy the city (38–39).

74. *New York Times*, 21 June 1861; Hicken, *Illinois in the Civil War*, 2–13.

75. Pitkin, "When Cairo Was Saved," 290. *Frank Leslie's Illustrated Newspaper*, 8 June 1861, 52–61, produced a series of drawings of Cairo and a brief article, declaring that Cairo's position "can hardly be overrated" (54).

76. Lansden, *History of the City of Cairo*, 134, 137.

77. See the *National Republican* (Washington, DC), 9 February 1861, for Cairo as a center for cotton exports northward "through Cairo and the Illinois Central railroad" (2), and Bigham, *Towns and Villages*, for Cairo as "the nexus of an extensive north-south rail network" (121).

78. Pitkin, "When Cairo Was Saved," 290. See also Trollope, *North America*, 2:90–91. For the impact of the blockade on the economies of Louisville and other river ports along the middle Ohio River Valley, see Jenness, "Tentative Relations," 144–51.

79. Wegner, "Little Egypt's Naval Station," 75; Kionka, *Key Command*, 46–48.

80. *Harper's Weekly*, 1 June 1861, reproduced in Pitkin, "When Cairo Was Saved," 301.

81. Kionka, *Key Command*, 74–102; Hays, "Way Down in Egypt Land," 120, 130; *Alton (IL) Telegraph*, 23 August 1861, 2; Jones, "Cairo of Maud Rittenhouse," 75.

82. Lansden, *History of the City of Cairo*, 209.

83. Merrill, "Cairo, Illinois," 243; Hays, "Way Down in Egypt Land," 120.

84. Dickens, *The Life and Letters of Martin Chuzzelwit*, 186.

85. Pitkin, "When Cairo Was Saved," 292.

86. Lansden, *History of the City of Cairo*, 129; *New York Times*, 8 June 1861.

87. Wegner, "Little Egypt's Naval Station," 75.

88. Pitkin, "When Cairo Was Saved," 298. See also Trollope, *North America*, 2:90–91, 93; Lansden, *History of the City of Cairo*, 129.

89. Lansden, *History of the City of Cairo*, 254.

90. Pitkin, "When Cairo Was Saved," 301–2; Hays, "Way Down in Egypt Land," 130. VanderCreek, "Economic Development," noted that transformation of Cairo into a military camp helped to produce some millionaires, but it also attracted land speculators and gamblers, and it drove up wages for those who had remained. See also Kionka, *Key Command*, who, perhaps tongue in cheek, described these as "morally destructive pastimes" (78–79). See Dexter, "Old Newspapers," 20, for a description of Cairo's prostitution trade during the Civil War.

91. Trollope, *North America*, 2:93.

92. Ramold, *Slaves, Sailors, Citizens*, 77–78.

93. Bureau of Naval Personnel, *Register*, 5. See also Buchanan, *Slaves, Free Blacks*, 66–68, for work assignments on board ships. Tomblin, *Blue Jackets and Contrabands*, noted that the navy often assigned black recruits "as mess boys, stewards, and wardroom attendants, menial jobs the navy considered more appropriate for persons of color" (17).

94. *Indianapolis (IN) Freeman* (AA), 19 October 1889, 1.

95. Lansden, *History of the City of Cairo*, 209; Hays, "Way Down in Egypt Land," 147.

96. Cole, *Era of the Civil War*, 331. See also Bigham, *On Jordan's Banks*, 85. Population figures for Cairo show a significant increase in percentage of black residents. For 1865 Cairo's reported population was 8,569, of which 2,083 were blacks, or 24 percent. In 1870 those figures were 6,267, of which 1,849 (29 percent) were blacks. For 1880 the

figures were 9,011, of which 3,349 were blacks, or 37 percent. The percentage of blacks in the population stabilized at 35 percent for 1890 and 39 percent for 1900. Population data are taken from Portwood, "African-American Politics," 15.

97. *Cairo (IL) Gazette*, 19 August 1862. For more on contrabands in Cairo, see Voegeli, *Free but Not Equal*, 60–61; Eaton, *Grant, Lincoln and the Freedmen*.

98. Wegner, "Little Egypt's Naval Station," 76.

99. Ramold, *Slaves, Sailors, Citizens*, 67–68, 76; Bigham, *On Jordan's Banks*, 54.

100. Noyes, "Contraband Camp," 210.

Chapter 1. A Gambler's World of Liquor, Vice, and Hometown Politics in the Post–Civil War Era

1. Hays, "Way Down in Egypt Land," 135–36.

2. Light, "Ethnic Vice Industry," noted that "transients were preponderant consumers of vice services" (470).

3. Hays, "Way Down in Egypt Land," 137–38.

4. Lantz, *Community in Search*, 68–72.

5. Lansden, *History of the City of Cairo*, 209; Hays, "Way Down in Egypt Land," 147.

6. Lansden, *History of the City of Cairo*, 146. See also Gleeson, *Illinois Rebels*, for Cairo as a southern town, a "part of the 'Upper South,' or 'Upper Dixie'" (2).

7. Portwood, "African-American Politics," 13; Wheeler, "Together in Egypt," 64. Wheeler, however, studied the housing and commercial patterns of Cairo between 1860 and 1920 and makes a convincing case that blacks and whites frequented each other's businesses, that mixed marriages were permitted, and that housing units often contained persons of both races.

8. Lansden, *History of the City of Cairo*, 146.

9. Ibid., 147.

10. Bradsby, "History of Cairo," 55.

11. *Indianapolis (IN) Freeman* (AA), 19 October 1889, 1; *Cairo (IL) Daily Democrat*, 25 January 1866; Hays, "Way Down in Egypt Land," 322–25.

12. Dexter, "Old Newspapers," 21. *Alexander County Profiles* noted that the 1864 school "was a result of the Negro sentiment toward the White people; they were quite sensitive on the pigment points. However, their attitude changed in the 1880s" (29). For the Freedman hospital, see Pearson, "Historic Hospitals," 28.

13. Atherton, Badgley, and McMunn, *Where They Sleep*, 3:80.

14. U.S. Census of 1870, Illinois, Alexander County, series 593, roll 188, p. 10, NARA. Scott's son, William E., remains a mysterious figure in this narrative. His name did not appear in census records for Alexander County, Illinois, until 1900. Records of the 1890 census no longer exist. Nor did his name appear in census records for Licking County, Ohio, unless the census enumerator in 1870 erred in listing William (three years old) in the joined households of Lucy and Henry Scott as William Semons (son of Anna Scott Semons) instead of as William Scott (see U.S. Census of 1870, Ohio, Licking County, Newark, series M593, roll 1233, p. 359, NARA). The earliest known record linking him to W. T. Scott is a notice in the *Cairo (IL) Bulletin* of 14 May 1882. William E. (born in

January 1863 in Ohio) and his wife, Annie (born in April 1869 in Tennessee), had four children as of 1900: William B. (born in 1888 in Missouri), Henry T. (born in 1890 in Missouri), Lizinker (born in 1893 in Illinois), and Estella J. (born in 1895 in Illinois). Ebel, *Cairo City Directory*, 173, listed Wm. E. Scott as bartender for W. T. Scott and his residence as the same as that given for W. T. Scott. Cairo's city directories for 1887 and 1893 identify William E. as working in his father's tavern, a clear linkage to William T. Scott. I am indebted to Shirley J. Portwood for the references in the 1887 and 1893 city directories. In *Daily Telegram's Cairo City Directory for 1895-96*, 148, 203, William E. Scott is listed as restaurateur. For reference to William E. Scott in the 1900 census record, see U.S. Census for 1900, Illinois, Alexander County, series T623, roll 236, p. 69, NARA.

15. *Cairo (IL) Evening Bulletin*, 30 June 1869, 1. There were no newspaper ads for the hair salon after 1869.

16. *Daily Illinois State Journal*, 29 January 1905. See also U.S. Census of 1870, Illinois, Alexander County, series 593, roll 188, p. 10; *Lincoln Evening News*, 30 January 1905; *Indianapolis (IN) Freeman* (AA), 19 October 1889, 1.

17. *Cairo (IL) Daily Bulletin*, 22 March 1870. See also *East Saint Louis (IL) Daily Journal*, 8 July 1904.

18. *Indianapolis (IN) Freeman* (AA), 19 October 1889, 1.

19. *Lincoln (NE) Evening News*, 30 January 1905, 2. Joens, *From Slave to State Legislator*, noted that John W. E. Thomas of Chicago, who had become the first black American to be elected to the Illinois General Assembly in 1876, also was a "professional bailer," a lawyer, and a real estate investor who became "the wealthiest African American in the city when he died in 1899" (53–56).

20. *Cincinnati (OH) Daily Gazette*, 5 March 1866, 4.

21. Kionka, *Key Command*, 117–18. See "Cairo, Illinois, During the Civil War," http://www.angelfire.com/wi/wisconsin42nd/cairo.html, accessed 21 December 2012, for photographs of Cairo.

22. Lansden, *History of the City of Cairo*, 202–7. Comparisons of dated dollar values to 2010 dollars were obtained at http://www.measuringworth.com/uscompare/, accessed 9 July 2012.

23. *Daily Illinois State Journal* (Springfield), 29 January 1905.

24. *Morning Star* (Springfield, IL), 23 September 1899, 1.

25. U.S. Census of 1870, Illinois, Alexander County, series 593, roll 188, p. 10.

26. Bigham, *On Jordan's Banks*, 225; U.S. Census of 1870, Illinois, Alexander County, series 593, roll 188, p. 44.

27. *Cairo (IL) Daily Bulletin*, 22 March 1870. Oberly was a Democrat from Tennessee who had opposed secession and had migrated to Cairo at the beginning of the Civil War. He became editor of the *Cairo Bulletin* in 1868 and served as Cairo's mayor from 1869 to 1871. He left Cairo in 1877, moving to Bloomington, Illinois, where he edited the *Bloomington Bulletin*. During Grover Cleveland's administration, Oberly served as commissioner of Indian schools. For Oberly, see Brister, *Centennial History of the City*, 182.

28. See Cha-Jua, *America's First Black Town*, 164–69, for types of businesses that were popular and available for blacks in towns with large black settlement.

29. Ibid., 188.

30. Reed, *Black Chicago's First Century*, 1:292.

31. For a description of how a bondsman operated, see *Chicago (IL) Tribune*, 11 December 1887, 25, as quoted in Joens, *From Slave to State Legislator*, 54.

32. See Herd, "Paradox of Temperance," for "alcohol the enslaver" and "alcohol the disinhibitor."

33. See Keire, *For Business & Pleasure*, 3–4, for the attitude transition from tolerance to opposition after the Civil War.

34. Lantz, *Community in Search*, 68.

35. Light, "Ethnic Vice Industry," 470.

36. Lantz, *Community in Search*, 70–71. See Light, "Ethnic Vice Industry," 470–72, for a discussion of three types of prostitutes: independents who worked occasionally and generally quit when they married; full-time sex workers who were associated with the "pimp system" (pimps identified and defended territory and solicited clients in saloons); and full-time workers who lived in brothels. See Blair, *I've Got to Make My Livin'*, 34–38, for similar treatment of ages at which women worked in the vice commerce of late nineteenth-century Chicago.

37. *Cairo (IL) Bulletin*, 21 October 1883.

38. Lantz, *Community in Search*, 71.

39. Ibid., 69–70.

40. Quoted in Grossman, *Democratic Party and the Negro*, 17, emphasis cited in Grossman.

41. *Cairo (IL) Evening Bulletin*, 30 July 1869, 1. Grossman, *Democratic Party and the Negro*, 24–25, noted that Democrats in the North had universally opposed ratification of the Fifteenth Amendment and were convinced that a vast majority of Americans opposed it.

42. Hays, "African American Struggle," 274–75.

43. Hays, "Way Down in Egypt Land," 353. Dexter, "Old Newspapers," 21, noted that Frederick Douglass had spoken at Cairo's Atheneum Theater in 1867. Quality of schools was a common theme of Douglass's lectures.

44. *Proceedings of the Illinois State Convention of Colored Men*, 2–3. Of the fifty-six delegates, twenty-four (42 percent) represented Galesburg and nearby Monmouth. Ten delegates came from Chicago. The Reverend Strothers was the only official delegate from Cairo.

45. Quoted in Hays, "Way Down in Egypt Land," 355. For the grammar school sit-in, see also Blocker, *A Little More Freedom*, 94.

46. Bird had been active in statewide black politics in Cairo since 1866, when he was listed as one of the thirty-three members of the Committee of Correspondence for the Illinois State Convention of Colored Men, which met in Galesburg, Illinois, on 16 October. For Bird at the 1866 convention, see *Proceedings of the Illinois State Convention of Colored Men*, 2. The U.S. Census of 1870, Illinois, Alexander County, series M593, roll 188, p. 46, however, indicates that Bird's two sons were born in Canada in 1866 and 1868, which contradicts the above account, unless Bird's family remained in Canada when he moved to Cairo.

47. University of Illinois, *Semi-centennial Record*, 970. It is possible that Bird and Scott may have known each other in Ohio.

48. *Cairo (IL) Evening Bulletin*, 10 August 1869, 3.

49. Lansden, *History of the City*, 181–82. See also Cha-Jua, *America's First Black Town*, 20–21, for a summary for Brooklyn, Illinois, where whites within the Republican Party dominated politics until 1886.

50. *Cairo (IL) Daily Bulletin*, 4 February 1871.

51. Ibid., 11 February 1871, 3.

52. Ibid., 15 February 1871, 3.

53. Ibid.

54. Ibid., 26 February 1871, 3.

55. Ibid., 1 March 1871, 1.

56. Ibid., 25 April 1872, 4.

57. Atherton, Badgley, and McMunn, *Where They Sleep*, 3:90; *Cairo (IL) Bulletin*, 28 November 1876.

58. *Cairo (IL) Daily Bulletin*, 24 September 1871, 4.

59. Ibid., 19 October 1871, 4.

60. Ibid., 7 November 1871, 4.

61. Ibid., 8 February 1871 and 3 April 1872.

62. Bridges, "Equality Deferred," 95–97.

63. *Cairo (IL) Daily Bulletin*, 3 April 1870.

64. Ibid.

65. Ibid., 23 July 1870. For a description of Democratic tactics during the 1872 campaign, see Grossman, *Democratic Party and the Negro*, 30–35.

66. *Cairo (IL) Daily Bulletin*, 19 July 1872, 4.

67. Ibid., 21 July 1872, 4.

68. Ibid., 3 August 1872.

69. Ibid.

70. Ibid., 23 July 1872, 4.

71. Oberly also composed a sonnet, with Scott as one of its main characters, to commemorate what he believed to be a major split in black voters.

72. *Cairo (IL) Bulletin*, 28 November 1872, 4, 21 December 1872, 4, and 21 March 1873, 4.

73. Ibid., 21 March 1873, 4, and 8 August 1873; *Janesville (WI) Gazette*, 20 March 1873, 1.

74. *Cairo (IL) Bulletin*, 21 March 1873, 4. The *Daily Register* (Ironton, OH), 21 March 1873, 1, reported Scott's loss at $10,000.

75. *Cairo (IL) Bulletin*, 21 March 1873, 4. Wheeler, "Together in Egypt," wrote that "by the end of the 1870s Cairo had become synonymous with liquor, homicide, prostitution, and other forms of vice" (115).

76. *Cairo (IL) Daily Bulletin*, 22 March 1873, 4.

77. *Cairo (IL) Bulletin*, 18 July 1873, 4.

78. Ibid., 16 April 1873, 4. According to Portwood, "African-American Politics," 15, Bird was reelected in 1877 but resigned in 1879.

79. Dexter, "Old Newspapers," 21; *Cairo (IL) Bulletin*, 15 April 1873, 4.

80. *Cairo (IL) Bulletin*, 5 June 1873, 2.

81. Bridges, "Equality Deferred," 98. Joens, *From Slave to State Legislator*, noted that many black Republicans believed that they had not received their "fair share of jobs from Republican officeholders" (36). According to University of Illinois, *Semi-centennial Record*, Bird served as trustee of the university, received his formal education in Cincinnati, worked for the U.S. Postal Service from 1881 to 1912, and "organized the first free sch. System for negroes in Ill., and was Supt." (970). Lusk, *Politics and Politicians*, noted that Bird was the "first colored person to receive recognition from the Executive of the State" (341). Bird's appointment as trustee was more than symbolic. According to "Report of the Trustees," Bird, along with the president of the board of trustees, gave a formal "address" to the meeting of the board.

82. *Cairo (IL) Bulletin*, 17 March 1874, 3. Williams was a barber, and Gladney was a police constable.

83. Ibid., 14 April 1874, 4. Col. Daniel W. Munn was a lawyer and a leading Radical Republican in Cairo. He was elected to the Illinois Senate in 1866 and was one of Illinois's electors in 1868. Patrick H. Pope migrated to Cairo from New York State and practiced law as a partner in the firm of Cleaver and Pope. He also was a leader in Cairo's Republican Party.

84. Ibid., 11 May 1873, 2, and 22 April 1874, 4. See Hays, "Way Down in Egypt Land," 342–46, for a description of Cairo's "midnight subculture."

85. *Cairo (IL) Bulletin*, 16 April 1874, 4, and 19 April 1874, 4.

86. Ibid., 12 August 1874, 4.

87. Personal communication with Shirley J. Portwood, 29 June 2011.

88. *Cairo (IL) Bulletin*, 12 August 1874, 4.

89. Ibid., 11 October 1874, 2.

90. Ibid., 8 January 1875, 3.

91. Ibid., 16 September 1875, 3. For Scott's saloon and billiard hall at 76 Commercial Avenue, see Gardner and Gaines, *Cairo City Directory*, 119, 158.

92. *Cairo (IL) Bulletin*, 24 December 1875, 3.

93. Joens, "Ulysses S. Grant," 311. According to a report appearing in the *Racine County (WI) Argus* (Democrat), 27 July 1876, Bird and Scott were the heads of a Hayes and Wheeler Club in Cairo in 1876, while "most of the white republicans . . . declared for Tilden and reform" (2). See also Grossman, *Democratic Party and the Negro*, 51–54, for the 1876 election.

94. *Cairo (IL) Evening Bulletin*, 6 July 1876.

95. Hays, "Way Down in Egypt Land," 241–43; *Daily Inter Ocean* (Chicago), 14 July 1876, 5.

96. *Cairo (IL) Evening Bulletin*, 28 November 1876.

97. Bridges, "Equality Deferred," 99–100; Bigham, *On Jordan's Banks*, 189.

98. Joens, *From Slave to State Legislator*, xi.

99. Bridges, "Equality Deferred," 99.

100. Ibid., 99–100.

101. Cha-Jua, *America's First Black Town*, 188.

102. *Cairo (IL) Daily Democrat*, 25 January 1866 and 31 January 1866.

103. *Cairo (IL) Bulletin*, 9 March 1871.

104. Ibid., 20 January 1880, and numerous other issues.

105. Ibid., 26 December 1879. Light, "Ethnic Vice Industry," 472–74, identified "resort" as a polite term for brothel.

106. *Cairo (IL) Daily Bulletin*, 24 September 1871, 4, 19 October 1871, 4, 4 March 1873, 4, and 5 December 1873, 2.

107. *Cairo (IL) Bulletin*, 5 December 1873, 2.

108. See Haynes, *Third Party Movement*, 30–40 for Liberal Republicans, 51–66 for farmer parties, and 91–100 for the growth of Greenback strength in nearby Iowa.

109. Bridges, "Equality Deferred," 90.

110. Hays, "Way Down in Egypt Land," 212.

111. Quoted in Carlson, "Black Migration," 45.

Chapter 2. Covering His Past with Rebellion and Journalism, the Early 1880s

1. According to Hays, "African American Struggle," 275, George McKeaig, Cairo's postmaster and a Republican whom Scott had often supported, in 1879 had publicly and angrily refused to add any blacks to his staff.

2. *Christian Recorder* (AA, Philadelphia), 16 May 1878.

3. Bigham, *Towns and Villages*, 121.

4. *Daily Illinois State Journal* (Springfield), 29 January 1905, 1.

5. *Decatur (IL) Daily Republican*, 21 April 1880, 3.

6. See Joens, "John W. E. Thomas: A Political Biography," 137–38, for background on Colored Conventions in Illinois.

7. Quoted in Joens, *From Slave to State Legislator*, 36.

8. Ibid., 58.

9. For the 1880 Illinois state convention and the Chicago convention, see Joens, "Ulysses S. Grant," 310–30.

10. Peskin, *Garfield*, 263. For the 1880 convention and the confusion surrounding the final balloting, see Ackerman, *Dark Horse*, 98–122. Ackerman noted that the Negro National Republican Committee had placed the name of Blanche Bruce, black senator from Mississippi, in nomination for the office of vice president (130).

11. *Illinois State Journal* (Springfield), 20 July 1880, 2.

12. *Decatur (IL) Daily Review*, 22 July 1880, 4; *New York Times*, 21 July 1880. The *Cairo (IL) Bulletin*, 25 July 1880, 4, noted simply that the convention had been "called for the purpose of demanding of the Republican party a proportionate share of the loaves and fishes."

13. Joens, *From Slave to State Legislator*, 63.

14. *Boston Advocate*, quoted in Beatty, *Revolution Gone Backward*, 49. For an elaborate discussion of "Independence" in the Midwest, see ibid., 45–59.

15. Grossman, *Democratic Party and the Negro*, 94–95.

16. *Daily Arkansas Gazette* (Little Rock), 23 July 1880, 4; *Illinois State Journal* (Springfield), 21 July 1880, 5.

17. *Illinois State Journal* (Springfield), 21 July 1880, 5.

18. *Boston Daily Advertiser*, 21 July 1880.

19. *Decatur (IL) Daily Review*, 22 July 1880, 4. See also *Daily Arkansas Gazette* (Little Rock), 23 July 1880, 4; *Boston Daily Advertiser*, 21 July 1880, 2. The *Decatur (IL) Daily Republican*, 26 July 1880, reported that one delegate from Mattoon had not been seated "on account of an entire want of reliability as a republican" (3). According to the *Daily Illinois State Journal* (Springfield), 25 July 1880, 3, the convention had addressed the question of Democratic Party sponsorship of the convention in a separate resolution, had disclaimed "any intention or purpose to give aid or comfort to the Democracy," and had reaffirmed its "devotion to said [Republican] party, and pledge it our hearty and unanimous support in the present campaign."

20. *Salt Lake (UT) Herald*, 22 July 1880, 2; *Sacramento (CA) Daily Record-Union*, 22 July 1880, 1; *Decatur (IL) Daily Record*, 24 July 1880, 4; Bigham, *On Jordan's Banks*, 190; Bridges, "Equality Deferred," 100; Joens, *From Slave to State Legislator*, 83–84.

21. *Salt Lake (UT) Herald*, 22 July 1880, 2. For accounts of the 1880 Springfield conference, see Hays, "Way Down in Egypt Land," 359; Bigham, *On Jordan's Banks*, 190; Bridges, "Equality Deferred," 100; Hays, "African American Struggle," 282. The accounts in the *Quincy (IL) Daily Whig*, 21 July 1880, 4, and 22 July 1880, 4, mentioned only Bird, who had been elected one of five vice presidents.

22. *Illinois State Journal* (Springfield), 21 July 1880, 5. The *Illinois State Register* (Springfield), 21 July 1880, 4, and 22 July 1880, 4, noted that black Greenbackers and Democrats were denied delegate status at the convention. See also the *Inter Ocean* (Chicago), 22 July 1880, 2, for another report of the convention.

23. *Illinois State Journal* (Springfield), 20 July 1880, 2.

24. Bigham, *On Jordan's Banks*, 189–90, 390–91; *Cairo (IL) Bulletin*, 27 October 1880. For Oberly as chairman of the Democratic state central committee of Illinois in 1885, see *Chicago Times*, 14 February 1885, 5.

25. Bigham, *On Jordan's Banks*, 190.

26. *Cairo (IL) Bulletin*, 28 July 1880, 4.

27. Bridges, "Equality Deferred," 101, noted that the Colored Garfield Wide-Awake Club of McLean County had described Bird and Scott as "designing politicians" and unworthy of black support. Cairo's black Republicans also condemned the endorsement of Oberly.

28. *Cairo (IL) Bulletin*, 17 October 1880. See also Joens, "John W. E. Thomas," 200–216.

29. Bigham, *On Jordan's Banks*, 297. The *Inter Ocean* (Chicago), 8 March 1876, 2, indicated that Cairo's "colored school" had four grades and four teachers.

30. Wheeler, "Together in Egypt," 115. See also Hays, "African American Struggle," 267; Bigham, *On Jordan's Banks*, 222.

31. Hays, "African American Struggle," 266–70; Wheeler, "Together in Egypt," 119–20.

32. For a thorough review of changes that occurred in black communities along the Ohio River, see Bigham, *On Jordan's Banks*.

33. *Cairo (IL) Bulletin*, 9 August 1882.

34. Penn, *Afro-American Press*, 128. See also Walker, "Promised Land," 13; Hays, "African American Struggle," 276; Bigham, *On Jordan's Banks*, 221; *Brooklyn (NY) Daily Eagle*, 16 June 1882, 1. Belles, "Black Press," 346, indicates that Scott purchased the *Gazette* in 1881. See Ayer, *N. W. Ayer & Son's American Newspaper Annual*, 80, which noted in 1888 that the *Gazette* was a four-page "independent" weekly newspaper with a circulation of 952. Rowell, *Rowell's American Newspaper Directory*, 139, listed it as a four-page weekly, 23 by 35 inches, $2 annual subscription, established in 1882.

35. Penn, *Afro-American Press*, 128.

36. *Christian Recorder* (AA, Philadelphia), 7 December 1882.

37. Bridges, "Equality Deferred," 101; *Barton's Free Press* (Carbondale, IL), 24 April 1883, 2. For the 1883 flood, see *Decatur (IL) Daily Republican*, 7 March 1883, 2.

38. *Cairo (IL) Daily Bulletin*, 1 September 1882.

39. *Cairo (IL) Bulletin*, 24 May 1882.

40. Ibid., 28 July 1880, 4.

41. *Indianapolis (IN) Freeman* (AA), 19 October 1889, 1; *Cairo (IL) Bulletin*, 16 June 1882.

42. *Indianapolis (IN) Sentinel*, 23 June 1882, 1; *Daily Inter Ocean* (Chicago), 23 June 1882, 5; *Cairo (IL) Bulletin*, 23 June 1882, 4.

43. *Cairo (IL) Bulletin*, 23 June 1882, 4.

44. Rittenhouse dairy, 2:36–39. See also Jones, "Cairo of Maud Rittenhouse," 74–85, for a description of the "special world of Cairo's economic and social elite" and a brief review of Cairo's history.

45. *Indianapolis (IN) Freeman* (AA), 19 October 1889, 1.

46. *Daily Inter Ocean* (Chicago), 14 July 1882, 1, and 23 June 1882, 5; *Indianapolis (IN) Sentinel*, 23 June 1882, 1.

47. *New York Times*, 9 August 1882. See also *Decatur (IL) Daily Republican*, 9 August 1882, 2; *Plain Dealer* (Detroit, MI), 8 August 1882, 1. For a discussion of the content of black newspapers during this period and the rise of racial militancy, see Simmons, *African American Press*, 16–24.

48. Hays, "African American Struggle," 267; Penn, *Afro-American Press*, 128.

49. Bigham, *On Jordan's Banks*, 297. For reports of the 1883 flood at Cairo, see *Decatur (IL) Daily Republican*, 7 March 1883, 2.

50. Bigham, *On Jordan's Banks*, 297, 309–10; Wheeler, "Together in Egypt," 125–26; Hays, "Way Down in Egypt Land," 360–61; Hays, "African American Struggle," 283–84.

51. Bigham, *On Jordan's Banks*, 310; *Cleveland (OH) Gazette* (AA), 24 May 1883, 2; *Cairo (IL) Bulletin*, 3 May 1883.

52. Quoted in *Washington (DC) Bee* (AA), 27 January 1883, 2.

53. Quoted in ibid., 10 February 1883, 3. The *Grit* (AA, New York), 16 February 1884, 2, reported that Scott had given notice that if Republican leaders did not provide "substantial rewards" to black voters, those voters would support another party. Beatty,

Looking Backward, 52, characterized the Arthur administration as supporting "lily-white Republicanism." Interestingly, Beatty attributed Leonard's warning to Arthur to the *Washington (DC) Bee* rather than the *Cairo (IL) Gazette*.

54. *Arkansas Mansion* (AA, Little Rock), 14 July 1883, 4.

55. *Daily Freeman* (AA, Waukesha, WI), 12 July 1883, 4; *Arkansas Mansion* (AA, Little Rock), 14 July 1883, 4; *New Orleans (LA) Daily Times-Picayune* (AA), 12 July 1883. The *New York Globe* (AA), 27 January 1883, reported that an editorial had appeared in the *Cairo (IL) Gazette* criticizing the Colored Press Association for electing a president who was not a journalist. The *Globe* explained that the Colored Press Association was "purely a fraternal association of men who are fond of their calling, of each other, and of good eating and drinking."

56. *New York Times*, 14 July 1883, 5; *Daily Dispatch* (Richmond, VA), 14 July 1883, 3.

57. *Cairo (IL) Bulletin*, 17 July 1883.

58. *Quincy (IL) Morning Herald*, 15 June 1883, 3. The *State Journal* (Harrisburg, PA), 18 October 1884, 1, reported that Scott had attended the biannual meeting of the GUOOF in Cincinnati. As noted in the preface, the topic of black fraternal orders or societies is complicated. Fraternal societies were enormously popular in all segments of African American culture during the second half of the nineteenth century. These secret organizations provided their members with benefits that ranged from early forms of insurance payable in times of need to helpful bridges between church congregations or political societies. They were also schools where black males acquired leadership skills. It was a time when males were likely to belong to one or more such organizations. Scott was a joiner, belonging to many, and reached high offices in some.

59. *Arkansas Mansion* (AA, Little Rock), 15 September 1883, 1, and 29 September 1883, 3; *Washington (DC) Bee* (AA), 15 December 1883, 2.

60. McFeely, *Frederick Douglass*, 315.

61. *Springfield (MA) Republican*, 27 September 1883, 4; McFeely, *Frederick Douglass*, 315. The *Conservator* (Chicago), 8 September 1883, warned that the "younger element" had rejected the convention even before it took place.

62. *New York Globe* (AA), 29 September 1883, 2. For additional accounts, see the *New York Herald*, 26 September 1883, 6; *Kalamazoo (MI) Gazette*, 26 September 1883, 4.

63. *New Orleans (LA) Daily Times-Picayune* (AA), 25 September 1883, 1; *National Republican* (Washington, DC), 25 September 1883, 1. For a slightly different reconstruction of the first session, see Blassingame and McKivigan, *Frederick Douglass Papers*, 5:85.

64. *Saint Paul (MN) Daily Globe* (AA), 26 September 1883, 4; *Abilene (KS) Reflector*, 27 September 1883, 2; *Plain Dealer* (AA, Cleveland, OH), 27 September 1883, 2.

65. *Saint Paul (MN) Daily Globe* (AA), 26 September 1883, 4. For the full text of Douglass's speech, see Blassingame and McKivigan, *Frederick Douglass Papers*, 5:86–110. McFeely, *Douglass*, also reported that Douglass later, in an interview with the press, said: "I cannot see how any honest colored man, who has brains enough to put two ideas together, can allow himself, under the notion of independence, to give aid and comfort to the Democratic Party in Ohio or elsewhere" (316).

66. *New York Globe* (AA), 29 September 1883, 1.

67. Ibid. The *Augusta (GA) Chronicle*, 26 September 1883, 1, reported that Douglass had been "sarcastically severe upon the government and incidentally so upon the Republican party." See also the *Western Recorder* (AA, Lawrence, KS), 5 October 1883, 2, for conference proceedings and resolutions passed by the convention.

68. *Washington (DC) Bee* (AA), 29 December 1883, 2.

69. Joens, "John W. E. Thomas: A Political Biography," 146–47. For accounts of this day's activities, see also *Cairo (IL) Bulletin*, 20 October 1883; *Chicago Times*, 16 October 1883, 8; *Springfield (IL) Register*, 16 October 1883, 3; *Illinois State Journal* (Springfield), 16 October 1883, 7; *Chicago Evening Journal*, 16 October 1883, 1; *Saint Louis (MO) Globe-Democrat*, 16 October 1883, 2. See Joens, *From Slave to State Legislator*, 86–88, for a detailed description of the convention's struggle to select a permanent chair.

70. Joens, *From Slave to State Legislator*, 89; *Illinois State Journal* (Springfield), 16 October 1883, 7.

71. Ex-Senator Blanche Bruce had said that "nothing has occurred since the war to embarrass and discourage them as much as the decision of yesterday" (*Quincy [IL] Daily Whig*, 17 October 1883, 2). For accounts of the Colored Convention and condemnation of the Supreme Court decision, see ibid., 18 October 1883, 4, 20 October 1833, 4, and 23 October 1883, 3; *Quincy (IL) Herald*, 23 October 1883, 3.

72. Quoted in Higginbotham, *Shades of Freedom*, 106.

73. Joens, "John W. E. Thomas: A Political Biography," 149.

74. Joens, *From Slave to State Legislator*, 112.

75. *Chicago Evening Journal*, 17 October 1883, 1.

76. Ibid.

77. *Cairo (IL) Bulletin*, 20 October 1883, mentioned only that Scott had introduced such a resolution at an earlier Cairo convention but that "it was couched in language less open."

78. *Springfield (IL) State Register*, 17 October 1883, 3.

79. *Cairo (IL) Bulletin*, 6 November 1883.

80. *Chicago Evening Journal*, 18 October 1883, 1. Joens, *From Slave to State Legislator*, labeled the *Evening Journal*'s comment as "unfair and untrue" and concluded that "the convention was merely a battle in a war that the factions would wage for the next two years" (91–92).

81. *Daily Illinois State Journal* (Springfield), 24 November 1883, 2. See Joens, *From Slave to State Legislator*, 207, for Mitchell.

82. *Cairo (IL) Bulletin*, 6 November 1883.

83. *Washington (DC) Bee* (AA), 22 December 1883, 2, and 29 December 1883, 2; *Cleveland Gazette* (AA), 22 December 1883, 3; *People's Advocate* (AA, Washington, DC), 22 December 1883, 2; *Cairo (IL) Bulletin*, 29 December 1883.

84. *People's Advocate* (AA, Washington, DC), 22 December 1883, 2.

85. *Chicago Times*, 30 January 1884, 3.

86. Ibid., 31 January 1884; *New York Globe* (AA), 16 February 1884, 4, and see 23 February 1884, 2, for the full text of the resolution adopted at the meeting.

87. *Cleveland (OH) Gazette* (AA), 22 March 1884, 1.

88. Ibid., 29 March 1884, 2.

89. *Chicago Times*, 30 April 1884, 5.

90. Ibid., 1 May 1884, 7.

91. Joens, *From Slave to State Legislator*, 94–95.

92. See Grossman, *Democratic Party and the Negro*, 65–68, for Cleveland's term as mayor of Buffalo and governor of New York State.

93. *Daily Illinois State Journal* (Springfield), 16 October 1885, 4.

94. Joens, *From Slave to State Legislator*, 119.

95. *Daily Illinois State Journal* (Springfield), 17 October 1885, 4.

96. Ibid., 16 October 1885, 4.

97. Ibid., 17 October 1885, 4.

98. Ibid.

99. Ibid.

Chapter 3. Reinvention as a Respectable Democrat, 1884 to 1893

1. Scott offered a resolution at the 1885 Illinois Colored Convention that commended the "North, Central and South American Exposition," otherwise known as the New Orleans Cotton Exposition, "for placing the exhibits of colored persons on the same footing with those of white persons." That resolution passed unanimously (*Daily Illinois State Journal* [Springfield], 17 October 1885, 4).

2. Grossman, *Democratic Party and the Negro*, 81.

3. Taylor, *America's First Black Socialist*, 6–7.

4. Grossman, *Democratic Party and the Negro*, 101–2.

5. *Washington (DC) Bee* (AA), 27 January 1883, 2, and 21 June 1884, 3. In the *Appeal* (AA, Saint Paul, MN), 12 October 1889, 1, Bird was listed as second vice president of the Colored Men's State League of Illinois, which was a Republican league.

6. *Daily Illinois State Journal* (Springfield), 17 October 1885, 4. Houser was still working for Scott in 1886 (*Western Kansas World* [AA, WaKenney], 25 December 1886). In 1887 Houser was appointed as clerk in the Recorder of Deeds Office in Washington, DC (*Western Appeal* [AA, Minneapolis, MN], 12 March 1887, 1). Houser would become the editor of the *Negro World* of Minneapolis in 1892 and would play a prominent role in Democratic politics at the turn of the century. In 1892 C. H. J. Taylor of Kansas City had already identified Houser as one of Illinois's most effective orators (*Times-Picayune* [AA, New Orleans], 30 July 1892). Houser originally was from Chicago (*Saint Paul [MN] Daily Globe*, 12 December 1887, 4).

7. *Washington (DC) Bee* (AA), 21 June 1884, 3. Painter, "Black Journalism," 37, noted that the first black daily newspaper was the *Colored Citizen* of Cincinnati, which was printed between 1863 and 1865, with a small circulation to Union soldiers. Scott's *Cairo Gazette*, however, was the newspaper that obtained national notice and was considered by the black press of the late nineteenth century to have been the first black daily. According to Painter, "Black Journalism," 39, 154, black papers were being printed nationally in 1890.

8. *Indianapolis (IN) Freeman* (AA), 19 October 1889, 1; *Lincoln (NE) Evening News,* 30 January 1905.

9. Portwood, "African-American Politics," 13; *Quincy (IL) Daily Journal,* 25 August 1897, 7. Scott did not entirely escape controversy once he became politically active. In July 1884, for example, he was reported to have "shot and wounded one of his customers" at his Cairo saloon (*Cleveland [OH] Gazette,* 19 July 1884).

10. Ayer, *N. W. Ayer & Son's American Newspaper Annual,* 80.

11. Penn, *Afro-American Press,* 128.

12. Belles, "Black Press," 346; Scott, *Newspapers and Periodicals,* 37. Henritze, *Bibliographic Checklist,* 42, gave different years for the *Cairo (IL) Gazette* (1882–89), *Three States* (1887–88), and a third, the *Sentinel* (1892–95). The *Sentinel* was not listed in other sources.

13. *Decatur (IL) Review,* 11 August 1886, 2.

14. Bigham, *On Jordan's Banks,* 309–10. Hugh Davis, *We Will Be Satisfied,* 111, noted that Cairo's black voters "enabled the Republicans to be the dominant political force there from 1870 until the early twentieth century."

15. For a historical review of black fraternal and sororal associations in the Midwest, see Schwalm, *Emancipation's Diaspora,* 157–74. For Scott's remaining political influence, see *Cairo (IL) Citizen,* 3 May 1888.

16. *Cairo (IL) Bulletin,* 3 November 1874, 4. Greenbaum, "Comparison of African-American," noted that such organizations "also sponsored social, educational and cultural activities which reinforced ethnic networks and group identity, while providing for the common welfare" (95). Greenbaum also noted (99–100) that such benefit societies worked best when small and when everyone knew everyone. In effect, failure to pay dues meant that one lost membership in the group. The smaller the dues, the more likely that members would maintain payments and that the society would keep a steady "stream of revenue" from which to cover obligations and payments. Peck, "Life Insurance," described these as "Negro fraternal benevolent burial associations" and indicated that they provided modest health benefits, a "decent burial for the deceased," and prompt payment of benefits (154).

17. For a discussion of voluntary associations and benevolent societies, see Bigham, *On Jordan's Banks,* 261–64. Emery and Emery, *Young Man's Benefit,* 12, noted that premiums for burial insurance often amounted to as little as "a few cents a week" and were paid to "neighbourhood collectors," who made weekly rounds. They also noted (17) the stigma attached to burial in a pauper's grave, primarily because funerals were public events, and the burial process reflected upon the status of the family.

18. The *Daily Telegram's Cairo City Directory for 1893,* 35–44, listed twenty-two "secret associations" for black men: Masonic (Lincoln Lodge No. 5 and three other lodges); Grand Union Order of Odd Fellows (Egypt Lodge No. 1667); Grand Army of the Republic (James P. Foster Post No. 598 and one additional post); Knights of Tabor (Rising Son of Egypt Temple No. 14 and six additional temples); United Brothers of Friendship (Star of Egypt Temple No. 3 and five additional temples); Free Benevolent Sons of America; Marine Fireman No. 5655; and Improved Order of Red Men (Oneida Tribe No. 104).

19. Bigham, *On Jordan's Banks*, 266. Bigham also mentioned various aid societies, formal musical societies, and sports organizations. For similar societies along the upper Mississippi River, see Schwalm, *Emancipation's Diaspora*, 157–74; Mouser, *For Labor*, 83–84. For Pride of Egypt Tabernacle No. 8 of the Knights of Tabor, see *Indianapolis (IN) Freeman* (AA), 1 April 1893; *Illinois Record* (AA, Springfield), 21 May 1898, 3. For Scott's membership in United Brothers of Friendship, see *Morning Herald* (Baltimore, MD), 13 July 1898, 3.

20. Schwalm, *Emancipation's Diaspora*, 157; Trotter, "African American Fraternal Associations," 362–63.

21. Schwalm, "Emancipation Day Celebrations."

22. *Saint Louis (MO) Republican*, 24 November 1902, 4; *Indianapolis (IN) Freeman* (AA), 18 May 1895, 4, and 23 May 1891; *State Capital* (AA, Springfield, IL), 9 May 1891; *New Orleans (LA) Item*, 21 November 1902, 6.

23. *Cairo (IL) Evening Bulletin*, 25 June 1869, 3; *Cairo (IL) Daily Bulletin*, 26 June 1872, 4.

24. *Lincoln (NE) Evening News*, 30 January 1905.

25. *Christian Recorder* (AA, Philadelphia), 16 May 1878.

26. *Daily Illinois State Journal* (Springfield), 11 September 1880, 4, and 2 February 1881, 8. The *Daily Inter Ocean* (Chicago), 5 August 1881, 8, reported that Scott was elected grand master again in 1881.

27. *Cairo (IL) Bulletin*, 4 May 1873, 4, and 27 December 1873, 4.

28. Andrews, *Masonic Abolitionists*, 108–9. See also *Cairo Evening Bulletin*, 29 December 1877, for dates that differ slightly from Andrews' reconstruction.

29. Andrews, *Masonic Abolitionists*, 107, 109–10. For Scott's activities in Prince Hall Masonry, see *Proceedings of the Thirteenth Annual Communication*; and *Condensed Report of the Twelfth Annual Communication* (http://www.andrewspress.com/Research /Proceedings/MWPHGL_1878.pdf, accessed 3 March 2014). For Scott's election as grand master of the Grand United Order of Odd Fellows of Illinois, see *Cairo (IL) Bulletin*, 9 August 1882.

30. *Cleveland (OH) Gazette* (AA), 19 September 1885, 1.

31. *Indianapolis (IN) Freeman* (AA), 25 August 1888, 1, 29 October 1888, 2, and 19 October 1889, 1.

32. *New York Globe* (AA), 20 September 1884, 4; *New York Freeman* (AA), 23 July 1887, 2.

33. *Cleveland (OH) Gazette* (AA), 31 January 1885, 2, and 27 February 1886, 1.

34. *Washington (DC) Bee* (AA), 7 August 1886; *Decatur (IL) Review*, 16 October 1886, 2.

35. *Western Appeal* (AA, Saint Paul, MN), 2 July 1887, 1. See also *Washington (DC) Bee* (AA), 2 July 1887, 3, for the schedule of presentations.

36. *Washington (DC) Bee* (AA), 4 August 1888, 2.

37. The *Huntsville (AL) Gazette* (AA), 5 February 1885, 2, reported that the *Galveston (TX) Spectator* had been the first daily black newspaper and that the *People's Journal* of Jacksonville, Florida, was printing a daily in 1885.

38. Penn, *Afro-American Press*, 128.

39. *Cairo (IL) Citizen*, 21 November 1889. See also *Indianapolis (IN) Freeman* (AA), 15 June 1889, 4; *Cleveland (OH) Gazette* (AA), 20 July 1889, 1.

40. *Cleveland (OH) Gazette* (AA), 6 February 1886, 2. Editor Smith of the *Cleveland Gazette* and Scott and Leonard hurled insults at each other in 1887 and 1888.

41. *Cairo (IL) Bulletin*, 23 January 1879.

42. *New York Times*, 23 April 1888.

43. *Saint Paul (MN) Daily Globe*, 7 July 1888, 4.

44. *Galveston (TX) Daily News*, 3 July 1888, 11, dateline Pana, Illinois, reported part of a text that may have come from the Saint Louis convention. It suggested that delegates had "grown weary of the fraud and deception which has been the reward of their fealty [to the Republican Party]. . . . This [Republican] party gave manhood to the chattel, freedom to the man, but enslaved the mind and degraded the citizen by denying him the privilege of a conscientious exercise of his political convictions."

45. *Arkansas Gazette* (Little Rock), 19 August 1888, 3.

46. *Sun* (AA, New York), 7 June 1888, 3; *Wichita (KS) Eagle* (AA), 7 June 1888, 2; *Saint Louis (MO) Republic* (AA), 7 June 1888, pt. 2, 16.

47. *Galveston (TX) Daily News*, 3 July 1888, 1.

48. *Springfield (OH) Daily Republic*, 6 July 1888, 3. See also *Barton's Free Press* (Carbondale, IL), 14 July 1888, for Scott in Baltimore and Washington, DC.

49. *Washington (DC) Bee* (AA), 7 July 1888, 2.

50. Ibid. For a brief review of Chase's history in journalism, see Pride and Wilson, *History of the Black Press*, 98–102. James Monroe Trotter was born in 1842 and claimed to have obtained his secondary education at Gilmore School in Cincinnati. It is possible that they knew each other from their Cincinnati days. Trotter taught school in Chillicothe, Ohio, before enlisting in the Union army. During the final stages of the war, Trotter was the first black to be promoted to the rank of second lieutenant.

51. *Washington (DC) Bee* (AA), 7 July 1888, 2.

52. *New York Globe* (AA), 29 December 1883, 1; *Grit* (AA, New York), 16 February 1884.

53. *Newark (OH) Daily Advocate*, 9 July 1888, 4.

54. *Saint Louis (MO) Republic*, 19 July 1888.

55. *Washington (DC) Bee* (AA), 7 July 1888, 2.

56. *Saint Paul (MN) Daily Globe*, 25 July 1888, 4; *Plain Dealer* (AA, Cleveland, OH), 26 July 1888, 2; *Saint Louis (MO) Republic*, 25 July 1888; *Omaha (NE) Herald*, 26 July 1888, 5.

57. *Wichita (KS) Eagle* (AA), 5 April 1888, 2.

58. *Plain Dealer* (AA, Cleveland, OH), 26 July 1888, 1; *New Haven (CT) Register*, 26 July 1888, 3.

59. *Daily Illinois State Journal* (Springfield), 26 July 1888, 3.

60. *Saint Paul (MN) Daily Globe*, 25 July 1888, 4; *Plain Dealer* (AA, Cleveland, OH), 26 July 1888, 2; *Saint Louis (MO) Republic*, 25 July 1888; *Omaha (NE) Herald*, 26 July 1888, 5.

61. *New York Times*, 27 July 1888; *Omaha (NE) Herald*, 26 July 1888, 5.

62. *Washington (DC) Bee* (AA), 4 August 1888, 2. Blanche K. Bruce was a senator from Mississippi, and John R. Lynch was a congressman from Mississippi. The *Saint Louis (MO) Republic* (AA), 18 November 1902, 4, equated the term "boodle" with bribery or money paid on a monthly basis for services either rendered or not rendered.

63. *Washington (DC) Bee* (AA), 4 August 1888, 2. For other accounts of the Indianapolis conference, see *Broad Ax* (AA, Chicago and Salt Lake City, UT), 18 August 1888, 1 and 4; *Saint Paul (MN) Daily Globe*, 25 July 1888, 4; *New York Times*, 27 July 1888.

64. *Washington (DC) Bee* (AA), 18 August 1888, 1.

65. *Plain Dealer* (AA, Cleveland, OH), 26 July 1888, 1; *Saint Louis (MO) Republic*, 27 July 1888; *Kansas City (KS) Times*, 27 July 1888.

66. *Boston Journal*, 26 July 1888, 2; *Oregonian* (Portland, OR), 26 July 1888, 2; *Trenton (NJ) Evening Times*, 26 July 1888, 1; *Indianapolis (IN) Freeman* (AA), 6 April 1889, 4.

67. *Indianapolis (IN) Freeman* (AA), 6 April 1889.

68. Ibid., 15 June 1889, 4; *State Capital* (AA, Springfield, IL), 9 May 1891, 25 June 1892, and 1 April 1893; *Indianapolis (IN) Freeman* (AA), 1 April 1893.

69. See "A National Appeal," reproduced in Mouser, *For Labor*, 73–76.

70. For a brief review of Fortune's background and activities, see Pride and Wilson, *History of the Black Press*, 121–23; and King and Tuck, "De-centring the South," 213–15.

71. Mouser, *For Labor*, 64–66. For Fortune's plans in 1887, see Fishel, "Negro in Northern Politics," 483–86; Schwalm, *Emancipation's Diaspora*, 213–14; Alexander, "We Know Our Rights," 21–52. For the influence of New York politics on Fortune's scheme, see Swan, "Thomas McCants Stewart," 145–46.

72. *New York Freeman* (AA), 23 July 1887, 2.

73. Thornbrough, "National Afro-American League"; Mouser, *For Labor*, 66.

74. *Daily Illinois State Journal* (Springfield), 6 July 1891, 5.

75. Alexander, "We Know Our Rights," 108.

76. *Boston Daily Globe*, 20 June 1892, 8; *Saint Paul (MN) Daily Globe*, 20 June 1892, 5, and 22 June 1892, 5; *Evening Gazette* (Sterling, IL), 21 June 1892, 1; *New York Times*, 22 June 1892; *Wichita (KS) Daily Eagle* (AA), 22 June 1892, 2; *Omaha (NE) World Herald*, 21 June 1892; *State Capital* (AA, Springfield, IL), 25 June 1892 and 2 July 1892; Beatty, *Revolution Gone Backward*, 98.

77. *New York Times*, 22 June 1892.

78. *Appeal* (AA, Saint Paul, MN), 9 July 1892, 1.

79. *Atlanta (GA) Constitution* (AA insert), 15 May 1893, 1. See also *Alton (IL) Daily Telegraph*, 16 May 1893, 1.

80. *Morning Call* (Allentown, PA), 30 July 1893, 1.

81. *Daily Illinois State Journal* (Springfield), 6 July 1891.

82. Cha-Jua, *America's First Black Town*, 130–31; Cha-Jua, "'A Warlike Demonstration': Legalism, Armed Resistance," 70n39.

83. Cha-Jua, "'A Warlike Demonstration': Legalism, Violent Self-Help," 612.

84. *Illinois Record* (AA, Springfield), 24 September 1898; *Morning Call* (Allentown, PA), 10 July 1896, 6; *Daily Register Gazette* (Rockford, IL), 9 July 1896, 7.

85. *Illinois Record* (AA, Springfield), 24 September 1898.

86. *Appeal* (AA, Saint Paul, MN), 8 January 1898, 1. For the origins of the Protective League, see *Daily Inter Ocean* (Chicago), 24 August 1895.

87. Mouser, *For Labor*, 76–78; *Chicago Evening Post*, 27 June 1893, 2. For a detailed description of the exposition and black congresses that convened in Chicago in 1893, see Reed, *"All the World Is Here!"*

88. Cha-Jua, *America's First Black Town*, wrote that "political leaders were attracted to the [tavern] business because their wealth gave them a degree of economic independence and political influence" (188).

89. *New York Times*, 14 July 1883.

90. Strout, *Maud*, 5–6, 24–26, 41, 78, 113, 117, 410.

91. *Cairo (IL) Bulletin*, 26 August 1871.

92. The Partisan Prohibition Historical Society, http://www.prohibitionists.org /History/society/society.html and http://www.prohibitionists.org/History/votes/body_ votes.html, for candidates, accessed 9 April 2012; *Daily Journal and Republican* (Freeport, IL), 25 August 1885.

93. *Daily Journal and Republican* (Freeport, IL), 25 August 1885, 2.

94. Ibid.

Chapter 4. Scott's Frenetic Decade, 1893 to 1904

1. Hartshorn, *Era of Progress*, 471.

2. *State Capital* (AA, Springfield), 31 October 1891, 1; *Kalamazoo (MI) Gazette*, 9 November 1893, 5, and 5 July 1896, 4.

3. A single reference to Scott's residence in Chicago in 1893 is found in the *Saint Louis (MO) Palladium* (AA), 17 October 1893, 1, with reference to Scott "of Chicago" visiting in Saint Louis.

4. For a brief review of the causes and impact of the depression of 1893 by David O. Whitten, Auburn University, see Whitten, "The Depression of 1893," http://eh.net /encyclopedia/the-depression-of-1893/, accessed 28 February 2014.

5. Steeples and Whitten, *Democracy in Desperation*, 1; Ali, *In the Balance of Power*.

6. *Omaha (NE) World Herald*, 13 August 1894, 3.

7. *Muskegon (MI) Chronicle*, 2 June 1894, 6.

8. *Trenton (NJ) Evening Times*, 11 June 1894, 2.

9. *New York Herald*, 1 July 1894, 5.

10. Hays, "Way Down in Egypt Land," 395–97.

11. Lantz and Alix, "Occupational Mobility," 405–7.

12. Cha-Jua, "'A Warlike Demonstration': Legalism, Violent Self-Help," noted that blacks in Alton, Brooklyn, and Decatur also were challenging "white republican hegemony" in 1898.

13. *Cairo (IL) Citizen*, 25 October 1894, 27 October 1894, and 8 November 1894. In the 1894 election cycle, candidates for county offices listed themselves as Republican, Democrat, People's/Populist, People's Silver, and Independent. Republicans won all

offices. See also Ali, *In the Lion's Mouth*, 150–56, for the collapse of black Populism in the 1890s.

14. *Cairo (IL) Citizen*, 23 April 1896, reported that 281 votes had been cast in Scott's ward.

15. *Illinois Record* (AA, Springfield), 13 August 1898, 3.

16. Ibid., 24 September 1898.

17. Hays, "African American Struggle," 276–77; *Illinois Record* (AA, Springfield), 24 September 1898, 3.

18. *Cleveland (OH) Gazette* (AA), 13 November 1897, 1; *Cleveland (OH) Leader*, 23 September 1897, 2. According to the *Denver (CO) Post*, 23 September 1897, 5, in 1897 the national convention of colored veterans, G.A.R. Colored, in which Scott and John A. Ross of Buffalo, New York, were "moving spirits," had endorsed the ticket of Ohio's Negro Protective Party.

19. *Denver (CO) Rocky Mountain News*, 27 February 1898, 1.

20. *Cairo (IL) Citizen*, 10 November 1898, 1, and 17 November 1898. See also *Daily Illinois State Register* (Springfield), 10 November 1898; *Illinois Record* (AA, Springfield), 12 November 1898; Hays, "African American Struggle," 277.

21. *Daily Illinois State Register* (Springfield), 10 November 1898, 9.

22. Lansden, *History of the City of Cairo*, 146.

23. *Nevada State Journal* (Reno), 15 August 1896, 2; *Decatur (IL) Daily Review*, 17 June 1896, 2; *Saint Paul (MN) Globe* (AA), 12 August 1896, 3; *Daily Public Ledger* (Maysville, KY), 12 August 1896, 3; *Republican* (Seattle, WA), 22 August 1896; *Duluth (MN) News Tribune*, 12 August 1896, 2.

24. *Daily Inter Ocean* (Chicago), 13 August 1896, 7. The *Evening Star* (Washington, DC), 13 August 1896, reported that "an enraged minority, of gold men [delegates] fumed and claimed the convention was packed and the proceedings irregular" (8).

25. *Daily Inter Ocean* (Chicago), 12 August 1896, 3.

26. *Broad Ax* (AA, Chicago and Salt Lake City, UT), 22 August 1896; *Record-Union* (Sacramento, CA), 7 September 1896, 1; *Morning World Herald* (Omaha, NE), 8 September 1896; *New York Times*, 8 September 1896, 2.

27. *New York Times*, 10 August 1898, 5; *World* (New York), 11 August 1898, 7.

28. *Broad Ax* (AA, Chicago and Salt Lake City, UT), 22 August 1896, 1.

29. *Quincy (IL) Morning Whig*, 26 August 1897, 1. See also *Saint Louis (MO) Republic* (AA), 26 August 1897, 6, for a list of those attending the Quincy meeting.

30. *Quincy (IL) Daily Journal*, 18 August 1897, 1; *Quincy (IL) Morning Whig*, 21 August 1897.

31. *Saint Louis (MO) Republic*, 26 August 1897, 6. The *Quincy (IL) Daily Journal*, 25 August 1897, estimated that Scott was "probably the third wealthiest negro in Illinois" (7).

32. *Morning Star* (Springfield, IL), 10 July 1896; *Illinois Record* (AA, Springfield), 24 September 1898.

33. *Daily Register Gazette* (Rockford, IL), 9 July 1896, 7.

34. *Cairo (IL) Citizen*, 23 April 1896.

35. *Appeal* (AA, Saint Paul, MN), 8 January 1898, 1. For detailed treatment of this meeting, see Peavler, "African Americans in Omaha."

36. Peavler, "African Americans in Omaha," 348.

37. Ibid., 352.

38. *Indianapolis (IN) Freeman* (AA), 18 May 1895, 4.

39. *Daily Illinois State Journal* (Springfield), 1 April 1893 and 21 June 1893, 4.

40. *Denver (CO) Post*, 23 September 1897, 5.

41. *Morning Herald* (Baltimore, MD), 13 July 1898, 3.

42. *Broad Ax* (AA, Chicago and Salt Lake City, UT), 30 September 1899, 1; *Colored American* (AA, Washington, DC), 24 March 1900, 14. See also http://www.antiimperialist .com/the-leagues/leagues/13-leagues-under-activism/76-natnegroleague, accessed 28 February 2014, for a list of founding members of the Anti-Expansion League, also known as the National Negro League.

43. *Daily Herald* (Delphos, OH), 28 July 1900, 5. The *Sioux City (IA) Journal*, 27 June 1900, 1, reported that Scott also was president of the state league.

44. *Broad Ax* (AA, Chicago and Salt Lake City, UT), 8 September 1900, 1.

45. *Inter Ocean* (Chicago), 14 December 1896, 2; *Indianapolis (IN) Freeman* (AA), 25 March 1899, 5.

46. *Saint Louis (MO) Republic*, 23 July 1900 and 23 July 1901; *Colored American* (AA, Washington, DC), 1 October 1898, 5.

47. *Broad Ax* (AA, Chicago and Salt Lake City, UT), 9 June 1900, 1, and 7 July 1900, 1; *Times-Picayune* (AA, New Orleans), 12 August 1900, 22.

48. *Broad Ax* (AA, Chicago and Salt Lake City, UT), 7 July 1900, 1.

49. Ibid., 28 July 1900, 1; *American Citizen* (AA, Kansas City, KS), 6 July 1900, 1.

50. *Broad Ax* (AA, Chicago and Salt Lake City, UT), 7 July 1900, 1.

51. *New York Times*, 23 August 1900, 3; *Iowa State Bystander* (AA, Des Moines), 24 August 1900; *Times-Picayune* (AA, New Orleans), 23 August 1900, 2.

52. *Broad Ax* (AA, Chicago and Salt Lake City, UT), 15 September 1900; *New York Times*, 23 August 1900, 3.

53. *Dallas (TX) Morning News*, 23 August 1900, 8; *Savannah (GA) Tribune* (AA), 8 September 1900, 48; *Times-Picayune* (AA, New Orleans), 23 August 1900, 2.

54. *Cairo (IL) Evening Citizen*, 25 January 1901.

55. *Daily Miami (FL) Metropolis* (AA), 16 July 1904, 1.

56. *Saint Paul (MN) Appeal* (AA), 23 July 1904, 2.

57. Portwood, "African-American Politics," 16; *Cairo (IL) Citizen*, 23 April 1896.

58. *Daily Illinois State Journal* (Springfield), 11 April 1901, 2; *Saint Louis (MO) Palladium* (AA), 28 November 1903, 1; *Daily Public Ledger* (Maysville, KY), 11 April 1901, 3; *Saint Louis (MO) Republic*, 11 April 1901, 8.

59. *Cleveland (OH) Gazette* (AA), 15 July 1893, 2. See also Reed, "Black Presence"; and Reed, *Black Chicago's First Century*, 378–82, for extensive treatment of the 1893 exposition and discussion of opposition to Colored American Day.

60. *Saint Louis (MO) Republic*, 11 April 1901, 8; *Daily Public Ledger* (Maysville, KY), 11 April 1901, 3; *Daily Illinois State Journal* (Springfield), 11 April 1901, 2. For Scott as

"commissioner of Illinois" at the Louisiana American Exposition in 1884, see the *Times-Picayune* (AA, New Orleans), 12 September 1885.

61. *Broad Ax* (AA, Chicago and Salt Lake City, UT), 24 April 1901, 1. On 27 April 1901 the *Broad Ax* was especially critical: "If these gentlemen . . . are the representatives of the Negro, then the race is as hard up for representative men as the Democrats of St. Louis were in their late primaries. . . . These men are candidates for office after every election, and have been using the Negro ever since they were old enough to vote, and they have formed a combination for the purpose of keeping representative Negroes in the back." According to Parezo and Fowler, *Anthropology Goes to the Fair*, "there were no pavilions devoted to the lives and accomplishments of African Americans, because dark skin was equated with mental inferiority and inherent savagery, and due to the rampant Jim Crow racism of the time. . . . [The exposition] portrayed blacks stereotypically, as creatures of low intelligence" (255).

62. Wheeler, "Together in Egypt," 127–28.

63. *Saint Louis (MO) Republic*, 4 August 1901, 8.

64. The most complete treatments for blacks in East Saint Louis for the later half of the nineteenth century are Lumpkins, "Black East St. Louis"; and Lumpkins, *American Pogrom*.

65. Lumpkins, *American Pogrom*, 12–13.

66. Lumpkins, "Black East St. Louis," iii, 19.

67. *Belleville (IL) News Democrat*, 23 October 1902.

68. Lumpkins, "Black East St. Louis," 5.

69. Ibid., 56–58.

70. Lumpkins, *American Pogrom*, 18–19, 25–31, 55.

71. *Broad Ax* (AA, Chicago and Salt Lake City, UT), 9 February 1901, 1; *Saint Louis (MO) Republic*, 12 December 1901, 4. Walnut and Fourteenth Streets intersect, but Champa may have been a local name for a street between Thirteenth and Fifteenth that no longer exists.

72. For a physical description of Denver Side, see McLaughlin, *Power, Community*, 23–28. For a map of East Saint Louis showing the relative location of Denver Side, see Lumpkins, *American Pogrom*, 49.

73. *Belleville (IL) News Democrat*, 13 May 1903.

74. Ibid., 16 August 1901, 1.

75. Illinois, Saint Clair County, Clerk of Circuit Court, People vs. W. T. Scott, case 264, 1901, roll #267, sequence #100137.

76. Illinois, Saint Clair County, Clerk of Circuit Court, People vs. W. T. Scott, case 126, 1901, roll #287, sequence #100115.

77. *Belleville (IL) News Democrat*, 7 August 1901, 1.

78. Ibid.

79. Ibid., 16 August 1901, 1.

80. *Saint Louis (MO) Republic*, 12 December 1901, 4, and 14 July 1904. In the *Marshfield (WI) Times*, 17 February 1905, Scott explained the charges against him a bit differently.

He told an interviewer that the charge had involved "the character of its [the tavern's] customers' morals [which] was a matter of minor importance to the proprietor" (9).

81. *Lincoln (NE) Evening News*, 30 January 1905, 2; *East Saint Louis (IL) Daily Journal*, 8 July 1904. The *Daily Miami (FL) Metropolis* (AA), 16 July 1904, 1, noted that Scott's newspaper was named the *East Saint Louis Herald*. No copies of either newspaper have survived. The *Daily Illinois State Register* (Springfield), 17 June 1906, 2, reported that Scott was scheduled to begin publication on 5 July 1902.

Chapter 5. The National Negro Liberty Party and the Debacle of the 1904 Election

1. *New York Globe* (AA), 20 September 1884, 4.
2. *Cairo (IL) Daily Bulletin*, 3 August 1872.
3. Rittenhouse diary, 2:36–39.
4. Johnson, *All That Glitters*, 120.
5. Ibid., 124–25.
6. Ibid., 123–24.
7. Quoted in ibid., 125. See Schantz, "Pierre de Coubertin's Concept," for a detailed analysis of Coubertin's attitude about Social Darwinism.
8. For discussion of "black savagery," stereotypes of blacks at the turn of the century, the relationship of Darwinist ideology in the temperance movement, and the emergence of a "nightlife culture" that accompanied the migration of blacks from the rural South to the urban North, see Herd, "Paradox of Temperance," 364–71.
9. While removing himself at the national level, Scott remained active at the state level, becoming president of the Negro Democratic League of Illinois (*Muskegon [MI] Chronicle*, 18 June 1902, 6).
10. *Appeal* (AA, Saint Paul, MN), 14 November 1891, 1.
11. *Washington (DC) Times*, 15 April 1905, 4; *Colored American* (AA, Washington, DC), 28 April 1900, 1; *Akron Daily (OH) Daily Democrat*, 7 August 1901, 1.
12. The *Lincoln (NE) Evening News*, 4 January 1901, 1, estimated that the National Colored Personal Liberty League had a nationwide membership of one hundred thousand, with two thousand in Nebraska.
13. U.S. House, H.R. 11,119, 51st Cong., 1st sess., 24 June 1890, Cong. Rec. 21 (1889–90): 6464; U.S. Senate, S. 1289, 53rd Cong., 2nd sess., 8 January 1894, Cong. Rec. 26 (1894–95): 519; U.S. House, H.R. 8479, 55th Cong., 2nd sess., 21 February 1898, Cong. Rec. 31 (1898–99): 2010; U.S. Senate, S. 1176, 56th Cong., 1st sess., 11 December 1899, Cong. Rec. 33, pt. 1 (1899–1900): 180–84; U.S. House, H.R. 11,404, 57th Cong., 1st sess., 17 February 1902, Cong. Rec. 35, pt. 4 (1901–2): 1841. The provisions of these bills were identical.
14. *Atlanta (GA) Constitution* (AA insert), 5 February 1903; *Denton (MD) Journal*, 29 August 1903, 2. The *New York Times*, 30 November 1900, estimated that one hundred thousand persons had become victims to these schemes.
15. Berry, *My Face Is Black*; *Atlanta (GA) Constitution* (AA insert), 14 February 1903, 6. See Smythe, *Obsolete American Securities*, 362, for legal action to block associations

from use of U.S. mail. The Ex-Slave Petitioners' Assembly was banned on 11 August 1899.

16. Fleming, *Ex-Slave Petition Frauds*, 7–8. For Walton and the beginnings of his movement, see Watson, "'Black Phalanx'"; Mouser, *For Labor*, 109; Davidson, "Encountering the Ex-Slave Reparations Movement."

17. Berry, "Reparations for Freedom," 224–25; *Alton (IL) Evening Telegraph*, 23 September 1899, 4; *Tyrone (PA) Daily Herald*, 28 February 1901, 10.

18. See "Stanley P. Mitchell."

19. Ibid.

20. *Atlanta (GA) Constitution* (AA insert), 5 February 1903, 1; *Washington (DC) Bee* (AA), 3 September 1903, 1. For a conference called for Cincinnati on 24 May 1903, see *Davenport (IA) Daily Republican*, 7 January 1903, 2.

21. *Atlanta (GA) Constitution* (AA insert), 27 July 1903, 1; Mouser, *For Labor*, 110. This group should not be confused with the National Colored Personal Liberty League, whose headquarters were in Washington, DC. For the latter, see *New Castle (PA) News*, 7 August 1901, 20.

22. *Decatur (IL) Daily Review*, 26 May 1904, 9. Scott issued a call for the Negro State League to meet in Springfield on 14 June to discuss the "feasibility of nominating and running a full state ticket composed of representative colored men, and also to discuss the nomination of negro candidates for Congress in the Seventeenth, Twenty-second, Twenty-fourth and Twenty-fifth districts, where the negro vote is the balance of power."

23. *Cleveland (OH) Gazette* (AA), 9 July 1904, 2.

24. *Decatur (IL) Daily Review*, 26 May 1904, 9.

25. *New York Times*, 31 March 1904 and 5 May 1904; *Post-Standard* (Syracuse, NY), 31 March 1904, 1. Both reports indicated that Mitchell was president of the new party and the Reverend P. L. Walton was vice president.

26. *Daily Progress* (Petersburg, VA), 6 May 1904, 1.

27. *Marysville (OH) Tribune*, 5 May 1904, 1; *Minneapolis (MN) Journal*, 31 March 1904, 2.

28. *Daily Progress* (Petersburg, VA), 6 May 1904, 1.

29. *Palestine (TX) Daily Herald*, 11 April 1904, 2.

30. *Wichita (KS) Searchlight* (AA), 2 July 1904, 1.

31. *Indianapolis (IN) Freeman* (AA), 9 July 1904, 2.

32. *Appeal* (AA, Saint Paul, MN), 23 July 1904, 2.

33. *Daily Review* (Decatur, IL), 26 May 1904, 9; *Daily Illinois State Register* (Springfield), 14 June 1904, 1, and 15 June 1904, 6.

34. *Atlanta (GA) Constitution* (AA insert), 12 May 1904.

35. For Chase, see *Washington (DC) Bee* (AA), 30 July 1904, 1, 4.

36. *Grand Rapids Tribune* (Grand Rapids, WI), 13 July 1904, 6.

37. Mouser, *For Labor*, 111–12.

38. *Jersey Journal* (Jersey City, NJ), 8 July 1904, 4; *Saint Louis (MO) Palladium* (AA), 16 July 1904, 1.

39. *Jersey Journal* (Jersey City, NJ), 8 July 1904, 4; *Washington (DC) Bee* (AA), 3 September 1904, 1.

40. *Jersey Journal* (Jersey City, NJ), 8 July 1904, 4; *Logansport (IN) Reporter*, 7 July 1904; *Indiana (PA) Progress*, 13 July 1904. The *Indianapolis (IN) Freeman* (AA), 31 May 1913, 7, reported that the July meeting had consisted of four hundred delegates from thirty-seven states.

41. *Ogden (UT) Standard*, 8 July 1904, 6; *Salt Lake (UT) Tribune*, 9 July 1904, 2; *San Francisco Call*, 9 July 1904, 5; *Los Angeles Times*, 9 July 1904, 3; *Springfield (OH) Daily Republican*, 8 July 1904, 13; *Morning Olympian* (Olympia, WA), 9 July 1904, 1. The *Broad Axe* (AA, Chicago and Salt Lake City, UT), 3 February 1917, 1, reported that 475 had attended the second session.

42. *Grand Rapids (WI) Tribune*, 13 July 1904, 6; *Oxford Mirror* (Oxford Junction, IA), 14 July 1904, 3; *Elkhart (IN) Daily Review*, 8 July 1904, 2; *Appeal* (AA, Saint Paul, MN), 9 July 1904, 2.

43. *Muskogee (OK) Cimeter* (AA), 14 July 1904, 1.

44. *East Saint Louis (IL) Daily Journal*, 8 July 1904; *Washington (DC) Post*, 21 July 1904; *Landmark* (Statesville, NC), 22 July 1904, 2; *Appeal* (AA, Saint Paul, MN), 23 July 1904, 2; *Daily Miami (FL) Metropolis* (AA), 16 July 1904, 1; *Saint Louis (MO) Republic*, 8 July 1904, pt. 1, 3.

45. *Plaindealer* (AA, Topeka, KS), 15 July 1904, 1.

46. *Palladium* (AA, Saint Louis, MO), 16 July 1904, 1; *Daily Miami (FL) Metropolis* (AA), 16 July 1904, 1. See also *East Saint Louis (IL) Daily Journal*, 8 July 1904, 3, for a brief review of Scott's activities in East Saint Louis.

47. *Landmark* (Statesville, NC), 22 July 1904, 2. The *Tucson (AZ) Daily Citizen*, 26 July 1904, 1, reported, curiously, that "the party's candidate for Vice President, a deputy sheriff at Memphis, Tenn., was killed in a gambling raid shortly after his nomination." This was the only report indicating that Payne was not the initial choice of the convention.

48. *Saint Louis (MO) Republic*, 9 July 1904, 3; Dyal, Carpenter, and Thomas, *Historical Dictionary*, 110.

49. *Colored American* (AA, Washington, DC), 23 July 1904, 5; *Muskogee (OK) Cimeter* (AA), 14 July 1904, 1.

50. *Appeal* (AA, Saint Paul, MN), 23 July 1904, 2.

51. *Saint Louis (MO) Palladium* (AA), 16 July 1904, 1.

52. *Landmark* (Statesville, NC), 22 July 1904, 2; *Muskogee (OK) Cimeter* (AA), 14 July 1904, 1.

53. *Appeal* (AA, Saint Paul, MN), 23 July 1904, 2.

54. *Saint Louis (MO) Republic* (AA), 14 July 1904, 13.

55. *Daily Illinois State Register* (Springfield), 14 July 1904. See also *Daily Illinois State Journal* (Springfield), 15 July 1904; *Stevens Point (WI) Daily Journal*, 16 July 1904, 1; *Marshfield (WI) Times*, 19 February 1905, 3. According to the *Saint Louis (MO) Republic*, 24 April 1904, pt. 1, 8, the term "disorderly house" referred to houses of prostitution and were located in the "'red light' district."

56. *Stevens Point (WI) Daily Journal*, 14 July 1904, 4; *Decatur (IL) Review*, 16 July 1904, 1. For other accounts of his rearrest, see *Palladium* (AA, Saint Louis, MO), 16 July 1904, 1; *Daily Californian* (Bakersfield), 14 July 1904, 7; *Washington (DC) Herald*, 14 July 1904, 1; *New York Times*, 14 July 1904; *Lincoln (NE) Evening News*, 30 January 1905. In an interview with the *Daily Illinois State Journal* (Springfield), 29 January 1905, Scott claimed that in 1901 he had "obtained a settlement upon the payment of $50."

57. *Decatur (IL) Review*, 14 July 1904, 4.

58. *Cedar Rapids (IA) Republican*, 21 July 1904; *Ottumwa (IA) Evening Democrat*, 21 July 1904.

59. *Washington (DC) Post*, 21 July 1904. Similar language was used in the *Colored American* (AA, Washington, DC), 23 July 1904, 5.

60. *Washington (DC) Bee* (AA), 3 March 1917, 7.

61. *Indianapolis (IN) Freeman* (AA), 19 October 1889, 1.

62. *Daily Illinois State Journal* (Springfield), 29 January 1905.

63. *Cedar Rapids (IA) Republican*, 21 July 1904; *Ottumwa (IA) Evening Democrat*, 21 July 1904; *Washington (DC) Post*, 25 July 1904. See also Luker, *Social Gospel*, 242, for Scott's removal from the party's ticket. According to an account in the *Cairo (IL) Evening Citizen*, 31 January 1905, Scott spent only nine days in the Belleville jail and was released on 22 July 1904.

64. *Ottumwa (IA) Daily Courier*, 22 July 1904, 6.

65. For detailed treatment of Taylor's life, see Mouser, *For Labor*.

66. Mouser, "Taylor and Smith"; Mouser, "George Edwin Taylor."

67. *Marshfield (WI) Times*, 17 February 1905, 9; *Washington (DC) Post*, 25 July 1904.

68. *Saint Louis (MO) Palladium* (AA), 5 November 1904, 1.

69. Ibid.

70. Mouser, *For Labor*, 125–28.

71. *Davenport (IA) Tri-City Evening Star*, 10 January 1905; *Lincoln (NE) Evening News*, 30 January 1905.

72. *Saint Louis (MO) Republic*, 4 January 1905, 8; *Davenport (IA) Tri-City Evening Star*, 10 January 1905, 6. That appointment required that he be in Springfield. He was paid $3 per day.

73. *Cairo (IL) Citizen*, 23 April 1896.

Chapter 6. Hard Landing and
Slow Recovery in Springfield

1. This referred to Booker T. Washington, who dined in the White House on 16 October 1901. Scott criticized Washington for accepting that invitation. For Scott's criticism of Washington, see *Daily Illinois State Journal* (Springfield), 29 January 1905.

2. Ibid. Scott also claimed that the party's candidate for president had been on the ballot in Tennessee, Iowa, West Virginia, and Alabama.

3. Ibid., 29 August 1905, 2.

4. Ibid., 31 August 1905, 6.

5. Ibid., 29 August 1905, 2.

6. Ibid., 10 August 1905, 7, 30 August 1905, 4, 10 September 1905, 7, 14 September 1905, 5, and 13 December 1905, 5.

7. For detailed descriptions of Maceo, see Foner, *Antonio Maceo*; Helg, *Our Rightful Share*; Scott, *Degrees of Freedom*.

8. *Voice of the Negro* (AA, Atlanta, GA), November 1904, 480; *Colored American* (AA, Washington, DC), November 1900, 54.

9. *Indianapolis (IN) Freeman* (AA), 25 March 1899, 5, and 27 February 1909; *Richmond (VA) Planet* (AA), 4 August 1900, 1; *Appeal* (AA, Saint Paul, MN), 5 August 1899, 3; *Saint Paul (MN) Globe*, 2 August 1899, 2; *Daily Illinois State Journal* (Springfield), 17 August 1905, 5; *Baltimore (MD) American* (AA), 2 December 1905, 13.

10. *Daily Illinois State Journal* (Springfield), 5 September 1905, 5. The "colored" Union Giants of Springfield competed regionally and were recognized as one of the best baseball teams in the Midwest.

11. *Marshfield (WI) Times*, 17 November 1905, 3; *Daily Illinois State Journal* (Springfield), 29 January 1905, 1.

12. Ibid.

13. *Daily Illinois State Register* (Springfield), 18 October 1914, 1.

14. *Daily Illinois State Journal* (Springfield), 29 November 1905, 9, 13 December 1905, 5, and 20 December 1905, 8.

15. *Daily Illinois State Register* (Springfield), 21 December 1905, 14.

16. *Daily Illinois State Journal* (Springfield), 5 September 1905, 5.

17. Ibid., 20 November 1906, 7, and 8 November 1907, 10; Bateman, *Historical Encyclopedia*, 749. The first mention of Scott and the *Springfield Leader* in Springfield's city directories was in its 1908 edition. The *Leader* was mentioned in the 1910, 1911, and 1912 editions, but not in that for 1913. It was listed again in the 1916 edition. For these references, see Polk, *Springfield City Directory for . . . 1908*, 746; Polk, *Springfield City Directory for . . . 1910*, 771; Polk, *Springfield City Directory for . . . 1911*, 765, 1026; Polk, *Springfield City Directory for . . . 1912*, 850; Polk, *Springfield City Directory for . . . 1916*, 835, 1155.

18. *Daily Illinois State Journal* (Springfield), 3 April 1908, 9. This also was known as the Colored Voters' Municipal Ownership and Personal Liberty League.

19. *Daily Illinois State Register* (Springfield), 28 April 1908. The *Omaha (NE) World Herald*, 21 January 1904, identified the Ambidexter Institute as "a colored industrial school of Springfield . . . interested in the uplifting of the colored race" (8).

20. *Lincoln (NE) Evening News*, 30 January 1905; *Daily Illinois State Journal* (Springfield), 29 January 1905, 1.

21. *Daily Illinois State Register* (Springfield), 18 October 1914, 1.

22. *Daily Register Gazette* (Rockford, IL), 28 October 1907, 4.

23. *Lincoln (NE) Evening News*, 30 January 1905; *Daily Illinois State Journal* (Springfield), 29 January 1905, 1.

24. *Broad Ax* (AA, Chicago and Salt Lake City, UT), 20 June 1908, 1–2. Julius Taylor, editor of the *Broad Ax*, attended the Denver Convention. See *Denver (CO) Post*, 10 July 1908, 9, for Taylor in Denver.

25. *Cedar Rapids (IA) Evening Gazette*, 27 June 1908, 1.

26. *Evening News* (Ada, OK), 27 June 1908, 3; *Daily Illinois State Journal* (Springfield), 26 June 1908, 5. The convention call also indicated that the convention would "declare against degrading a soldier of the United States Army without the preliminary of a trial, and announce for a strict adherence to the constitution and all its amendments, discuss the feasibility of nominating a candidate for president on the civil liberty party ticket, or vote direct for the Denver nominees and issue an address to the colored citizens of the nation." For similar announcements, see *Galveston (TX) Daily News*, 3 August 1908; *Leavenworth (WA) Echo*, 17 July 1908, 1; *Pullman (WA) Herald*, 3 July 1908, 6.

27. *Daily Illinois State Register* (Springfield), 26 June 1908, 5.

28. *Grand Forks (ND) Herald*, 11 July 1908, 3. Scott also had traveled to Denver as the president of the National Negro Anti-Expansion League, promising to deliver two hundred thousand votes to whichever candidate the convention chose to champion. The *Cairo (IL) Evening Citizen*, 10 August 1908, sarcastically noted, however, that Scott "is strong on 'delivery,' that is at conventions, but when election comes round 'Bill' is nowhere to be seen." A decade earlier, the *Cairo (IL) Citizen*, 19 October 1893, had even harsher words for Scott: "The colonel was in the thickest of the fight when a ten dollar bill was in view."

29. *Denver (CO) Post*, 8 July 1908, 11, and 11 July 1908, 5.

30. *Baltimore (MD) Sun*, 15 July 1908, 1; *Omaha (NE) World Herald*, 15 July 1908, 3; *San Diego (CA) Union*, 15 July 1908, 2.

31. *Daily Herald*, 4 September 1908, 2; Senechal, "Springfield Race Riot," 25. The *Chicago Examiner*, 15 August 1908, described it as a "drunken, crazy mob" (1). See also Crouthamel, "Springfield Race Riot," 161–81, for a full description of circumstances leading to the riot.

32. Senechal, "Springfield Race Riot," 22; *Daily Herald* (Chicago), 4 September 1908, 2; *Broad Ax* (AA, Chicago and Salt Lake City, UT), 22 August 1908, 1–2, and 29 August 1908, 1–2. See the *Quincy (IL) Daily Journal*, 15 and 16 August 1908, for extensive coverage of the riots and the observations of National Guardsmen from Quincy who arrived to occupy Springfield. These articles detailed the flight of blacks from Springfield. The *Chicago Examiner* gave the riot extensive coverage in its 15, 17, and 18 August 1908 issues.

33. Senechal, *Sociogenesis*.

34. Krohe, *Springfield Reader*, 139. See also Krohe, "Summer of Rage," for a review of Springfield before and during the 1908 riot.

35. Senechal, "Springfield Race Riot," 24–25.

36. Senechal, *Sociogenesis*, 21. For an elaborate view of the saloon/vice complex as it operated in Springfield immediately before the 1908 riot, see Clark, *Hell at Midnight*.

37. Senechal, "Springfield Race Riot," 23.

38. Ibid., 24–25; Senechal, *Sociogenesis*, 20–22.

39. Stokes, *D. W. Griffith's "The Birth of a Nation,"* 37–47. Senechal, *Sociogenesis*, 23–25, raised the same issue, but from black middle-class values that were critical of miscegenation, which they believed to incite white hatred. Thomas Dixon also wrote a play based on *The Clansman*, which captured white audiences more firmly than did the novel.

40. Senechal, "Springfield Race Riot," 22, 25–27.

41. *Albuquerque (NM) Journal*, 9 January 1910, 6.

42. *Daily Herald* (Chicago), 4 September 1908, 2; *Broad Ax* (AA, Chicago and Salt Lake City, UT), 31 October 1908, 2; *Oakland (CA) Tribune*, 17 August 1908, 6; *Star Publications* (Chicago), 3 September 1908, 3. The *Chicago Examiner*, 15 August 1908, wrote that it was "the culmination of years of unrestricted view in the black and levee districts, a territory more notorious and disreputable than ever has been allowed to run in any city of the size of Springfield" (1). The *Examiner* added: "It has had police and political protection." For an elaborate essay that was critical of newspaper coverage of the riot and that had a significant impact among white intellectuals, see Walling, "Race War."

43. Mouser, *For Labor*, 132–33; Childs, *Leadership*, 3–30; Bennett, "Niagara Movement," 134; Scott, "Their Faces Were Black," 318–19; James, *Transcending*, 18–33.

44. Du Bois, *Autobiography*, 157.

45. Spear, *Black Chicago*, 87–88.

46. Ibid., 85, noted that Charles Bentley and James Madden of Chicago, who also were members of Chicago's Equal Opportunity League, attended the first Niagara conference in Ontario, Canada.

47. See *Daily Illinois State Register* (Springfield), 8 November 1909. For *The Red Moon*, see *Afro-American Ledger* (AA, Baltimore, MD), 8 May 1909, 7; Robinson, "The Pekin."

48. *Daily Illinois State Journal* (Springfield), 15 October 1909, 5, and 8 November 1909, 5. See ibid., 9 November 1909, 1, and 17 November 1909, 5, for a preliminary hearing regarding the raid. Defendants claimed that "they have a legal right to establish a club and run it for social purposes." For use of the term "restaurant," see ibid., 19 November 1909, 5.

49. Ibid., 27 November 1909, 5, and 28 November 1909, 5.

50. Ibid., 9 November 1909, 1, 2 March 1910, 8, 7 June 1910, 6, 7 July 1910, 2, 25 December 1911, 6, 28 January 1912, 10, 11 February 1912, 17, 2 December 1912, 2, 9 December 1912, 6, 8 December 1913, 8, 9 March 1914, 6, 17 August 1915, 2, and 5 January 1916, 11.

51. Ibid., 27 November 1909, 5.

52. Ibid., 11 February 1912.

53. U.S. Census of 1910, Illinois, Sangamon, series T624, roll 325, p. 254.

54. *Daily Illinois State Journal* (Springfield), 1 December 1909, 3.

55. Lantz, *Community in Search*, 68–72; Cooper, "Some Political Results," 19–21; *Cairo (IL) Bulletin*, 11 May 1873, 2. See also Cha-Jua, *America's First Black Town*, 198–204, for reformist movements at the turn of the century in Brooklyn, Illinois. See *Daily Illinois State Register* (Springfield), 4 April 1908, 1, for the debate between the Personal Liberty League and the Anti-Saloon League regarding local option in the Springfield area.

56. *Daily Illinois State Journal* (Springfield), 6 October 1913, 7, 6 July 1914, 5, 26 June 1915, 13, and 4 July 1915, 12; *Broad Ax* (AA, Chicago and Salt Lake City, UT), 10 July 1915.

57. *Broad Ax* (AA, Chicago and Salt Lake City, UT), 9 September 1911, 1.

58. Ibid.

59. Ibid.

60. *Daily Illinois State Journal* (Springfield), 6 October 1911, 6.

61. Ibid., 3 January 1916, 4, and 4 January 1916, 3.

62. *Broad Ax* (AA, Chicago and Salt Lake City, UT), 6 July 1912, 1–2.

63. Ibid., 9 May 1914, 2, and 15 August 1914, 2.

64. *Daily Illinois State Register* (Springfield), 12 and 14 July 1912.

65. Ibid., 8 August 1913.

66. *Alaska Citizen* (Fairbanks), 27 January 1913, 8.

67. *Broad Ax* (AA, Chicago and Salt Lake City, UT), 22 March 1913, 2.

68. Ibid., 1. For more detail concerning Walters's role in the London Pan-African Conference in 1900 and his tour of Liberia and the Cape Coast of West Africa in 1910, see Walters, *My Life and Work*, 149–67, 253–63. For Walters's nomination by the National Negro Liberty Party in 1904, see Mouser, *For Labor*, 12.

69. *Daily Register Gazette* (Rockford, IL), 21 May 1913, 9; *Indianapolis (IN) Freeman* (AA), 31 May 1913, 7; *Washington (DC) Bee* (AA), 26 April 1913, 4.

70. *Cairo (IL) Citizen*, 8 December 1893.

71. *Albuquerque (NM) Journal*, 17 March 1913, 4.

72. *Washington (DC) Bee* (AA), 23 May 1914, 4.

73. Editorial in *Cleveland Daily Plain Dealer*, 23 September 1913, as cited in *Cleveland (OH) Gazette* (AA), 27 September 1913, 2.

74. *Oregonian* (Portland, OR), 7 September 1913.

75. *Daily Illinois State Register* (Springfield), 8 August 1813.

76. *Appeal* (AA, Saint Paul, MN), 19 April 1913, 2; *Adair County News* (Columbia, KY), 25 June 1913, 2; *Indianapolis (IN) Freeman* (AA), 3 May 1913, 4, and 31 May 1913, 7; *San Francisco Call*, 18 April 1913; *Washington (DC) Bee* (AA), 26 April 1913, 4; *San Diego (CA) Union*, 18 April 1913, 1.

77. *Broad Ax* (AA, Chicago and Salt Lake City, UT), 9 May 1914, 2, 15 August 1914, 2, and 21 November 1914, 1; *Daily Illinois State Journal* (Springfield), 3 May 1914, 6.

78. *Broad Ax* (AA, Chicago and Salt Lake City, UT), 15 August 1914.

79. *Daily Illinois State Register* (Springfield), 18 October 1914, 1. For the origins of the league, see ibid., 6 October 1911, 6, which listed Scott as chairman of its executive committee and as "grand organizer."

80. Ibid., 6 October 1911, 6.

81. *Broad Ax* (AA, Chicago and Salt Lake City, UT), 12 June 1915, 1; *Leader* (AA, Springfield, IL), 12 June 1915, reprinted in *Broad Ax* (AA, Chicago and Salt Lake City, UT), 19 June 1915, 1.

82. *Broad Ax* (AA, Chicago and Salt Lake City, UT), 10 July 1915, 4.

83. Ibid., 21 August 1915, 4.

84. *Saint Louis (MO) Argus* (AA), 16 June 1916, 1. For Scott's activity in the state league, see *Broad Ax* (AA, Chicago and Salt Lake City, UT), 9 April 1914, 2; *Saint Louis (MO) Republic* (AA), 25 May 1916, 2.

85. No probate record was found in Sangamon County records.

86. For Shelby, see *Daily Illinois State Register* (Springfield), 7 October 1916, 3.

87. *Saint Louis (MO) Argus* (AA), 27 January 1917, 5; *Jonesboro (IL) Gazette*, 2 February 1917; *Broad Ax* (AA, Chicago and Salt Lake City, UT), 3 February 1917, 1; *Macon (GA)*

Telegraph, 11 February 1917; *Cairo (IL) Evening Citizen*, 27 January 1917; *Cairo (IL) Bulletin*, 27 January 1917; *Washington (DC) Bee* (AA), 17 February 1917, 7; *Savannah (GA) Tribune* (AA), 2 March 1917, 1. According to the *Illinois State Journal* (Springfield), 24 January 1917, 7, and the *Chicago Defender* (AA), 3 February 1917, Scott was survived by one niece, Miss Estella Scott, and two nephews, William H. Scott and William E. Scott. It is likely that William E. was W.T.'s son and that Estella (Estella J.) and William H. (William B.) were grandchildren (see U.S. Census of 1900, Illinois, Alexander County, series T623, roll 236, p. 69; U.S. Census of 1910, Illinois, Alexander County, series T624, roll 230, p. 163). According to the 1900 census, Scott had two other grandchildren, Henry T. Scott (born 1890) and Lizenker Scott (born 1893).

Bibliography

Newspapers

Searchable newspaper databases used in this study included NewspaperArchives.com, Genealogybank.com, ChroniclingAmerica.org, and African American Newspapers 1827–1998. In nearly all cases, databases identified newspapers according to titles used in their headers. Most newspapers published a single edition, but some printed varying formats and contents in morning, evening, daily, and/or weekly editions. In several cases, databases differed with respect to exact newspaper titles. The titles listed here reflect database designations, with the addition of the state abbreviation in parentheses. Newspapers noted in databases as African American are noted as "AA." Some major newspapers contained sections printed specifically and in some cases separately for black customers, and they are designated collectively as "AA insert." In most cases, however, so-called Jim Crow inserts are not identified separately in databases. Several small-town newspapers regularly carried African American news but were not identified in databases as African American newspapers.

Abilene (KS) Reflector
Adair County News (Columbia, KY)
Afro-American Ledger (AA, Baltimore, MD)
Akron (OH) Daily Democrat
Alaska Citizen (Fairbanks)
Albuquerque (NM) Journal
Alton (IL) Evening Telegraph
Alton (IL) Telegraph
American Citizen (AA, Kansas City, KS)
Appeal (AA, Saint Paul, MN)
Arkansas Gazette (Little Rock)
Arkansas Mansion (AA, Little Rock)

Atlanta (GA) Constitution (AA insert)
Augusta (GA) Chronicle
Baltimore (MD) American (AA)
Baltimore (MD) Sun
Barton's Free Press (Carbondale, IL)
Belleville (IL) News Democrat
Boston Daily Advertiser
Boston Daily Globe
Boston Journal
Broad Ax (AA, Chicago and Salt Lake City, UT)
Brooklyn (NY) Daily Eagle
Cairo (IL) Bulletin
Cairo (IL) Citizen
Cairo (IL) Daily Bulletin
Cairo (IL) Daily Democrat
Cairo (IL) Evening Bulletin
Cairo (IL) Evening Citizen
Cairo (IL) Gazette
Cairo (IL) Gazette (AA)
Cedar Rapids (IA) Evening Gazette
Cedar Rapids (IA) Republican
Chicago Daily Tribune
Chicago Defender (AA)
Chicago Evening Journal
Chicago Evening Post
Chicago Examiner
Chicago Times
Chicago Tribune
Christian Recorder (AA, Philadelphia)
Cincinnati (OH) Daily Gazette
Cleveland (OH) Gazette (AA)
Cleveland (OH) Herald
Cleveland (OH) Leader
Colored American (AA, Washington, DC)
Conservator (AA, Chicago)
Coshocton (OH) County Democrat
Daily Arkansas Gazette (Little Rock)
Daily Californian (Bakersfield)
Daily Dispatch (Richmond, VA)
Daily Freeman (AA, Waukesha, WI)
Daily Globe (AA, New York)
Daily Herald (Chicago)
Daily Herald (Delphos, OH)

Daily Illinois State Journal (Springfield)
Daily Illinois State Register (Springfield)
Daily Inter Ocean (Chicago)
Daily Journal and Republican (Freeport, IL)
Daily Miami (FL) Metropolis (AA)
Daily Progress (Petersburg, VA)
Daily Public Ledger (Maysville, KY)
Daily Register (Ironton, OH)
Daily Register Gazette (Rockford, IL)
Daily Review (Decatur, IL)
Dallas (TX) Morning News
Davenport (IA) Daily Republican
Davenport (IA) Tri-City Evening Star
Decatur (IL) Daily Record
Decatur (IL) Daily Republican
Decatur (IL) Daily Review
Decatur (IL) Review
Denton (MD) Journal
Denver (CO) Post
Denver (CO) Rocky Mountain News
Duluth (MN) News Tribune
East Saint Louis (IL) Daily Journal
Elkhart (IN) Daily Review
Enterprise (AA, Omaha, NE)
Evening Gazette (Reno, NV)
Evening Gazette (Sterling, IL)
Evening News (Ada, OK)
Evening Star (Washington, DC)
Frank Leslie's Illustrated Newspaper (New York)
Galveston (TX) Daily News
Grand Forks (ND) Herald
Grand Rapids (WI) Tribune
Grit (AA, New York)
Harper's Weekly (New York)
Huntsville (AL) Gazette (AA)
Illinois Record (AA, Springfield)
Illinois State Journal (Springfield)
Illinois State Register (Springfield)
Indiana (PA) Progress
Indianapolis (IN) Freeman (AA)
Indianapolis (IN) Sentinel
Inter Ocean (AA insert, Chicago)
Iowa State Bystander (AA, Des Moines)

Janesville (WI) Gazette
Jersey Journal (Jersey City, NJ)
Jonesboro (IL) Gazette
Kalamazoo (MI) Gazette
Kansas City (KS) Times
Landmark (Statesville, NC)
Leader (AA, Springfield, IL)
Leavenworth (WA) Echo
Lincoln (NE) Evening News
Logansport (IN) Journal
Logansport (IN) Reporter
Los Angeles Herald
Los Angeles Times
Macon (GA) Telegraph
Marshfield (WI) Times
Marysville (OH) Tribune
Milwaukee (WI) Sentinel
Minneapolis (MN) Journal
Morning Call (Allentown, PA)
Morning Herald (Baltimore, MD)
Morning Olympian (Olympia, WA)
Morning Star (Springfield, IL)
Morning World Herald (Omaha, NE)
Muskegon (MI) Chronicle
Muskogee (OK) Cimeter (AA)
National Republican (Washington, DC)
Nevada State Journal (Reno)
Newark (OH) Advocate
Newark (OH) Daily Advocate
New Castle (PA) News
New Haven (CT) Register
New Orleans (LA) Daily Times-Picayune (AA)
New Orleans (LA) Daily True Delta
New Orleans (LA) Item
New Orleans (LA) Times
New York Freeman (AA)
New York Globe (AA)
New York Herald
New York Times
New York Tribune
Oakland (CA) Tribune
Ogden (UT) Standard
Omaha (NE) Herald

Omaha (NE) World Herald
Oregonian (Portland, OR)
Ottumwa (IA) Daily Courier
Ottumwa (IA) Evening Democrat
Oxford Mirror (Oxford Junction, IA)
Palestine (TX) Daily Herald
Palladium (AA, Saint Louis, MO)
Palladium of Liberty (AA, Columbus, OH)
People's Advocate (AA, Washington, DC)
Plain Dealer (AA, Cleveland, OH)
Plain Dealer (AA, Detroit, MI)
Plaindealer (AA, Topeka, KS)
Post-Standard (Syracuse, NY)
Pullman (WA) Herald
Quincy (IL) Daily Journal
Quincy (IL) Daily Whig
Quincy (IL) Herald
Quincy (IL) Morning Herald
Quincy (IL) Morning Whig
Racine County (WI) Argus
Record-Union (Sacramento, CA)
Republican (AA, Seattle, WA)
Richmond (VA) Planet (AA)
Sacramento (CA) Daily Record-Union
Saint Louis (MO) Argus (AA)
Saint Louis (MO) Globe-Democrat
Saint Louis (MO) Palladium (AA)
Saint Louis (MO) Republic
Saint Louis (MO) Republican
Saint Paul (MN) Daily Globe (AA)
Saint Paul (MN) Globe
Salt Lake (UT) Herald
Salt Lake (UT) Tribune
San Diego (CA) Union
San Francisco Call
Savannah (GA) Tribune (AA)
Sioux City (IA) Journal
Southern Illinoisan (Carbondale)
Springfield (IL) Register
Springfield (IL) State Register
Springfield (MA) Republican
Springfield (OH) Daily Republic
Star Publications (Chicago)

State Capital (AA, Springfield, IL)
State Journal (Harrisburg, PA)
Stevens Point (WI) Daily Journal
Sun (AA insert, New York)
Times-Picayune (AA, New Orleans)
Trenton (NJ) Evening Times
Tucson (AZ) Daily Citizen
Tyrone (PA) Daily Herald
Voice of the Negro (AA, Atlanta, GA)
Washington (DC) Bee (AA)
Washington (DC) Herald
Washington (DC) Post
Washington (DC) Times
Western Appeal (AA, Saint Paul, MN)
Western Kansas World (AA, WaKenney)
Western Recorder (AA, Lawrence, KS)
Wichita (KS) Daily Eagle (AA)
Wichita (KS) Eagle (AA)
Wichita (KS) Searchlight (AA)
World (AA, Saint Louis, MO)
World (New York)
Zainesville (OH) Courier

Primary and Secondary Works Cited

Ackerman, Kenneth D. *Dark Horse: The Surprise Election and Political Murder of President James A. Garfield.* New York: Carroll & Graf, 2003.

Alexander, Shawn L. "We Know Our Rights and Have the Courage to Defend Them." PhD dissertation, University of Massachusetts, Amherst, 2004.

Alexander County Profiles. Cairo: Woman's Club and Library Association, 1968.

Ali, Omar H. *In the Balance of Power: Independent Black Politics and Third-Party Movements in the United States.* Athens: Ohio University Press, 2008.

————. *In the Lion's Mouth: Black Populism in the New South, 1886–1900.* Jackson: University of Mississippi Press, 2010.

Andrews, Daryl Lamar. *Masonic Abolitionists: Freemasonry and the Underground Railroad in Illinois.* Chicago: Andrews Press, 2010.

Arnold, Samuel Greene. *Biographical Sketches of Distinguished Jerseymen.* Trenton: Press of the Emporium, 1845.

————. *The Life of George Washington.* New York: T. Mason and G. Lane, 1840.

————. *The Life of Patrick Henry of Virginia.* N.p.: Auburn, Buffalo, Miller, Orton & Mulligan, 1854.

————. *Memoir of Hannah More.* New York: T. Mason and G. Lane, 1839.

Atherton, Wanda, Glenna Conant Badgley, and Martha W. McMunn. *Where They Sleep: Cemetery Inscriptions of Pulaski County, Illinois.* 3 vols. Carterville: Genealogy Society of Southern Illinois, 1993.

Ayer, N. W. *N. W. Ayer & Son's American Newspaper Annual . . . 1888.* Philadelphia: N. W. Ayer & Co., 1888.

Baily, Marilyn. "From Cincinnati, Ohio to Wilberforce, Canada: A Note on Antebellum Colonization." *Journal of Negro History* 58, no. 4 (October 1973): 427–40.

Barber, A. D. "Report on the Condition of the Colored People of Ohio." Paper read before the Ohio Anti-Slavery Society at its Fifth Anniversary at Massillon, 27 May 1840. Copy in author's possession.

Bateman, Newton, ed. *Historical Encyclopedia of Illinois.* Vol. 2:1. Chicago: Munsell Publishing Co., 1912.

Beatty, Bess. *A Revolution Gone Backward: The Black Response to National Politics, 1876–1896.* New York: Greenwood Press, 1987.

Belles, A. Gilbert. "The Black Press in Illinois." *Journal of the Illinois State Historical Society* 68, no. 4 (September 1975): 344–52.

Bennett, Kevin. "Granville's Big Historical Moment Was a Riot! . . . or Was It?" *Historical Times: Newsletter of the Granville, Ohio, Historical Society* 19, no. 1 (February 2005): 1–4.

Bennett, Lerone, Jr. "The Niagara Movement." *Ebony,* May 1976, 130–40.

Berry, Mary F. *My Face Is Black Is True: Callie House and the Struggle for Ex-slave Reparations.* New York: Alfred A. Knopf, 2005.

———. "Reparations for Freedom, 1890–1916: Fraudulent Practices or Justice Deferred?" *Journal of Negro History* 57, no. 3 (1972): 219–30.

Bigham, Darrel E. *On Jordan's Banks: Emancipation and Its Aftermath on the Ohio River Valley.* Lexington: University Press of Kentucky, 2006.

———. *Towns and Villages of the Lower Ohio.* Lexington: University Press of Kentucky, 1998.

Blair, Cynthia M. *I've Got to Make My Livin': Black Women's Sex Work in Turn-of-the-Century Chicago.* Chicago: University of Chicago Press, 2010.

Blassingame, John W., and John R. McKivigan, eds. *The Frederick Douglass Papers, Series One.* Vol. 5 (1881–95). New Haven, CT: Yale University Press, 1992.

Blocker, Jack S. *A Little More Freedom: African Americans Enter the Urban Midwest, 1860–1930.* Columbus: Ohio State University Press, 2008.

Blyden, Edward W. "The Fifth President of the Republic of Liberia." *African Repository* 46 (1870): 121–24.

Bradsby, H. C. "History of Cairo." In *History of Alexander, Union and Pulaski Counties, Illinois,* edited by William Henry Perrin, 11–220. Chicago: O. L. Baskin, 1883.

Bridges, Roger D. "Equality Deferred: Civil Rights for Illinois Blacks, 1865–1885." *Journal of the Illinois State Historical Society* 74, no. 2 (Summer 1981): 82–108.

Brister, E. M. P. *Centennial History of the City of Newark and Licking County, Ohio.* Chicago: S. J. Clarke, 1909.

Buchanan, Thomas C. "Rascals on the Antebellum Mississippi: African American Steamboat Workers and the St. Louis Hanging of 1841." *Journal of Social History* 34, no. 4 (Summer 2001): 797–816.

———. "The Slave Mississippi: African-American Steamboat Workers, Networks of Resistance, and the Commercial World of the Western Rivers, 1811–1880." PhD dissertation, Carnegie Mellon University, 1998.

———. *Slaves, Free Blacks, and the Western Steamboat World*. Chapel Hill: University of North Carolina Press, 2004.

Bureau of Naval Personnel. *Register of Commissioned and Warrant Officers of the United States Navy and Marine Corps and Reserve Officers of Active Duty*. Washington, DC: Bureau of Naval Personnel, 1870.

Bushnell, Henry. *The History of Granville, Licking County, Ohio*. Columbus: Hann and Adair, 1889.

"Cairo, Illinois, During the Civil War." http://www.angelfire.com/wi/wisconsin42nd /cairo.html. Accessed 21 December 2012.

Carlson, Shirley J. "Black Migration to Pulaski County, Illinois, 1860–1900." *Illinois Historical Journal* 80, no. 1 (Spring 1987): 37–46.

Chafetz, Henry. *Play the Devil: A History of Gambling in the United States from 1492 to 1955*. New York: Bonanza Books, 1960.

Cha-Jua, Sundiata Keita. *America's First Black Town, Brooklyn, Illinois, 1830–1915*. Urbana: University of Illinois Press, 2000.

———. "'A Warlike Demonstration': Legalism, Armed Resistance, and Black Political Mobilization in Decatur, Illinois, 1894–1898." *Journal of Negro History* 83, no. 1 (Winter 1998): 52–72.

———. "'A Warlike Demonstration': Legalism, Violent Self-Help, and Electoral Politics in Decatur, Illinois, 1894–1898." *Journal of Urban History* 26, no. 5 (July 2000): 591–629.

Childs, John B. *Leadership, Conflict, and Cooperation in Afro-American Social Thought*. Philadelphia: Temple University Press, 1989.

Childs, Marquis W. *Mighty Mississippi: Biography of a River*. New Haven: Ticknor & Fields, 1982.

Clark, William Lloyd. *Hell at Midnight in Springfield, or a Burning History of Sin and Shame of the Capital of Illinois*. Milan, IL: William Clark, 1924.

Cole, Arthur Charles. *The Era of the Civil War, 1848–1870*. Springfield: Illinois Centennial Commission, 1919.

Cooper, T. V. "Some Political Results." *Our Banner . . . Devoted to the Principles of the Reformed Presbyterian Church* 15 (January 1888): 19–24.

Crouthamel, James L. "The Springfield Race Riot of 1908." *Journal of Negro History* 45, no. 3 (July 1960): 164–81.

Daily Telegram's Cairo City Directory for 1893. Cairo: Telegram Directory Publishers, 1893.

Daily Telegram's Cairo City Directory for 1895-96. Cairo: Telegram Directory Publishers, 1895.

Davidson, James M. "Encountering the Ex-slave Reparations Movement from the Grave: The National Industrial Council and National Liberty Party, 1901–1907." *Journal of African American History* 97, nos. 1–2 (Winter 2012): 13–38.

Davis, Hugh. *We Will Be Satisfied with Nothing Less: The African American Struggle for Equal Rights in the North during Reconstruction*. Ithaca, NY: Cornell University Press, 2011.

Devol, George H. *Forty Years a Gambler on the Mississippi*. New York: Henry Holt and Company, 1926.

Dexter, Darrel. "Old Newspapers Reveal Surprises from Cairo's Forgotten Past." *Genealogy Society of Southern Illinois, Newsletter* 39, no. 3 (March 2011): 19–22.

Dickens, Charles. *The Life and Adventures of Martin Chuzzlewit.* New York: J. Alden, 1935.

Du Bois, W. E. B. *The Autobiography of W. E. B. Du Bois.* New York: International Publishers, 1968.

Dyal, Donald H., Brian B. Carpenter, and Mark A. Thomas. *Historical Dictionary of the Spanish American War.* Westport, CT: Greenwood Publishing, 1996.

Eaton, John. *Grant, Lincoln and the Freedmen: Reminiscences of the Civil War.* 1909. Reprint, New York: Negro Universities Press, 1969.

Ebel, Charles O. *Cairo City Directory for 1884–85.* Cairo: Chas. O. Ebel and Co., 1884.

Emery, George, and J. C. Herbert Emery. *A Young Man's Benefit: The Independent Order of Odd Fellows and Sickness Insurance in the United States and Canada, 1860–1929.* Montreal: McGill-Queen's University Press, 1999.

Findlay, John M. *People of Chance: Gambling in American Society from Jamestown to Las Vegas.* New York: Oxford University Press, 1986.

Finkelman, Paul. *An Imperfect Union: Slavery, Federalism and Comity.* Chapel Hill: University of North Carolina Press, 1981.

———. "John Bingham and the Background to the Fourteenth Amendment." *Akron Law Review* 36, no. 671 (2003): 671–92.

———. "The Strange Career of Race Discrimination in Antebellum Ohio." *Case Western Reserve Law Review* 55, no. 373 (Winter 2004): 372–408.

Fishel, Leslie H., Jr. "Negro in Northern Politics, 1870–1900." *Mississippi Valley Historical Review* 42, no. 3 (1955): 466–89.

Fitzgerald, Michael W. "Republican Factionalism and Black Empowerment: The Spencer-Warner Controversy and Alabama Reconstruction, 1860–1880." *Journal of Southern History* 64, no. 3 (August 1998): 473–94.

Fleming, Walter L. *Ex-slave Petition Frauds.* Baton Rouge, LA: Ortlieb's Printing, 1910.

Foner, Philip Sheldon. *Antonio Maceo: The "Bronze Titan" of Cuba's Struggle for Independence.* New York: Monthly Review Press, 1978.

Gardner & Gaines. *Cairo City Directory . . . 1875–76.* Cairo: Gardner & Gaines, 1875.

Gerber, David. *Black Ohio and the Color Line, 1860–1915.* Urbana: University of Illinois Press, 1976.

Gilje, Paul A. *Rioting in America.* Bloomington: Indiana University Press, 1996.

Gleeson, Ed. *Illinois Rebels: A Civil War Unit History of G Company, 15th Tennessee Regiment Volunteer Infantry.* Carmel: Guild Press of Indiana, 1996.

Graham, A. A. *History of Licking County, Ohio, Its Past and Present.* Newark, OH: A. A. Graham, 1881.

"The Granville Riot." *Historical Times: Newsletter of the Granville, Ohio, Historical Society* 12, no. 3 (Summer 1998): 1–3.

Greenbaum, Susan D. "A Comparison of African-American and Euro-American Mutual Aid Societies in 19th Century America." *Journal of Ethnic Studies* 19, no. 3 (1991): 95–119.

Grossman, Lawrence. *The Democratic Party and the Negro: Northern and National Politics, 1868–92.* Urbana: University of Illinois Press, 1976.

Hartshorn, W. H. *An Era of Progress and Promise, 1863–1910*. Boston: Priscilla Publishing, 1910.

Haynes, Fred E. *Third Party Movement since the Civil War*. Iowa City: State Historical Society of Iowa, 1916.

Hays, Christopher K. "The African American Struggle for Equality and Justice in Cairo, Illinois, 1865–1900." *Illinois Historical Journal* 90, no. 4 (Winter 1997): 265–84.

———. "Way Down in Egypt Land: Conflict and Community in Cairo, Illinois, 1850–1930." PhD dissertation, University of Missouri–Columbia, 1996.

Helg, Aline. *Our Rightful Share: The Afro-Cuban Struggle for Equality, 1886–1912*. Chapel Hill: University of North Carolina Press, 1995.

Henritze, Barbara K. *Bibliographic Checklist of African American Newspapers*. Baltimore, MD: Genealogical Publishing Co., 1997.

Herd, Denise. "The Paradox of Temperance: Blacks and the Alcohol Question in Nineteenth-Century America." In *Drinking and Belief in Modern History*, edited by Susanna Barrows and Robin Room, 354–57. Berkeley: University of California Press, 1991.

Hicken, Victor. *Illinois in the Civil War*. Urbana: University of Illinois Press, 1991.

Higginbotham, A. Leon, Jr. *Shades of Freedom: Racial Politics and the Presumptions of the American Legal Process*. New York: Oxford University Press, 1996.

Holsoe, Svend E. "A Portrait of a Black Midwestern Family during the Early Nineteenth Century: Edward James Roye and His Parent." *Liberian Studies Journal* 3, no. 1 (1970–71): 41–52.

Howard, Johnathan S. "Changing the Law; Fighting for Freedom: Racial Politics and Legal Reform in Early Ohio, 1802–1860." MA thesis, Ohio State University, 2011.

Howe, Henry. *Historical Collections of Ohio*. 2 vols. Norwalk: Laning Printing, 1896.

Irwin, Ned. "Willard Warner." *Encyclopedia of Alabama*. http://www.encyclopediaofalabama.org. Accessed 1 April 2011.

James, Joy. *Transcending the Talented Tenth: Black Leaders and American Intellectuals*. New York: Routledge, 1997.

Jenness, Timothy M. "Tentative Relations: Secession and War in the Central Ohio River Valley, 1859–1862." PhD dissertation, University of Tennessee, 2011.

Joens, David A. *From Slave to State Legislator: John W. E. Thomas, Illinois' First African American Lawmaker*. Carbondale: Southern Illinois University Press, 2012.

———. "John W. E. Thomas and the Election of the First African American to the Illinois General Assembly." *Journal of the Illinois State Historical Society* 94, no. 2 (Summer 2001): 200–216.

———. "John W. E. Thomas: A Political Biography of Illinois' First African American State Legislator." PhD dissertation, Southern Illinois University–Carbondale, 2009.

———. "Ulysses S. Grant, Illinois, and the Election of 1880." *Journal of the Illinois State Historical Society* 97, no. 4 (Winter 2004/5): 310–33.

Johnson, William B. *All That Glitters Is Not Gold: The Olympic Game*. New York: G. P. Putnam's Sons, 1972.

Johnson, Wm. D. "Educational Work of the African M.E. Church." *African Methodist Episcopal Church Review* 8, no. 4 (1892): 391–400.

Jones, Johnetta. "The Cairo of Maud Rittenhouse." *ICarbS* 3, no. 1 (Summer–Fall 1976): 74–85.

Keire, Mara L. *For Business & Pleasure: Red-Light Districts and the Regulation of Vice in the United States, 1890–1933.* Baltimore, MD: Johns Hopkins University Press, 2010.

Kemp, Daniel F. "Civil War Reminiscences." http://www.sunsite.utk.edu/civil-war /kemp.html. Accessed 1 July 2011.

King, Desmond, and Stephen Tuck. "De-centring the South: America's Nationwide White Supremacist Order after Reconstruction." *Past and Present* (Oxford), no. 194 (February 2007): 213–53.

King, Horace. "The Abolitionists in Granville." *Historical Times: Newsletter of the Granville, Ohio, Historical Society* 3, no. 1 (1989): 1–4.

Kionka, T. K. *Key Command: Ulysses S. Grant's District of Cairo.* Columbia: University of Missouri Press, 2006.

Krohe, James, Jr., ed. *A Springfield Reader: Historical Views of the Illinois Capital, 1818–1976.* Springfield: Sangamon County Historical Society, 1976.

———. "Summer of Rage: The Springfield Race Riot of 1908." Springfield: Sangamon County Historical Society, 1973.

Lansden, John M. *A History of the City of Cairo, Illinois.* Chicago: R. R. Donnelley and Sons, 1910.

Lantz, Herman R. *A Community in Search of Itself: A Case History of Cairo, Illinois.* Carbondale: Southern Illinois University Press, 1972.

Lantz, Herman R., and Ernest K. Alix. "Occupational Mobility in a 19th Century Mississippi Valley River Community." *Social Science Quarterly* 51, no. 2 (1970): 404–8.

Light, Ivan. "The Ethnic Vice Industry, 1880–1944." *American Sociological Review* 42 (June 1977): 464–79.

Love, E. F. "Registration of Free Blacks in Ohio: The Slaves of George C. Mendenhall." *Journal of Negro History* 69, no. 1 (Winter 1984): 38–47.

Lovett, Otto Arnold. "Black Laws of Ohio." MA thesis, Ohio State University, 1929.

Luker, Ralph E. *The Social Gospel in Black and White: American Racial Reform, 1885–1912.* Chapel Hill: University of North Carolina Press, 1991.

Lumpkins, Charles L. *American Pogrom: The East St. Louis Race Riot and Black Politics.* Athens: Ohio University Press, 2008.

———. "Black East St. Louis: Politics and Economy in a Border City, 1860–1945." PhD dissertation, Pennsylvania State University, 2006.

Lusk, David W. *Politics and Politicians: A Succinct History of the Politics of Illinois from 1856 to 1884.* Springfield: H. W. Rokker, 1884.

Matthews, Samuel. "John Isom Gaines: The Architect of Black Public Education." *Queen City Heritage* 45, no. 1 (Spring 1987): 41–48.

McFeely, William S. *Frederick Douglass.* New York: Norton and Company, 1991.

McLaughlin, Malcolm. *Power, Community, and Racial Killing in East St. Louis.* New York: Palgrave Macmillan, 2005.

Merrick, George B. *Old Times on the Upper Mississippi: The Recollections of a Steamboat Pilot from 1854 to 1863.* Saint Paul: Minnesota Historical Society Press, 1987.

Merrill, James M. "Cairo, Illinois: Strategic Civil War River Port." *Journal of the Illinois State Historical Society* 76, no. 4 (Winter 1983): 242–56.

Middleton, Stephen. *The Black Laws: Race and the Legal Process in Early Ohio.* Athens: Ohio University Press, 2005.

Moody, Minnie Hite. "Both Men Were Teachers." *Newark Advocate,* 8 December 1970.

———. "Too Many Questions." *Newark Advocate,* 7 December 1970, 18.

Mouser, Bruce L. *For Labor, Race, and Liberty: George Edwin Taylor, His Historic Run for the White House, and the Making of Independent Black Politics.* Madison: University of Wisconsin Press, 2011.

———. "George Edwin Taylor and Wayland: Leaving His Mark." *Greetings* (July 2010): 14–19.

———. "Taylor and Smith: Benevolent Fosterage." *Past, Present & Future: The Magazine of the La Crosse County Historical Society* 32, no. 1 (August 2010): 1–3.

Noyes, Edward. "The Contraband Camp at Cairo, Illinois." In *Historical Papers: Selected Proceedings,* edited by Lysle E. Myer, 203–17. Moorhead, MN: History Department of Moorhead State University, 1971.

Ohio State Centennial Educational Committee. "History of the Schools of Newark." In *Historical Sketches of Public Schools in Cities, Villages and Townships in the State of Ohio,* n.p. Columbus, OH: State Commissioner of Common Schools, 1876. http://archive.org/stream/cu31924031821055#page/n5/mode/2up. Accessed 27 February 2014.

Painter, Nell. "Black Journalism, the First Hundred Years." *Harvard Journal of Afro-American Affairs* 2, no. 2 (1971): 30–42.

Parezo, Nancy J., and Don D. Fowler. *Anthropology Goes to the Fair: The 1904 Louisiana Purchase Exposition.* Lincoln: University of Nebraska Press, 2007.

The Partisan Prohibition Historical Society. http://www.prohibitionists.org/History/society/society.html. Accessed 27 February 2014.

Pearson, Emmet F. "The Historic Hospitals of Cairo." *Journal of the Illinois State Historical Society* 77, no. 1 (Spring 1984): 21–32.

Peavler, David J. "African Americans in Omaha and the 1898 Trans-Mississippi and International Exposition." *Journal of African American History* 93, no. 3 (2008): 337–61.

Peck, Dennis L. "Life Insurance as Social Exchange Mechanism." In *Handbook of Death and Dying,* edited by Clifton D. Bryant, 148–57. Thousand Oaks, CA: Sage Publications, 2003.

Penn, Irving G. *The Afro-American Press and Its Editors.* Springfield, MA: Willey & Co., 1891.

Peskin, Allan. *Garfield: A Biography.* Kent, OH: Kent State University Press, 1978.

Pitkin, William A. "When Cairo Was Saved for the Union." *Journal of the Illinois State Historical Society* 52, no. 3 (Autumn 1958): 284–305.

Polk, R. L. *Springfield City Directory for . . . 1908.* Springfield: Rokker, 1908.

———. *Springfield City Directory for . . . 1910.* Springfield: Rokker, 1910.

———. *Springfield City Directory for . . . 1911.* Springfield: Rokker, 1911.

———. *Springfield City Directory for . . . 1912*. Springfield: Rokker, 1912.

———. *Springfield City Directory for . . . 1916*. Springfield: Rokker, 1916.

Portwood, Shirley J. "African-American Politics and Community in Cairo and Vicinity, 1863–1900." *Illinois History Teacher* 3, no. 2 (1996): 13–21.

Price, Robert. "Further Notes on Granville's Anti-abolition Disturbances of 1836." *Ohio History: The Scholarly Journal of the Ohio Historical Society* 45, no. 4 (1936): 365–68.

———. "The Ohio Anti-slavery Convention of 1836." *Ohio History: The Scholarly Journal of the Ohio Historical Society* 45, no. 2 (1936): 173–88.

Pride, Armistead S., and Clint C. Wilson II. *A History of the Black Press*. Washington, DC: Howard University Press, 1997.

Proceedings of the Illinois State Convention of Colored Men. Chicago: Church, Goodman and Donnelly, 1867.

Proceedings of the Thirteenth Annual Communication of the Most Worshipful Grand Lodge of Free and Accepted Ancient York Masons, for the State of Illinois. Chicago: G. H. Bryant, 1880.

Quillin, Frank U. *The Color Line in Ohio: A History of Race Prejudice in a Typical Northern State*. Ann Arbor: George Wahr, 1913.

Ramold, Steven J. *Slaves, Sailors, Citizens: African Americans in the Union Navy*. DeKalb: Northern Illinois University Press, 2002.

Reed, Christopher R. *"All the World Is Here!": The Black Presence at White City*. Bloomington: Indiana University Press, 2000.

———. *Black Chicago's First Century*. Vol. 1, *1833–1900*. Columbia: University of Missouri Press, 2005.

———. "The Black Presence at 'White City': African and African American Participation at the World's Columbian Exposition, Chicago, May 1, 1893–October 31, 1893." Paul V. Galvin Library Digital History Collection. http://columbus.iit.edu/reed2 .html. Accessed 26 June 2011.

"Report of the Trustees, Principal, Treasurer, etc. of the Southern Illinois Normal University Located at Carbondale December 1874." Board of Trustees, Carbondale, IL, 1874.

Ridella, Tyler, deputy clerk, Clerk of Courts, Licking County, Ohio, to Bruce Mouser, 10 June 2011.

Rittenhouse, Maud. Diary, MS 305, "Republican Convention at Opera House, 14 July 1882," 2:36–39. Special Collections, Morris Library, Southern Illinois University-Carbondale.

Robinson, Edward A. "The Pekin: The Genesis of American Black Theater." *Black American Literature Forum* 16, no. 4 (1982): 136–38.

Rowell, Geo. P. *Rowell's American Newspaper Directory*. New York: Geo. P. Rowell & Company, 1887.

Sandlin, Lee. *Wicked River: The Mississippi When It Ran Wild*. New York: Pantheon Books, 2010.

Schantz, Otto J. "Pierre de Coubertin's Concept of Race, Nation, and Civilization." In *The 1904 Anthropology Days and Olympic Games: Sport, Race, and American Imperialism*, edited by Susan Brownell, 156–88. Lincoln: University of Nebraska Press, 2008.

Schwalm, Leslie A. "Emancipation Day Celebrations: Former Slaves in the Upper Midwest." *Annals of Iowa* 62 (Summer 2003): 291–332.

———. *Emancipation's Diaspora: Race and Reconstruction in the Upper Midwest*. Chapel Hill: University of North Carolina Press, 2009.

Scott, Daryl M. "Their Faces Were Black, but the Elites Were Untrue." *Journal of African American History* 91, no. 3 (2006): 318–22.

Scott, Frank W. *Newspapers and Periodicals of Illinois, 1814–1879*. Chicago: R. R. Donnelley and Sons, 1911.

Scott, Rebecca. *Degrees of Freedom: Louisiana and Cuba after Slavery*. New York: Belknap Press, 2005.

Senechal, Roberta. *The Sociogenesis of a Race Riot: Springfield, Illinois, in 1908*. Urbana: University of Illinois Press, 1990.

———. "The Springfield Race Riot of 1908." *Illinois History Teacher* 3, no. 2 (1996): 22–32.

Sheller, J. Reuben. "The Struggle of the Negro of Ohio for Freedom." *Journal of Negro History* 31, no. 2 (April 1946): 208–26.

Shimansky, Karl K. "The Granville Riot." *Hamilton Daily Republican*, 29 July 1914, 2.

Simmons, Charles A. *The African American Press: With Special References to Four Newspapers, 1827–1965*. London: McFarland and Co., 1997.

Smith, Grace Partridge. "Negro Lore in Southern Illinois." *Midwest Folklore* 2, no. 3 (Autumn 1952): 159–62.

Smythe, B. G. "Recollections of Newark." *Newark Advocate*, 20 May 1924, 14.

Smythe, Ronald M. *Obsolete American Securities and Corporations*. New York: Trow Press, 1911.

Spear, Allan H. *Black Chicago: The Making of a Negro Ghetto, 1890–1920*. Chicago: University of Chicago Press, 1967.

"Stanley P. Mitchell." Notable Kentucky African Americans Database. https://www.uky.edu/Libraries/NKAA/record.php?note_id=2444. Accessed 26 June 2011.

Steeples, Douglass, and David O. Whitten. *Democracy in Desperation: The Depression of 1893*. Westport, CT: Greenwood Press, 1998.

Steinglass, Steven, and Gino Scarselli. *The Ohio State Constitution: A Reference Guide*. Westport, CT: Praeger, 2004.

Stokes, Melvyn. *D. W. Griffith's "The Birth of a Nation": A History of "The Most Controversial Motion Picture of All Time."* New York: Oxford University Press, 2008.

Strout, Richard Lee. *Maud*. New York: Macmillan, 1939.

Swan, Robert J. "Thomas McCants Stewart and the Failure of the Mission of the Talented Tenth in Black America, 1880–1923." PhD dissertation, New York University, 1990.

Swanson, Leslie C. *Riverboat Gamblers of History*. Moline, IL: Leslie Swanson, 1989.

Taylor, Nikki M. *America's First Black Socialist: The Radical Life of Peter H. Clark*. Lexington: University Press of Kentucky, 2013.

———. *Frontiers of Freedom: Cincinnati's Black Community, 1802–1868*. Athens: Ohio University Press, 2005.

Terzian, Barbara. "Ohio's Constitutions: An Historical Perspective." *Cleveland State Law Review* 51 (2004): 359–94.

Thornbrough, Emma Lou. "National Afro-American League, 1887–1908." *Journal of Southern History* 27, no. 4 (1961): 494–512.

Tomblin, Barbara Brooks. *Blue Jackets and Contrabands: African Americans and the Union Navy*. Lexington: University Press of Kentucky, 2009.

Trollope, Anthony. *North America*. 2 vols. New York: Harper & Brothers, 1862. http://www.gutenberg.org/files/1866/1866-h/1866-h.htm. Accessed 27 February 2014.

Trotter, Joe William, Jr. "African American Fraternal Associations in American History: An Introduction." *Social Science History* 28, no. 3 (Fall 2004): 355–66.

———. *River Jordan: African American Urban Life in the Ohio Valley*. Lexington: University Press of Kentucky, 1998.

University of Illinois. *The Semi-centennial Record of the University of Illinois*. Chicago: Donnelley and Sons, 1918.

VanderCreek, Drew E. "Economic Development and Labor in Civil War Illinois." http://dig.lib.niu.edu/civilwar/economic.html. Accessed 27 February 2014.

Voegeli, V. Jacque. *Free but Not Equal: The Midwest and the Negro during the Civil War*. Chicago: University of Chicago Press, 1967.

Walker, Juliet E. K. "The Promised Land: The Chicago *Defender* and the Black Press of Illinois, 1862–1970." In *The Black Press in the Middle West, 1865–1985*, edited by Henry L. Suggs, 9–20. Westport, CT: Greenwood Press, 1996.

Walling, William English. "The Race War in the North." *Independent*, 3 September 1908, 529–34.

Walters, Alexander. *My Life and Work*. New York: Fleming H. Revell Co., 1917.

Watson, Bobby. "'Black Phalanx': The National Liberty Party of 1904." MS 00-10, Series VI—Law and Politics, A–B, box 1, file 12. Tom D. Dillard Arkansiana Collection, University of Arkansas Library.

Wegner, Dana M. "Little Egypt's Naval Station." *United States Naval Institute Proceedings* 98 (1972): 74–76.

Wheeler, Joanne. "Together in Egypt: A Pattern of Race Relations in Cairo, Illinois, 1865–1915." In *Toward a New South? Studies in Post–Civil War Southern Communities*, edited by O. C. Burton and R. C. McMath Jr., 103–34. Westport, CT: Greenwood Press, 1982.

Whitten, David O. "The Depression of 1893." http://eh.net/encyclopedia/the-depression-of-1893. Accessed 28 February 2014.

Woodson, Carter. "The Negro in Cincinnati prior to the Civil War." *Journal of Negro History* 1, no. 1 (1916): 2–13.

Index